... Superbly organized, astutely detailed, and wonderfully written; this Christian publication is inspirational, deeply informative, and an excellent addition to the library of Christian writings ...

*Kenneth D. Jones, M.D. (Psychiatrist)
former Deacon at Curtis Baptist Church, Augusta, GA*

Henry Summerall asked me to read his manuscript of a proposed book on basic Christian doctrine. I found it refreshing in a number of respects. It has all the essentials of a book about doctrine. It is characterized by biblical authority, clarity, and applicability. Furthermore, it has one other absolute essential ... readability! A lot of books have biblical weight, some are clear, and a few are applicable; but not all are readable. A book is of little use if people won't read it! This book is readable. Any Christian pastor or lay leader will be able to teach the basic tenets of our faith with this book. Recovery of basic doctrinal integrity now has a tool!

*Rev. Larry Scales
Pastor of Levels Baptist Church, Aiken, SC
and former Southern Baptist missionary to Tanzania*

SUCH A GREAT SALVATION

SUCH A GREAT SALVATION

An Overview of the Christian Faith

Henry Summerall, Jr.

TATE PUBLISHING & *Enterprises*

Such a Great Salvation
Copyright © 2009 by Henry Summerall, Jr. All rights reserved.

No part of this publication may be reproduced, stored in a retrieval system or transmitted in any way by any means, electronic, mechanical, photocopy, recording or otherwise without the prior permission of the author except as provided by USA copyright law.

Except for Part Two where NIV is the basic Scripture quoted, all Scripture quotations not otherwise indicated are taken from *The New King James Version* / Thomas Nelson Publishers, Nashville: Thomas Nelson Publishers. Copyright © 1982. Used by permission. All rights reserved.

Scripture quotations marked "RSV" are taken from the *Revised Standard Version of the Bible*, Copyright © 1952 by the Division of Christian Education of the National Council of the Churches of Christ in the United States of American. Used by permission. All rights reserved.

Scripture quotations marked "NRSV" are taken from *The Holy Bible: New Revised Standard Version* / Division of Christian Education of the National Council of Churches of Christ in the United States of America, Nashville: Thomas Nelson Publishers, Copyright © 1989. Used by permission. All rights reserved.

Scripture quotations marked "NIV" are taken from the *Holy Bible, New International Version* ®, Copyright © 1973, 1978, 1984 by International Bible Society. Used by permission of Zondervan Publishing House. All rights reserved.

This book is designed to provide accurate and authoritative information with regard to the subject matter covered. This information is given with the understanding that neither the author nor Tate Publishing, LLC is engaged in rendering legal, professional advice. Since the details of your situation are fact dependent, you should additionally seek the services of a competent professional.

The opinions expressed by the author are not necessarily those of Tate Publishing, LLC.

Published by Tate Publishing & Enterprises, LLC
127 E. Trade Center Terrace | Mustang, Oklahoma 73064 USA
1.888.361.9473 | www.tatepublishing.com

Tate Publishing is committed to excellence in the publishing industry. The company reflects the philosophy established by the founders, based on Psalm 68:11,
"The Lord gave the word and great was the company of those who published it."

Book design copyright © 2009 by Tate Publishing, LLC. All rights reserved.
Cover design by Leah LeFlore
Interior design by Stefanie Rooney

Published in the United States of America

ISBN: 978-1-60696-641-9
1. Religion, Christian Theology, Systematic
09.05.05

Dedicated to the glory of God,
Father, Son, and Holy Spirit

*"How shall we escape
if we ignore such a great salvation?"*
(Hebrews 2:3, NIV)

ACKNOWLEDGMENTS

There is no possible way I can express proper appreciation for the many people who have influenced my understanding of the Christian faith. As the Apostle Paul asked, "And what do [we] have that [we] did not receive?" (1 Cor. 4:7).

To my parents, I owe the gift of life itself and their example of Christian faith persevering through difficult times. They dedicated me to the Lord while I was still in my mother's womb.

Through the thirty-seven years of our marriage, my wife June (the former June Love Smith) showed me the love of God through her strong love for God and for me and through her indomitable faith in Jesus Christ, even during many difficult years of illness. May God grant her blessed sleep in Jesus and bring her to the glorious resurrection unto eternal life.

Through being a father to our children, Anne and Mark, God has taught me something of what God's fatherly love is, and how far human love falls short. They bless my life immeasurably.

Then there are so many others who witnessed a real and living Christian faith to me, such as:

The pastors at my home church, First Baptist Church, Aiken, SC, especially Rev. Amplus D. Howard who received my profession of faith and baptized me when I was eight years old and Dr. Robert L. Cate who encouraged me and spoke words of wisdom to me when I was going through seminary.

My pastors when I was a college student at Madison, Wis., especially Rev. George ("Shorty," 6'6" tall) Collins, the Baptist student pastor, and Rev. Charles R. Bell, the pastor of First Baptist Church.

The Rev. Howard M. Hickey, Rector of St. Thaddeus Episcopal Church, Aiken, SC, who instructed my wife June and me in confirmation class, introduced us to the exciting story of Christianity down through the centuries, and led us into a closer walk with the Lord through liturgical worship and the Holy Communion. Later he presented me for ordination.

Dr. John Rodgers at Virginia Theological Seminary (Episcopal), at Alexandria, Va, who was my major professor and adviser through seminary, who introduced me to St. Augustine, Luther, Calvin, evangelical theology, a deeper understanding of the Bible, and the importance of prayer, and led me into the study of the work of Dr. Regin Prenter, the leading theologian in the Church of Denmark (Lutheran), through his book, *Creation and Redemption,* which shaped my thinking about the Christian faith to a considerable degree. (Dr. Rodgers is now a Bishop in the traditional Anglican movement, serving in the Anglican Mission to America). I thank him specially for writing the Foreword.

The Rev. Peter R. Doyle, then Rector of St. James Episcopal Church in Leesburg, Va., now Senior Minister of Trinity Presbyterian Church, Auburn-Opelika, Alabama, through whose counseling and preaching of the Reformed doctrines of sin and grace, the Holy Spirit worked a conversion in my life from being a "church Christian" to being a "Jesus Christ-ian."

Dr. R. C. Sproul, Director of Ligonier Ministries, Orlando, Fl, whom I have never met in person, but who through his books, teaching tapes, and daily Bible study material (*Tabletalk*) has given me a deeper understanding of the Christian faith from the Reformed perspective.

Rev. Barry T. Antley, Pastor of St. James Lutheran Church, Graniteville, SC, my friend and pastor, through whose teaching centered on "The Kingdom of God" I came into a more comprehensive understanding of the Christian faith than ever before.

My brothers in Christ, the Wednesday morning Bible study group: Fred Christensen, Ric Bozzone, Jesse Goldman, George

Alexander, Christopher Davies, Ron Maury, and Bob Henry, for their encouragement, support, and suggestions.

Then, there are those to whom I owe a special debt of gratitude for their time-consuming detailed analysis of this book and their many helpful suggestions, especially my friends who worked over the manuscript, Lane Rogers the first four Parts and Bob Henry the fifth Part. Betty Christensen, Jean Henry, and Joan Bozzone each proofread portions of the manuscript, and Diane Maury helped immensely by proofreading the entire manuscript. And I owe a particular debt of gratitude to my dear friend Rita Stout, herself a published author, who has not only helped edit this book but has also encouraged me tremendously. The help of all these folks has made this book much better than it would otherwise have been, and I appreciate it tremendously.

For whatever in this book is an accurate expression of God's truth, all the credit and praise is due to God the Father, Jesus Christ the Son, and God the Holy Spirit. All the inaccuracies, misunderstandings, and mistakes are mine.

TABLE OF CONTENTS

19	*Foreword by Bishop John H. Rodgers, Jr.*
21	*Introduction*
25	PART ONE: GOD CREATING
27	A. "In the beginning God created the heavens and the earth"
30	B. How Did God Create the Heavens and the Earth?
33	C. What Kind of Creation Is It?
33	1. God's Creation Is Good
37	2. God's Creation Is Orderly
40	3. God's Creation Is Dependable
43	4. God Creates Man and Woman
47	PART TWO: MANKIND SINNING
49	A. The Fall of Mankind
56	B. Consequences of the Fall
64	1. Effects of the Fall: Summary
66	C. The Corruption of Human Nature
69	D. God's Promise of Salvation
71	INTRODUCTION TO PARTS THREE, FOUR, AND FIVE: GOD SAVING: PAST, PRESENT, AND FUTURE
77	PART THREE: GOD HAS SAVED HIS PEOPLE
79	A. The Virgin Birth of Jesus Christ
84	B. Jesus' Hidden Years
88	C. Jesus' Baptism and Temptation
92	D. The Earthly Ministry of Jesus
92	1. Jesus Preaching
94	2. Jesus Teaching
100	3. Jesus' Healing Miracles

104	4. Jesus Casting Out Evil Spirits
105	5. Jesus Exercising his Power Over Nature
108	6. Jesus Raising the Dead
110	7. Jesus Training His Disciples
113	E. The Turning Point
116	F. Jesus at Jerusalem
122	G. The Meaning of Jesus' Crucifixion
123	1. Sacrifice for Sins
129	2. Passover Lamb
131	3. Propitiation for Sin
134	4. Reconciliation
135	5. Redemption
138	6. Payment of Our Sin Debt
139	7. Triumph Over the Devil
142	H. The Burial of Jesus
144	I. The Resurrection of Jesus Christ
144	1. The Direct Evidence
147	2. The Indirect Evidence
153	J. The Ascension of Jesus
159	**PART FOUR: GOD IS SAVING HIS PEOPLE**
161	A. Pentecost
164	B. Who Is The Holy Spirit?
166	C. How Does Salvation Come To Us?
170	D. Human Response to the Message of Salvation
171	1. Repentance
173	2. Faith
174	3. Baptism
179	a. The Individual Christian and the Local Church
182	E. The Christian at War
182	1. The Devil
185	2. The World
187	3. The Flesh
192	F. God's Work Behind the Scenes
194	1. God Foreknew His People

196	2. God Predestined His People
199	a. Responding to a Question About Election and Predestination
201	3. God Called His People
203	4. God Justified His People
205	5. God Glorified His People
208	G. The Goal of the Christian Life: Becoming Like Jesus
209	1. Love
211	2. Joy
212	3. Peace
213	4. Patience
213	5. Kindness
214	6. Goodness
215	7. Faithfulness
216	8. Gentleness
217	9. Self-control
220	H. Spiritual Gifts
220	1. The Word of Wisdom
221	2. The Word of Knowledge
222	3. Faith
222	4. Gifts of Healing
223	5. Working of Miracles
224	6. Prophecy
226	7. Discerning of Spirits
228	8. Speaking in Different Kinds of Tongues
229	9. Interpretation of Tongues
229	10. Some Additional Spiritual Gifts
232	I. Some Other Work of the Holy Spirit
237	PART FIVE: GOD WILL SAVE HIS PEOPLE
239	A. The Second Coming of Jesus Christ
239	1. The Reality of His Return
244	2. The Signs of His Coming
244	a. The preaching of the Gospel to all the world

245	b. Persecution of Christians
248	c. Apostacy
250	d. Disasters
255	e. The Antichrist
258	f. The conversion and ingathering of the Jews
262	g. Disorder and chaos in the universe
263	3. Are we living in the Last Days?
264	4. What should be our attitude toward Jesus' Second Coming?
267	B. The Resurrection of the Dead
272	C. The Final Judgment
272	1. What will the judgment be?
277	a. Saved by Faith, Judged by Works?
280	2. The urgency of being prepared for the Final Judgment
287	3. How can we escape condemnation and be acquitted at the Last Judgment?
292	D. Hell
293	1. A real place
295	2. Some characteristics of hell
297	E. Heaven
298	1. Some glimpses of what heaven is like
299	2. Some things that will not be in heaven
302	3. Some things that will be in heaven
307	*Conclusion*
309	*About the Author*
311	*Selected Bibliography*
313	*Endnotes*

FOREWORD

It is a privilege and honor to write a foreword to this excellent, concise summary of the Christian faith and life. The author is a beloved colleague, a brother in the Lord, and a former student. It is good when a teacher is surpassed by his students.

What sets this book apart from other attempts to outline the heart of the Christian faith is not only the clarity of the writing or the comprehensiveness of its scope, but the depth of its impact. Before one is through an initial reading of this book, one is lifted up in praise and gratitude to God for *Such a Great Salvation* and finds oneself looking forward to rereading this book again and again. The reader's heart and spirit are touched as the mind is being instructed and transformed.

Another characteristic of this book that is worthy of special mention is its dependence upon and faithfulness to Holy Scripture. This is evident in the general structure of the book around the past, present, and future aspects of God's great salvation. It is evident as well in the flow of the book's narrative, which follows the basic narrative of Scripture itself. It is found also in its remarkably apt use of Scriptural citation. Time and time again just the right verse is chosen to ground and sum up the point under discussion. The texts are so illuminating that the reader would do well to be guided by this book in memorizing Scripture.

Lastly, I want to refer to the practicality of this book. To a far greater extent than I have ever seen in a concise summary, faith and life, grace and fruit are wedded together in a very practical and encouraging way. Brief summaries, informative definitions and applications challenge and guide the reader. This is a book to be used as a resource and reference on Christian living, as well as on Christian doctrine, for the two belong together.

In short, this book gives wonderful and worthy expression to the great salvation that is offered in Christ Jesus to all who will receive and grow in it. May this book help many to do so.

The Right Rev. John H. Rodgers, Jr., ThD.
Bishop in the Anglican Mission in America,
Former Dean/President and Professor of
The Trinity Episcopal School for Ministry,
Ambridge, PA.

INTRODUCTION

Here's how this book came about. Back when I was a seminary student, my major professor, friend, and mentor, Dr. John Rodgers, once made the remark that he wished there was a book that gave an overall view of the Christian faith that could be put into the hands of new Christians and people inquiring about the faith, but he knew of none that met the need. That remark was the germ of the idea for this book which has been brewing for many years.

These pages which have resulted after all these years are a distillation of trying to teach the Bible and elements of the Christian faith as a minister and teacher, first in the Episcopal Church, then in the Traditional Anglican Church, and more recently as a layman in the Lutheran Church. These efforts included Confirmation classes, Bible classes for adults, and Sunday School classes for teenagers and for adults.

Of course, no teaching involving the Bible or the Christian faith is brand new; if it were, it would be heresy. My effort here is simply to set forth as well as I can an over-view of the heart of the Christian faith.

The sources of some of the research embodied in this effort are listed in the Bibliography. Part One about creation follows the thought of Dr. Regin Prenter to a considerable extent. Also, some ideas came from *Maker of Heaven and Earth* by Prof. Langdon Gilkey, whose faith was "tried in the fires of affliction" as a prisoner in a Japanese internment camp for "enemy nations" in World War II.

Part Two about sin and the Fall entitled "Mankind Sinning" is based largely on Martin Luther's exposition of the third chapter of Genesis in his *Lectures on Genesis*. The alternate interpretation of God's casting Adam and Eve out of the Garden of Eden came from Pastor Antley.

The organization of the material on the life, ministry, death, and resurrection of Jesus in Part Three ("God Has Saved his People") is based on the article by Prof. J. W. Bowman in *Peake's Commentary on the Bible*, p.733ff., and particularly his interpretation of The Sermon on the Mount. The sections in Part Three on "The Meaning of Jesus' Crucifixion" were greatly influenced by Dr. John Rodgers' seminary course on The Atonement in which he insisted that we get away from theologians' theories and see what the New Testament itself has to say on the subject.

Part Four ("God Is Saving his People") was influenced by many different writings on living the Christian life. The germ of the idea for the drama of justification came from a teaching by Dr. R. C. Sproul of Ligonier Ministries.

The part of this book that has been the most difficult to write is Part Five, "God Will Save his People," which deals with the Last Things. There are so many diverse interpretations of the Second Coming and the end of the world that I decided to do something drastic: to see what Jesus and his Apostles had said. So I went through the New Testament writings, verse by verse, and listed each verse under the subtopics (The Second Coming of Jesus Christ, including the signs and the appearance of antichrist; the Resurrection of the Dead; the Last Judgment; Hell; and Heaven), jotting down the key words that would remind me of the text. Then under each subtopic, I tried to summarize the New Testament teaching. Often, the best approach was simply to let the Scriptures speak for themselves. That is why there are so many direct quotations from the Bible in Part Five. In working through this material, I found some key thoughts from the writings of Dr. Regin Prenter to be most helpful. In regard to the section on the Final Judgment, the subsection entitled "The Urgency of Being Prepared for the Final Judgment" is largely based on the article on *krino* (judgment) in *Theological Dictionary of the New Testament* (Gerhard Kittel, Editor; translated by Geoffrey W. Bromiley), vol. III, pages 936–941.

This book is not church-specific nor denomination-specific.

Obviously, I write from my own perspective as an Evangelical Christian. It is my hope, however, that whatever one's religious or church background, he or she will be led by the Holy Spirit through this book to search the Scriptures "to see whether these things [are] so" (Acts 17:11) and to come into a personal, life-giving relationship with Jesus Christ the Lord and only Savior.

Part One:
God Creating

"IN THE BEGINNING GOD CREATED THE HEAVENS AND THE EARTH."

This is the first verse of the first chapter of the first book of the Holy Bible, Genesis 1:1. It is a foundational statement, the truth that underlies everything that follows.

What is the difference between "the heavens" and "the earth"? Psalm 115:16 tells us: "The heaven, even the heavens, are the Lord's; But the earth he has given to the children of men." Thus, heaven is God's dwelling place; the earth is that portion of the created universe which God has put under the control and dominion of mankind. Together, "the heavens and the earth" make up the total created universe, everything that exists.

What does it mean to say that God is the creator of everything that exists? To answer this question, we must first look at our common understanding of the word "create."

We use the words "create" and "creative" frequently with reference to people. We say that a person is a creative cook; that one is a creative woodworker. When we analyze what we mean by using the word "creative" in these ways, however, we find that it means the new or unusual arrangement of pre-existing components. When a creative cook whips up a new dish, he or she does not originate the ingredients, but rather combines them in a new and tasty way. Even though we say a woodworker created a piece of furniture, he did not create the wood he works with; the wood itself already existed. He simply arranged it in a new form.

In short, when human beings create, they simply re-arrange pre-existing materials into a different form.

When God created, however, he did something quite different: He brought into existence the very materials themselves which did not exist before. God created out of nothing. "In the beginning God created the heavens and the earth" out of nothing. Out of the void, out of the infinite emptiness, out of nothing, God created and brought into being the very physical elements which did not exist before.

God "calls into existence the things that do not exist" (Rom. 4:17, RSV). "It is by faith that we understand that the world was created by one word from God, so that no apparent cause can account for the things we can see" (Heb.11:3, Jerusalem Bible). "Look at the heaven and the earth and see everything that is in them, and recognize that God made them out of things that did not exist" (II Maccabees 7:28, RSV *Apocrypha*).

In the Hebrew language, in which the Old Testament was originally written, the word translated "created" (*barah*) is a very special word because it is never used with anyone but God for its subject. This means that God is the only truly creative Being. God is the only one who really creates. To speak of human beings as creative is only a figure of speech.

All the religions in the world have some doctrine of creation, of how the world began. However, except for the biblical doctrine of creation, most of the other doctrines of creation mean the forming and shaping of matter which already exists. It is only the biblical doctrine of creation that really goes to the root of the matter, namely, that God created the entire physical universe out of nothing.

Where there was nothing, only an infinite emptiness, God spoke his mighty and creative word, and the universe came into being, beginning with the creation of light itself. "Then God said, 'Let there be light; and there was light'" (Gen. 1:3).

What does it mean for our lives that God created everything that exists out of nothing? The truth of God's creation means:

(1) God alone is the source of everything that exists; He is the source of our lives, and we are completely dependent upon him. We owe to him the very fact that we are alive, for "It is he who has made us, and not we ourselves" (Ps. 100:3).

(2) God's action in creation was an intentional action with meaning and purpose. Therefore, in God's plan, our lives have meaning and purpose, even though we may not sense it or feel it or may even feel worthless and meaningless. But God's truth is that our lives do have meaning and purpose. It is part of the adventure of living the Christian life to discover God's plan for our individual lives. As God said to the Prophet Jeremiah: "Before I formed you in the womb I knew you; Before you were born I sanctified you; And I ordained you a prophet to the nations" (Jer. 1:5).

(3) Because we have been given our very lives by God as a free gift, we are meant to live with a constant attitude of gratitude and thankfulness toward God. Our very life and existence is a gift from him, and therefore we should be truly grateful. Every morning when we first wake up from sleep, we should thank God for the gift of life. With the psalmist David we say: "Bless the Lord, O my soul; And all that is within me bless his holy name! Bless the Lord, O my soul, And forget not all his benefits" (Ps. 103:1).

B

HOW DID GOD CREATE THE HEAVENS AND THE EARTH?

Since God's original creation began before there were any human beings on the earth, creation would be a complete mystery to us, if God had not revealed some of his truth to us. By revelation, God has given us a glimpse of the mystery of creation.

The way in which God created was through speaking his Word (in Greek, the *logos*). God spoke his mighty Word of Command and the universe came into being, out of nothing. As the psalmist wrote: "By the word of the Lord the heavens were made, And all the host of them by the breath of his mouth." (Ps. 33:6).

As expressed by one of the leading theologians of modern times: "The creation is the miracle that out of nothing something comes into being simply through a Word of God."[1]

What is this Word of God through which the heavens and the earth were created?

In the Holy Scriptures, God opens the door wide enough for us to have a glimpse of this overwhelming and awe-inspiring mystery: this Word of God (the *Logos*) was God the Son, the Second Person of the Holy Trinity. He was the agency or instrumentality through Whom the creation took place. As set forth in sublime language by St. John:

> "In the beginning was the Word, and the Word was with God, and the Word was God. He was in the beginning with God. All things were made through him, and without him nothing was made that was made."
>
> (Jn. 1:1–3)

And wonder of wonders, when God's time was right, this same creative and all-powerful Word of God took human flesh in the womb of the Virgin Mary, begotten by the Holy Spirit, and became a human being, Jesus Christ, truly and completely human and truly and completely God!

This staggers our imagination. It is something we could not have known or figured out on our own. God himself had to reveal this tremendous truth: the creation took place through a Person that we know as Jesus Christ. As St. Paul expresses it:

> "He [Jesus Christ] is the image of the invisible God, the firstborn over all creation. For by him all things were created that are in heaven and that are on earth, visible and invisible, whether thrones or dominions or principalities or powers. All things were created through him and for him. And he is before all things, and in him all things consist."
>
> (Col. 1:15–17)

The doctrine of creation answers the questions: Why is there anything at all? Why does the world exist? On the personal level: Why am I here? Why do I exist? Why am I living?

God has shown us the answer to these questions: because of Jesus Christ! Out of God's great and overflowing love, he created us, and he did it through Jesus Christ. Very simply, you are living because God loves you. You are a walking miracle. You are living, breathing proof that "God is love" (1 Jn. 4:8). The very fact that you are alive is proof that God loves you in and through Jesus. God has created you because he loves you.

Therefore, with the angels and archangels, the saints, the elders of the Old Israel and the elders of the New Israel, worship and bless God because he created this world and because he created you:

> "You are worthy, O Lord,
> To receive glory and honor and power;
> For You created all things,
> And by Your will they exist and were created."
>
> (Rev. 4:11)

What Kind of Creation Is It?

We need to stress three characteristics of God's Creation: It is good; it is orderly; it is dependable. We can remember these as an acrostic on the word "God":

Good

Orderly

Dependable

1. GOD'S CREATION IS GOOD

In the biblical view of creation, creation is good because God Who created it is good, and his creation reflects that aspect of himself. "The heavens declare the glory of God; And the firmament shows his handiwork" (Ps. 19:1). "Ever since the creation of the world [God's] eternal power and divine nature, invisible though they are, have been understood and seen through the things he has made" (Rom. 1:20, NRSV). "You are good, and do good" (Ps. 119:68).

This point seems so obvious to us that we take it for granted. We assume that the created world is good, and we should enjoy it. And yet, the reason we take the goodness of the material universe for granted is that this is a cultural assumption which grows from biblical roots.

Many non-biblical religions and philosophies of the world do not believe that the physical, material world is good. They think the created material universe is evil and bad. They consider the soul and spiritual things to be good, while material and physical things, especially the human body, are evil. According to such thinking, as epitomized by the Greek philosopher Plato, the problem with humanity is that our souls, which are considered good and pure, are trapped and imprisoned in physical bodies, which are considered evil. Hence, according to such thinking, salvation must lie in the soul's being set free from the "prison house" of the body.

This view is called *dualism*, and is taught in many religions of the world. It teaches that the soul is good and the body is bad; that the spiritual life is good, and the physical life is evil.

People who hold this view tend to go to one of two extremes in their conduct. Either they deny the body by ascetical practices to attempt to purify the soul, or else they fall to the other extreme and indulge the body in vice, licentiousness, and perversions of all sorts since in their view the body does not matter, but only the soul or spirit is important.

Furthermore, those who hold to the religious philosophy of "dualism" believe that the soul is immortal and will live forever, while the body will die and disintegrate. They make a sharp split between the soul and the body.

What people believe about creation makes a tremendous difference in their attitude toward life itself. As proof of this point, consider those areas of the world where extremes of religious devotion exist side by side with the most abject suffering, misery, poverty, and indifference to the dignity of human life. This attitude grows out of the philosophy that only the soul is important, while the body and thus pain and suffering do not matter.

In contrast to these dualistic religions and philosophies,

Christianity is in many ways the most materialistic religion of all. Christianity teaches that not simply our souls, but our bodies as well, are good and were created by God as a unity; that everything which has being is good. In short, the creation is basically and essentially good because a good God created it. In Christian teaching the physical, material universe is good because it is the work of a loving Father through his well-beloved Son by the power of his Holy Spirit.

As the account of creation unfolds in the first chapter of Genesis, at the various stages of creation God considers what he has created through his Word and pronounces it to be good. After the creation of light, "God saw the light, that it was good" (Gen. 1:4). After the separation of the land from the waters and the creation of vegetation, "God saw that it was good" (Gen.1:10). After he created the sun and the moon and the stars, "God saw that it was good" (Gen.1:18). After God created an abundance of living creatures in the waters, and of winged birds, "God saw that it was good" and he blessed them (Gen. 1:21–22). After he created the living creatures on the earth, cattle, creeping things, and beasts of the earth, "God saw that it was good" (Gen. 1:25).

After the creation of humanity, the crowning glory of God's creation, which God created in his own image and likeness, "[t]hen God saw everything that he had made, and indeed it was *very good*" (Gen. 1:31).

This is God's verdict on creation: everything material, all things that have being, the physical universe, our human bodies including our sexuality, are *"very good."*

This sense of the goodness and majesty and wonder of God's creation is found many places in the Scriptures, especially in the Psalms and in the teachings of Jesus. The Psalmist sees the majesty of God revealed even in the awesome thunderstorm (Ps. 29). He senses the wonder of God's creation, the inter-connectedness between the various forms of life (Ps. 104). God sets forth his wisdom and power in creation in verse after verse in the voice from the whirlwind responding to Job's questions (Job chapters 38–41). In the teachings of Jesus, especially in the Sermon on the Mount and in the parables of growth, he sets before us the mystery and majesty of God's creation.

God's loving hand is over all he has made. God's creation is very good. The physical universe is good because a good God made it. It is the work of the loving Father.

What does it mean for our lives that God's creation is good, very good? It means that it is to be *used, but not abused.* Two illustrations of this principle are our attitude toward (1) food and (2) sex.

(1) *Food:* The food that we have is a gift from God, and we are to use it and enjoy it. "Go, eat your bread with enjoyment, and drink your wine with a merry heart; for God has long ago approved what you do" (Eccles. 9:7, NRSV).

The Old Testament distinction between clean and unclean foods is abolished for Christians. Jesus "declared all foods clean" (Mk. 7:19, RSV). "For everything created by God is good, and nothing is to be rejected, provided it is received with thanksgiving; for it is sanctified by God's word and by prayer" (1 Tim. 4:4–5, NRSV).

But we are not to abuse the good gift of food God gives us. That would be the sin of gluttony which is excessive indulgence in more food than we need, which can lead to poverty (Prov. 23:20–21) and is bad for our health (Prov. 25:16–17).

(2) *Sex:* Human sexuality is a great gift from God, to be used and enjoyed within the limits of his will and commandments, but not to be abused by being indulged outside of his will. God is the One who created human sexuality. He created humanity male and female (Gen.1:27). God said: "Therefore a man shall leave his father and mother and be joined to his wife, and they shall become one flesh" (Gen. 2:24). "He who finds a wife finds a good thing, And obtains favor from the Lord" (Prov. 18:22). "Let marriage be held in honor by all, and let the marriage bed be kept undefiled" (Heb. 13:4, NRSV). God's gift of sex in mar-

riage is not to be demeaned by obscene, silly, vulgar talk, but given and received with thanksgiving (Eph. 5:4).

God considers married human love so important that he devoted an entire book of the Holy Scriptures to it, the Song of Songs, also called the Song of Solomon or Canticles, which celebrates the joys and delights of married love.

However, sinful abuse of God's good gift of sexuality would be any expression of sex outside of marriage. One of God's foundational Commandments for his people is, "You shall not commit adultery" (Ex. 20:14; Deut. 5:18).

Further, God's Law prohibits fornication, which is sexual activity between persons who are not married (Eph. 5:3–5). God detests the sin of bestiality, that is, sex between a human being and an animal (Lev. 18:23; 20:15–16). And God abominates the sin against nature (homosexuality), that is, sex acts between persons of the same sex (Lev. 18:22; Gen.19; Rom. 1:24–27).

God intends for us to enjoy his good creation, to use it but not abuse it. For us to have the fullness of the joy and delight in his creation that God intends, we have to stay within the boundaries that God himself has set. He knows what is best for us and how we can have the greatest and highest enjoyment of the good world that he has created.

2. GOD'S CREATION IS ORDERLY

The doctrine of creation also means that God's creation is orderly. As Isaiah the prophet put it: "For thus says the Lord, who created the heavens (he is God!), who formed the earth and made it (he established it; he did not create it a chaos; he formed it to be inhabited!): 'I am the Lord, and there is no other'"(Is. 45:18, NRSV).

God has made this universe that he has created as an orderly universe, not a chaos. He has arranged it into an orderly whole so that it serves his purposes.

But what kind of an order is it?

There are two systems of order and organization: numbers

and words. When we think of the universe being an orderly place, we children of the 21st century cannot help thinking in scientific terms, of scientific formulas expressed in terms of numbers. However, there is another system of order besides that of numbers, that is, the orderliness of words. These two systems of organization are very basic to human thought. Even in children, usually either verbal aptitude or mathematical aptitude is greater, depending on which side of the brain is dominant in the child. All through the educational system, standardized tests are divided into verbal sections and mathematical sections.

Since these two systems for dealing with the reality of the physical universe, verbal and mathematical, are so basic, it should not surprise us to find both systems referred to in Holy Scripture. In the Bible we find many references to counting, number, numbers, numbering. This method of classifying and dealing with the reality of the physical universe is very helpful. It is the basis of the scientific enterprise which has been of such tremendous benefit to mankind.

As important as the scientific method of dealing with the physical universe is, however, it is not the primary way in which we are to think of the orderliness of God's creation. Rather, according to Scripture, the orderliness of God's creation is expressed primarily in terms of words, not numbers. The word "number" and its cognates appears in the Bible about 200 times, while the word "name" appears over 900 times.

This should not surprise us because creation itself took place through and by means of God's Word. God spoke, and it was done. "By the word of the Lord the heavens were made, And all the host of them by the breath of his mouth" (Ps. 33:6).

The numerical method of ordering reality and the verbal method are not in conflict. There is a wonderful verse in the Psalms which brings the two together: "He counts the number of the stars; He calls them all by name" (Ps. 147:4).

The primary way in which the orderliness of God's creation is expressed is by means of words. This is of tremendous importance to us humans. It means that we are not simply numbers, but individual persons each with our own names. Any system of identifying people primarily by numbers is ultimately dehumanizing, such as in the Nazi concentration camps where each prisoner had his or her assigned identification number tattooed on the wrist, and the administration and guards referred to them only by number, as "Prisoner Number ___." If the orderliness of God's creation as it affects human beings were primarily by number, then the universe would be a cold, impersonal, dehumanizing, and uncaring place. To God we are persons each with our own name. He calls his own sheep by name (Jn. 10:3). We are each separate and unique individuals of infinite worth and dignity. We are, each one of us, loved by God with an everlasting love.

It is because God loves you immensely that he has created you and given you the breath of life. He has brought you into a world that already existed, that was operating and running long before you were born. And God has preserved to this very moment the life he has given you, through many dangers. God has provided everything necessary for your life, at each and every instant of time.

God has created you not only to be his creature like the animals but to be in a person-to-person relationship with himself, to be his beloved child and his friend, to have fellowship and companionship with you and you with him. As St. Augustine wrote in his *Confessions:* "Thou hast created us for Thyself, and our hearts are restless until they find their rest in Thee."

Since God's creation is orderly, it stands to reason that God's Law underlies it and undergirds it. Since God made this world to be inhabited and not a chaotic place, there must be rules and regulations and guidelines as to how this orderliness is to be maintained. And that is exactly what we find, for God's laws are very closely connected with his creation. These laws, or commandments, are expressed not in the numerical formulas of science, but in understandable human words.

Here we refer to the moral law of God, summarized in the Ten Commandments. Our purpose here is not to go into a detailed exposition of the Ten Commandments, but simply to state that they summarize the moral law of God and are woven into the very fabric of God's creation. They are, as it were, the foundational constitution of God's creation.

In a sense, one cannot break God's Commandments, because the Commandments stand like a rock regardless of what we do, but one can certainly break himself or herself against them. If we live our lives in accordance with God's Commandments, we will find that our lives will be better, we will have more peace and stability, and we will be blessed by God.

As the Psalmist sang centuries ago: Those who delight in the law of the Lord and meditate on it day and night

> "shall be like a tree
> Planted by the rivers of water,
> That brings forth its fruit in its season,
> Whose leaf also shall not wither;
> And whatever he does shall prosper."
>
> (Ps. 1:3)

3. GOD'S CREATION IS DEPENDABLE

Closely akin to the orderliness of God's creation is the concept that the creation is dependable.

The order and dependability of the created universe make science and technology possible. For example, when a chemical experiment is repeated with the same chemicals in the same proportions under the same conditions, the same result occurs, time after time again. The ground rules of the universe do not change between experiments.

These factors of orderliness and dependability in the physical universe are the basis of science, technology, and modern civilization. Historically speaking, science and technology seem to grow better in soil which has been fertilized by the biblical doctrine of creation. If people do not believe that the creation is basically good, orderly and dependable, there would be no basis for engaging in the scientific enterprise. Rather, we would be like the pagan Hawaiians making sacrifices to Pele, whom they believe to be the passionate, volatile, and capricious goddess of volcanoes and fire.

We must not take the dependability of the universe for granted. God's universe is dependable because it was created by God himself, who is trustworthy and dependable. God himself said: "For I am the Lord, I do not change" (Mal. 3:6). "Jesus Christ is the same yesterday, today, and forever" (Heb. 13:8).

We are constantly amazed at the goodness and dependability of God himself which is reflected in his creation. At every change of seasons, at every change of day and night, through his actions, God speaks the same word to us as he originally did to Noah after the flood:

"While the earth remains,
Seedtime and harvest,
And cold and heat,
And winter and summer,
And day and night
Shall not cease."

(Gen. 8:22)

To the Christian, the rising of the sun every morning is not something that takes place automatically, but rather it is an amazing evidence of God's love and concern and care for us. When we first open our eyes in the morning, we should rejoice and give thanks to God that he has brought us to a new day. A Christian's response is to say, "This is the day which the Lord has made; We will rejoice and be glad in it" (Ps. 118:24).

Arising from the dependability of God's creation is the doctrine of God's providence. I had heard this word all my life without understanding what it meant until I realized that it is God's *provide-ence*. Then I knew that it means God provides for his people; He takes care of them; He protects them; He watches over them.

Not only did God create the universe ages ago, but he sustains it, he upholds it, he keeps it operating, at every instant of time. God's creation is a continuing, on-going process. From a Christian point of view, the sun did not come up this morning because of some "natural law." It did not happen automatically, but rather because God told the sun to come up this morning.

Years ago when the philosophy of Deism was fashionable, creation was compared with a gigantic but intricate timepiece (a watch) which God had made, had wound up and started running. But then, Deists believed, God left his universe to run itself in accordance with the natural laws he had put into place.

This idea of Deism is not the biblical doctrine of creation. The Scriptures teach that not only did God create the universe out of nothing at the beginning of time, but he also keeps it running and operating at every instant of time. He did not merely set it up and start it running and then leave it to operate on its own. No! As Jesus himself said: "My Father has been working until now, and I have been working" (Jn. 5:17). The Book of Hebrews tells us that God the Son upholds [present tense: *continues to uphold*] all things by his powerful Word (Heb. 1:3).

Our very lives, our existence, our being alive, depend at every instant of time upon God's upholding us, sustaining us, providing for us, taking care of us, and giving us the breath of life.

In surprising fashion Scripture also teaches that Jesus Christ himself is the cosmic force, so to speak, which holds together all of the atoms composing the physical universe. It is his power that holds everything together (Col. 1:17). It is because Jesus Christ is holding all things together that your physical body, the chair you are sitting in, the floor under your feet, does not explode, fall apart, and disintegrate. It is because of him that the tremendous explosive potential of the atoms is held together and not unleashed. It is Jesus Christ, God the Son, the Eternal Word of God, who is the cosmic force holding this universe together, at each and every instant of time, as long as it is God's will for this universe to continue.

This upholding of all things by Jesus Christ is expressed very concretely in the way God provides food for his creatures, both humans and animals, and upholds and sustains and renews his creation continuously (Ps. 104:27–30).

Our very lives at each instant of time are totally dependent upon God. The fact that we are alive, that our lives have been sustained up until now by air to breathe, food to eat and water to drink, is proof that God loves us and that his creation is dependable. Here we are as living proof.

Because God's creation is dependable, we can trust him. Because God will continue to provide for us just as he always has done, we can live in trust and without anxiety regarding the future. Following the lead of the Lord Jesus, we look at the physical universe around us and see how God takes care of the birds of the air and the lilies of the field, and know that we are infinitely more valuable in his sight than birds and flowers. Knowing this, we can trust him and live without anxiety (Mt. 6:25–34).

4. GOD CREATES MAN AND WOMAN

After the Fifth Day of Creation, God had completed the creation of the physical universe, except for its crowning glory. God had created light; the firmament dividing the waters above the earth from the waters below; the vegetation and plants; the sun, moon and stars; the creatures that move in the sea and the birds that fly in the heavens. Then on the Sixth Day, he created the cattle, creeping things, and beasts of the earth.

> "Then God said, 'Let Us make man in Our image, according to Our likeness; let them have dominion over the fish of the sea, over the birds of the air, and over the cattle, over all the earth and over every creeping thing that creeps on the earth.'" So God created man in his own image; in the image of God he created him; male and female he created them."
> (Gen. 1:26–27)

And this is the way he did it: "And the Lord God formed

man of the dust of the ground, and breathed into his nostrils the breath of life; and man became a living being" (Gen. 2:7).

God placed Adam (the Hebrew word "*adamah*" means dust or ground) in the Garden of Eden "to tend it and keep it" (Gen. 2:15). Thus, in the beginning mankind had work to do, but originally it was work that was fulfilling as well as necessary.

In the garden, God had planted every tree "that is pleasant to the sight and good for food" (Gen. 2:9). Also in the midst of the garden stood the Tree of Life, and the Tree of the Knowledge of Good and Evil. And God gave the man permission to eat the fruit of every tree of the garden, except the fruit of the Tree of Knowledge of Good and Evil. God specifically commanded the man not to eat of that tree, because, God explained, "in the day you eat of it you shall surely die" (Gen. 2:17).

God saw that it was not good for the man to be alone, and said that he would make man "a helper comparable to him" (Gen. 2:18).

Scripture tells us that God made a deep sleep to fall upon Adam, and while he was in the deep sleep, God took one of Adam's ribs and closed up the flesh in its place, and from the rib he made a woman, which he brought to Adam (Gen. 2:21–22). When Adam saw the woman, he exclaimed:

> "This is now bone of my bones
> And flesh of my flesh;
> She shall be called Woman,
> Because she was taken out of Man."
>
> (Gen. 2:23)

For many centuries Bible teachers have pointed out that God did not create woman from man's foot for him to trample her down, nor from man's head for her to rule over him, but God created woman from man's side for them to be close to each other, to love and honor and cherish each other. This is God's original intention for marriage, for husband and wife to be "heirs together of the grace of life" (1 Pet. 3:7). "And they were both naked, the man and his wife, and were not ashamed" (Gen. 2:25).

At this point in the Biblical account, man and woman have been created and are living in a beautiful married relationship with each other. God has provided them with the bountiful fruit of the garden and everything they need. They have fulfilling and enjoyable work to do. They have access to the Tree of Life, so they have abundant life and health. They walk and talk with God himself in the garden in the cool of the day, as friends meet and talk.

The only limitation upon them is God's command that they not eat fruit of the Tree of the Knowledge of Good and Evil.

At this point, they are living without sin, in unbroken and wonderful fellowship and communion with God himself and with each other. They were truly living in Paradise on earth, as God intended for it to be.

Part Two:
Mankind Sinning

Something dreadful has happened. It is obvious that we do not live in Paradise. The world we live in has little resemblance to the Garden of Eden. Some calamity of cosmic proportions has happened to spoil the idyllic life of man and woman in Paradise. Something drastic has ruined and polluted God's good creation. The beautiful picture of mankind's original life in Paradise has been smashed and shattered it into many jagged fragments.

What happened? Sin entered the world, and through sin, God's good creation has been contaminated and corrupted.

In the third chapter of the book of Genesis God has given us some insight into what happened. It is not only the account of what happened to Adam and Eve, the first man and woman, but it is also the story of what has happened to us in our own lives, in the life of every person who has ever lived on this earth, every person now living, and every person who will ever live, with one exception: Jesus of Nazareth.

THE FALL OF MANKIND

Here is what happened, as God has revealed it to us in Genesis chapter 3 (using New International Version translation):

Verse 1: "*Now the serpent was more crafty than any of the wild animals the Lord God had made.*" The Bible does not give us any rational explanation for the presence of sin, evil, and suffering in the world. We know that God is not the originator of evil, for he is good, he is love, he is light and in him is no darkness at all (1 Jn. 1:5). God who is good created a good, a very good, world. The serpent simply appears in the Garden. Evil, sin and suffering are present in our world, as a reality, as a plain fact.

Jesus made this same point in the Parable of the Wheat and the Tares. The farmer had planted good seed in his field and while he was sleeping, someone planted seeds of an evil poisonous weed. The farmer's servants asked him what had happened, for they had planted good seed, and the farmer (representing God in the parable) said simply, "An enemy has done this" (Mt. 13:24–30).

The fact of evil simply appearing in the midst of God's good creation is a mystery, "the mystery of iniquity," the Apostle Paul calls it. How could a good God allow evil, sin, and suffering to happen in this world which he created as a good and beautiful and happy place? We do not know the full answer to that question. The Christian faith does not provide a philosophically satisfactory answer to that question. However, Christianity does show the mighty actions that God has undertaken, is even now undertaking, and will undertake, to abolish sin, evil, and suffering and to set things right.

We know from other parts of the Bible that the serpent is the devil, Satan, the dragon, the destroyer, the tempter, the deceiver, the liar, the murderer (he has various names; Rev. 12:9; 20:2). He is the enemy, the adversary of mankind. It does say the serpent was originally a "beast of the field," that is, a four-footed animal that walked rather than creeping or crawling. The serpent must have originally been a charming and attractive animal because Adam and Eve were not afraid of its presence.

Verse 1 (cont'd): "*He [the serpent] said to the woman, 'Did God really say, "You must not eat from any tree in the garden?"'*" The serpent spoke in an insinuating tone of voice attempting to get the woman to doubt what God had said: "Did God really say that you and Adam cannot eat the fruit from any tree of the garden? All this wonderful fruit, and you are forbidden to eat any of it. What a pity and a shame that God would give such an absurd, unreasonable commandment to you and Adam!"

The devil attempts to get Adam and Eve to doubt God's goodness to them by making God's commandment appear much more restrictive and limited than it was. God's commandment to them had been very broad: "Of every tree of the garden you may freely eat, but of the tree of the knowledge of good and evil you shall not eat, for in the day that you eat of it you shall surely die" (Gen. 2:16–17). God had given them innumerable fruit trees for their food, even the Tree of Life, and nothing was forbidden except for one, the Tree of the Knowledge of Good and Evil.

Verses 2 and 3: "*The woman said to the serpent, 'We may eat fruit from the trees of the garden, but God did say, "You must not eat fruit from the tree that is in the middle of the garden, and you must not touch it, or you will die.'"* Uh, oh! The woman has been thinking about the forbidden tree; she has fixed her attention on it; she knows right where it is, "in the middle of the garden." Isn't that the way we humans are, forgetting and overlooking all the wonderful things God allows us to have and to do, and instead focusing our attention upon the relatively few things God forbids?

Furthermore, the woman has become so fixated upon and obsessed with the fruit of the forbidden tree that she adds to God's commandment. God had said not to eat it. Eve adds to what God has said by expanding upon God's prohibition: "Not only can we not eat it, we can't even touch it!" It is a sign of danger to us that we are getting close to violating God's commandments when we misstate them to make them more restrictive than they really are, or on the other hand, to make them broader and more permissive than they are. Both the Old Testament and the New Testament warn us against adding to, or taking away from, God's Word (Deut. 4:2, 12:32; Prov. 30:6; Rev. 22:18,19).

Moreover, the woman not only misstates God's command to make it more restrictive than it really is, she also casts doubt on the punishment God has decreed for violation of his command. What God had said was that if they ate of the forbidden fruit, " ... in the day that you eat of it you shall surely die" (Gen. 2:17). What the woman said, in the original Hebrew language, softens God's punishment, to say something like "if we eat of it, we may perhaps, possibly, die someday."

This shows that Eve "has turned from faith to unbelief. For just as a promise demands faith, so a threat also demands faith."[2]

Verses 4 and 5: *"You will not surely die,"* the serpent said to the woman. *"For God knows that when you eat of it your eyes will be opened, and you will be like God, knowing good and evil."* The devil now shifts from sly insinuation to direct attack on God's Word. God had told Adam that "in the day that you eat of it you shall surely die" (Gen. 2:17). But the devil flatly contradicts God, saying: "You will not surely die."

Moreover, the devil casts doubt on God's goodness, implying that God is trying to keep something good from Adam and Eve. The devil dangles before them the lure of secret, hidden knowledge: "God knows that when you eat of it, your eyes will be opened, and you will be like God, knowing good and evil." He insinuates that God wants to keep them in ignorance, jealous of his own prerogatives. The devil tempts them to think that God wants to hold power over them by withholding from them the knowledge of good and evil. He says, in effect, that once they are "enlightened," they will be equal with God, and God will no longer have control over them, and they will be free.

The false promise of the devil always is that if we sin, we will experience a wonderful freedom.

Verse 6: "*When the woman saw that the fruit of the tree was good for food and pleasing to the eye, and also desirable for gaining wisdom, she took some and ate it.*" At this point it is clear that even before she ate the forbidden fruit, Eve has already fallen away from faith in God. The tree and its fruit seem so desirable that she totally ignores what God has commanded. She no longer believes what God has said. She has turned from faith in God to unbelief.

The deepest sin of mankind, from which all other sins flow, is not believing what God has said, that is, disbelief of God's Word. Jesus taught the same thing when he told his disciples that when the Holy Spirit comes, "He will convict the world of sin ... because they do not believe in Me" (Jn. 16:8–9).

The acts and behaviors that we call "sins" are the outward visible signs of the underlying condition of "sin" (sinfulness) which begins inwardly in our hearts and minds with not believing what God has said. To use a medical analogy, the outward "sins" (the wrongful acts that people commit) are the symptoms of the underlying disease of sinfulness.

The woman is now in a spiritually blinded condition: she

sees as being desirable that which God has forbidden. She is believing a lie. She thinks that she knows better than God.

The sin of Adam and Eve was not simply the act of eating the forbidden fruit. That action was simply the manifestation of the root sin that was in their hearts, namely, disbelieving God's Word.

Worldly people ridicule the truth of God by focusing on the act of eating the fruit (an apple, they call it, although the Bible does not say so). They think it so unreasonable and arbitrary of God to give such importance to such an insignificant act as eating an apple. As we have seen, however, the act of eating the forbidden fruit is simply the outward manifestation of the sin of unbelief that lies deep in the heart. The sin in the heart is the root problem; it leads to the sinful actions and behaviors we call "sins." As Jesus himself said, "What comes out of a man is what makes him 'unclean.' For from within, out of men's hearts, come evil thoughts, sexual immorality, theft, murder, adultery, greed, malice, deceit, lewdness, envy, slander, arrogance and folly. All these evils come from inside and make a man 'unclean'" (Mk. 7:21–23, NIV).

Then, when the forbidden tree looked so attractive to Eve, so beautiful, so desirable, so fraught with the potential of having wisdom to understand the mysteries of the universe, the sin of disbelief in her heart led to the sinful action of eating the forbidden fruit.

> "The woman ate because she saw 'that the tree was to be desired to make one wise' (Gen.3:6). In feasting upon the fruit, Eve attempted to gain wisdom through her own efforts to know more than God had revealed...
>
> This temptation to achieve wisdom without the Lord is still present in all men and motivates non-believers to call Christians foolish (1 Cor. 1:18–31). It also leads believers to adopt practices and teachings that appease the culture at large."[33]

Verse 6b: "*She also gave some to her husband, who was with her, and he ate."* Adam and Eve were created by God to be joint heirs of the grace of life, and now they are co-conspirators against God and joint partners in sin, both equally guilty before God.

The man and the woman were both created in the image of God, but created male and female, so profoundly different.

Why did the devil through the serpent speak to Eve, enticing her first, rather than Adam? Each person, male or female, is a unique creation of God, but men and women have deeply diverse characteristics, physically, emotionally, mentally, and spiritually. In general, women are physically weaker than men; they are more vulnerable; they are more curious. Men are more likely to accept reality at face value, but women have a greater desire to understand the reason for things. Women are more apt to ask the question, "Why?" It is these general characteristics of women that led the devil to speak to the woman, to tempt her directly. Generally, men want to please their wives and will do what their wives ask, if at all possible. This is one of men's vulnerable points which the devil evidently knew and exploited.

In this first sin man and woman were both equally guilty. The man was just as guilty as the woman. In verse 6 we are told specifically that when the woman was tempted, the man was right there with her, all the time.

It was to Adam that God had given the instructions about the Tree of the Knowledge of Good and Evil, before Eve was created (Gen. 2:16–17). Undoubtedly, he had told Eve what God had said (Gen. 3:2–3). When his wife was being tempted by the devil through the serpent, why did Adam not speak up and remind her of God's command and the penalty for disobeying? It is a husband's duty to protect his wife from harm, to guide her into good and away from evil, to lead her. But when Eve was being tempted, Adam kept his mouth shut and did not speak up. By not doing so, he greatly sinned against her and against God. He failed her in her time of need.

Moreover, Adam failed and sinned against God in another particular. God had given Adam dominion over all the other creatures (Gen. 1:26). Why did Adam not exercise his God-given power and take dominion over the serpent and command it to go away? Instead, by his failure, he allowed the serpent to have free rein.

In any event, Adam sinned as profoundly as Eve did. The sins that beset men and women may be somewhat different, but they are equally deadly. God intended men and women to be "joint heirs of the gracious gift of life" (1 Pet. 3:7, NRSV), but by their sin, they have become joint heirs of death.

B
CONSEQUENCES OF THE FALL

Verse 7: "*Then the eyes of both of them were opened, and they realized they were naked; so they sewed fig leaves together and made coverings for themselves.*" What a profound shock Adam and Eve experienced! They had expected to receive some wonderfully liberating, deep knowledge when their eyes were opened, but all they saw was another shamefully naked, guilty person!

Before this, they had both been naked and not ashamed. Their nakedness had been their glory as the beautiful people God had created. Now their glory has been exchanged for shame, their innocence for guilt.

The bodily parts that had been created for the purpose of uniting them in a wonderful intimacy and for the godly purpose of procreation now appeared indecent to them. The bodily organs God had intended to be used for his glory in the godly work of procreation ("Be fruitful and multiply," Gen. 1:28) they now found to be disgraceful. That which had been beautiful they now saw as being ugly.

Now they felt an overwhelming need to cover up and hide that which had previously been open and visible. "So they sewed fig leaves together and made coverings for themselves."

Verse 8: *"Then the man and his wife heard the sound of the Lord God as he was walking in the garden in the cool of the day, and they hid from the Lord God among the trees of the garden."* Whereas before, Adam and Eve delighted in the presence of the Lord and looked forward eagerly to walking and talking with God in the cool of the day, now they are guilty and afraid and ran and tried to hide themselves from God.

The English language does not accurately convey the intensity of their action in hiding; in Hebrew it means something like "they scrambled around feverishly" trying to hide from God.

The philosophers of the world picture mankind as searching for God, writing books with such titles as *Man's Search for God* or *The Eternal Quest*. However, that is a false picture. The truth is that mankind is not eagerly searching for God, but on the contrary trying desperately to get away from him; not seeking him, but running to escape from him. Otherwise, why would God tell us over and over in his Holy Word to seek him, to seek his face? The fact that God has to tell us that shows that it is not something we do naturally.

Verse 9: *"But the Lord God called to the man, 'Where are you?'"* God knew where Adam was; He was not asking for information. When God called to Adam "Where are you?" he was summoning him into court, calling on him to present himself before the Court of the Lord for judgment.

For many reasons, we sinful humans try to hide from God, but we cannot hide from him (Jer. 23:24). He sees all the things we do (Prov. 15:3). He knows where we are and he knows what we have done. He even knows the secrets of our hearts (Ps. 44:21).

Verse 10: *"He [the man] answered, 'I heard You in the garden, and I was afraid because I was naked; so I hid.'"* Guilt has so clouded Adam's mind that he cannot think straight, and his excuses get more and more ridiculous. We can see this so clearly with our children. When they are caught doing something wrong, they come up with the most outlandish excuses. When we adults are caught in a sin, our excuses are more complicated and sophisticated than children's, but they are just as absurd.

If you were to interview convicted criminals in prison, often they have the most intricate and complicated stories about how they happened to be arrested even though it wasn't their fault and they were victims of circumstance. They just "happened to be in the wrong place at the wrong time," they say.

It is so easy for us sinners to spot lies and excuses other people give for their sins, but it is hard for us to accept and confess our own fault and guilt.

Verse 11: *"And he [God] said, 'Who told you that you were naked? Have you eaten from the tree that I commanded you not to eat from?'"* "It is as if God said: 'You know that you are naked, and for this reason you hid. But your nakedness is My creation. You are not condemning it as something shameful, are you? Therefore, it was not the nakedness that perplexed you, it was not My voice that frightened you; but your conscience convicted you of sin because you ate the fruit from the forbidden tree ... [Adam] was now terrified by God's voice, which previously he had heard with the utmost pleasure."[44]

Verse 12: *"The man said, 'The woman You put here with me—she gave me some fruit from the tree, and I ate it.'"* Under the pressure of being accused by God, which Adam in his conscience knew was a true accusation, now he is squirming and trying to come up with some explanation.

Adam points the finger at Eve and tries to shift the blame to her. He is willing to sacrifice her to save himself. He is willing to let her bear the punishment alone rather than honestly and manfully admitting his own guilt

Adam's sin goes much deeper than that. In effect, he is blaming God himself for his sin. Adam says, in effect, "God, You are at fault, because if You had not created the woman, she would not have given me the fruit, and I would not have eaten it." This is the height of presumption and blasphemy: to blame God for our sin, to accuse God of being the author of evil and sin in the world.

"This is the last step of sin, to insult God and to charge him with being the originator of sin."[55]

Verse 13: *"Then the Lord God said to the woman, 'What is this you have done?'"* God knew what she had done. She was before the Court of God's justice, charged like Adam with violating God's commandment. God put the question to her not to gain information, but to give her an opportunity to plead to the charge. When we are confronted and accused by our conscience of violating God's law, the issue is the same for us as it was for Eve: Are we guilty or not guilty?

Verse 13b: *"The woman said, 'The serpent deceived me, and I ate.'"* Like Adam, Eve does not admit and acknowledge her guilt; she pleads "not guilty" and tries to turn God's attention away from herself, pointing the finger of blame at the serpent. In effect, she says, "I couldn't help it. The serpent deceived me. The devil made me do it." Underlying her excuse is the implied accusation that if God had not created the serpent, it would not have been there to deceive her, and she would not have sinned. Today we might try to evade our responsibility by saying, "After all, I'm only human!"

This is the same abominable sin Adam had committed: to say that the All-Good, All-Wise, All-Loving God is the originator of sin. Like Adam, Eve's sin has become exceedingly, deeply, and profoundly sinful.

Verse 14: *"So the Lord God said to the serpent, 'Because you have done this, Cursed are you above all the livestock and all the wild animals!'"* The curse on the serpent will be finally and completely executed at the end of time when the devil will be thrown into the lake of burning sulfur where he will be tormented day and night forever and ever (Rev. 20:10). The devil's immediate punishment is this:

Verse 14b: *"'You will crawl on your belly and you will eat dust all the days of your life.'"* The serpent had originally been a four-footed wild animal, a "beast of the field," "a most beautiful little animal."[66] Now as punishment for its part in the sin of Adam and Eve, the serpent is changed into a snake that crawls on the ground, a creature which the vast majority of humanity finds to be extremely repulsive. Its attractive beauty is changed to repulsive ugliness. It is brought down from being upright on its four feet to slithering on the ground. It is fascinating that even today, many varieties of snakes have small vestigial feet attached to their spines inside their bodies.

Verse 15 is discussed later.

Verse 16: "*To the woman he [God] said: 'I will greatly increase your pains in childbearing; with pain you will give birth to children.'*" Producing offspring was a blessing from God before the Fall (Gen.1:28). However, with sin having entered the world, the nature of childbirth has changed. In the Garden of Eden, birthing a child would evidently have been a simple and relatively painless matter. However, now after the Fall, it becomes a much more painful and difficult process for the human mother. By contrast with the animals, such as cats and dogs, the kittens or pups usually seem to simply pop out of the mother's body easily and naturally.

Childbirth has also become a dangerous thing for women. In olden days, it was not unusual for women to die in childbirth. Even today, with modern medicine, injurious complications or death still sometimes occur.

Some Bible scholars think that words translated "greatly increase" or "greatly multiply" the woman's pain with regard to child-bearing refer not only to the process of delivering children but also to the sorrow and sighing and pain involved in raising them.[77]

The consequences of sin for the woman continue:
Verse 16b: God said: "*'Your desire will be for your husband, and he will rule over you'*"[87] (NIV). According to Dr. Walter Kaiser, eminent Old Testament scholar, a more accurate translation of the Hebrew words would be this: "You are turning away (from God) to your husband, and (as a result) he will rule over you (take advantage of you)."[98] Whichever translation is correct, the

point is that because of sin, the closeness and unity of the sexes and their right relationship to God and to each other have been drastically changed and impaired, to the detriment and injury of the woman.

Verse 17 and 18: *"To Adam he [God] said, 'Because you listened to your wife and ate from the tree about which I commanded you, "You must not eat of it," cursed is the ground because of you; through painful toil you will eat of it all the days of your life. It will produce thorns and thistles for you, and you will eat the plants of the field.'"* Adam sinned by not listening to what God said and heeding it, but rather listening to his wife and doing what she suggested. Also, he sinned in not exercising his God-given dominion over the serpent and commanding it to go away.

The consequences of his sin affected the man in one of the most vulnerable areas of his life: his work. Even before the Fall the man had work to do, dressing, keeping, and tending the fruit trees in the Garden. Then, it was satisfying and productive work; now, it will be difficult and frustrating toil. Before, his task was easy: gathering the abundant and delicious fruit God had provided. Now, his task is difficult: he has to work hard to produce food for himself and his family. And his work is hard and frequently non-productive; the ground will produce thorns and thistles rather than the grains and vegetables they would need for food outside the Garden.

God here curses the ground because of Adam's sin. We Christians in the 21st century should have a more profound understanding of this verse than all the generations that have gone before us. This is because of our deepened and much more extensive knowledge of the interconnection between mankind and the physical environment. Because of our mismanagement of God's creation, the ground, the water supply, the oceans, and the air and atmosphere are becoming increasingly polluted and poisoned. We are fouling our own nest. Our environment is being cursed because of our sin.

Verse 19: *"By the sweat of your brow you will eat your food until you return to the ground, since from it you were taken; for dust you are and to dust you will return."* As a result of sin, the nature of man's work changes from the easy matter of gathering abundant and delicious fruit to the hard, sweaty, difficult toil of wresting food from the accursed ground.

Not only that, but the original relationship of mankind to the earth is changed. Before the Fall, mankind had been immortal, having free and unhindered access to the Tree of Life; now, we are afflicted with mortality. We will die. God originally created humanity from the dust of the earth intending that we live forever; now he decrees that we must return to the dust from which we came. Our bodies were originally created incorruptible; now they are corruptible, as we age and our bodies deteriorate, and then finally when we die and lie in the bonds of death and decay.

Verse 20: *"Adam named his wife Eve, because she would become the mother of all the living."* Here, for the first time, the woman is given a proper name, Eve, which means "the mother of all the living." Interestingly, based on DNA studies, more and more life scientists are coming to believe that all human beings originally descended from one woman.

Notice a most significant thing here: God has given Adam and Eve a reprieve on the execution of their sentence. The human race would continue; Eve would be the mother of all the living. Originally, God had said that if they ate the forbidden fruit, on the very day that they did so, they would surely die. It is not stated explicitly, but it is implicit that God had changed his mind so that they not die immediately. Adam lived 930 years before he died (Gen. 5:5). In a number of passages of Scripture God is said to change his mind, to repent, to relent, but in each and every one of these passages, when God changes his mind, it is always without exception in the direction of mercy and blessing. It is his nature to have mercy (2 Chr. 30:9).

Here the Almighty Judge has graciously and mercifully granted Adam and Eve a delay. Yes, they would die, but not that very day.

Verse 21: *"The Lord God made garments of skin for Adam and his wife and clothed them."* God showed his heart of love and mercy toward mankind in this simple, practical act of making clothes for them from animal skins to replace the flimsy fig leaves they had hurriedly patched together for themselves. Apparently, the weather was colder outside the Garden and they would need clothes for their protection and comfort.

God is merciful and loving toward us even when we are in sin and rebellion against him. He loves us with an everlasting love (Jer. 31:3).

Verse 22: *"And the Lord God said, 'The man has now become like one of us, knowing good and evil. He must not be allowed to reach out his hand and take also from the tree of life and eat, and live forever.'"* This is one of verses which show that the doctrine of the Holy Trinity is prefigured in the Old Testament: *"like one of us."* One name for God in these early chapters of Genesis in Hebrew is *elohim* which is itself a plural word, literally meaning "mighty ones," often translated "gods." Although God is One in essence and being, there is a plurality of persons within the being of God: One God in three Persons, Father, Son and Holy Spirit.

God in his mercy had intended that mankind know only good; but in our sin and rebellion, we insisted on knowing evil as well as good. This made us like God in a limited sense, but we have to bear the consequences.

Verse 23: *"So the Lord God banished him from the Garden of Eden to work the ground from which he had been taken."* Now mankind is banished from the Garden of Eden and sent out into the cold, cruel world where he will have to toil and suffer. But God is still with us, even in the midst of our misery and sin.

Traditionally, God's banishment of mankind from the Garden of Eden has been seen as punishment for sin. However, there is another possible interpretation. Rather than being punitive, God's action was motivated by his love and mercy, for if mankind had continued to have access to the Tree of Life, we would likely have been content to live in our sin forever.

But God had something far better in mind for us: to live free of sin for eternity, restored to the fullness of life he originally intended us to have.

Verse 24: *"After he drove the man out, he placed on the east side of the Garden of Eden cherubim and a flaming sword flashing back and forth to guard the way to the tree of life."* Mankind is banished from the Garden and can never return there. Once we have lost our innocence, we cannot recover it. The gate to the Garden is shut and guarded by heavenly warriors and by a flaming sword which flashes every which way, to keep us from returning to the Garden, the state of original innocence.

By losing access to the Tree of Life, not only did mankind become subject to death, but also became subject to sickness and disease. The Bible tells us in other passages that the leaves of the Tree of Life were for healing (Ezek. 47:12; "the leaves of the tree are for the healing of the nations" Rev. 22:2). Being banished from the Garden, mankind no longer has access to the healing leaves of the Tree of Life and thus is subject to sickness and disease, and eventually to death.

[Note: This does not mean that if an individual person becomes sick, he or she is necessarily being punished for his or her particular sins. Jesus himself made this point very clear when he saw a man blind from birth. His disciples asked why the man had been born blind, whether it was the result of his own sins or those of his parents. Jesus replied that neither of those alternatives was true (Jn. 9:1–3; *see also*, Lk. 13:1–5). But it does mean that if mankind had not sinned, the human race would not be subject to sickness and disease.]

EFFECTS OF THE FALL: SUMMARY

The sin of Adam and Eve ("The Fall"), opening the door for sin to enter the world, has resulted in separation and broken relationships:

> *(1) Between God and Mankind:* The close and intimate relationship between mankind and God has been broken. Whereas,

originally, mankind rejoiced in the presence of God, as Adam and Eve looked forward eagerly and expectantly to walking and talking with God in the cool of the day, now they are separated from him and try to hide from him. Our sins and iniquities have separated us from God and have become barriers between us and him (Is. 59:2). Our sins have separated us from God, the source of goodness and blessing (Jer. 5:25).

(2) Between Man and Woman: The close and intimate relationship between man and woman has been distorted and corrupted. Suspicion has replaced trust; blame and recrimination have replaced unity. Instead of mutual delight in each other, now they have problems in their relationship, even in their sexual intimacy. Instead of being "joint heirs of the grace of life," they are now competitors, each trying to rule over the other and impose his or her will upon the other. They are not in the mutually loving relationship God intended them to have and which they had enjoyed in the Garden of Eden at first.

(3) Between Mankind and Nature: Sin has led mankind to pollute the environment that we were appointed to manage as trustees of God's good creation. ["Cursed is the ground because of you."] Women suffer in the process of pregnancy and the birthing and raising of children. Men's work has largely become toilsome and frustrating, rather than fruitful and enjoyable. Human beings are now subject to sickness, disease, and infirmity, since they no longer have access to the Tree of Life whose leaves are for healing. Then, finally, the ultimate separation of mankind from nature: death. Since mankind no longer has access to the Tree of Life, they are now subject to death.

THE CORRUPTION OF HUMAN NATURE:

Effect of the Fall on Successive Generations

Through the sin of Adam and Eve, human nature has been deformed and corrupted. The image of God in which mankind was created has not been completely obliterated but has been severely impaired. The Fall has adversely affected not only our bodies, but also our souls, our minds, our emotions, and our wills.

And this corruption has been passed on to all successive generations. How has the deadly disease of sin been transmitted from Adam and Eve to all the rest of mankind? There is a great deal we do not understand: it is a mystery. But God has revealed some clues to us: because all human beings are descendants of Adam and Eve, we have all inherited this corruption in our nature, this inclination toward evil and away from good. Western Christianity calls this "original sin;" Eastern Christianity calls it "the ancestral curse." This dread and deadly condition is like a genetic disorder, a congenital defect, passed down to us from our ancestors along with all of our other genetically acquired characteristics.

What does this disease-like condition called "sin" or "sinfulness" look like? St. Paul gives us a partial description of its symptoms, its outward manifestations, in a list of what he calls "the works of the flesh":

> "adultery, fornication, uncleanness, licentiousness, idolatry, sorcery, hatred, contentions, jealousies, outbursts of wrath, selfish ambitions, dissensions, heresies, envy, murders, drunkenness, revelries, and the like."
>
> (Gal. 5:19–21)

The Apostle Paul, quoting Scriptures, points out emphatically that all of humanity is under the power of sin, and it is not a pretty picture:

> "There is no one who is righteous, not even one;
> there is no one who has understanding,
> there is no one who seeks God.
> All have turned aside, together they have become worthless;
> there is no one who shows kindness, there is not even one."
> "Their throats are opened graves;
> they use their tongues to deceive."
> "The venom of vipers is under their lips."
> "Their mouths are full of cursing and bitterness."
> "Their feet are swift to shed blood;
> ruin and misery are in their paths,
> and the way of peace they have not known."
> "There is no fear of God before their eyes."
>
> (Rom. 3:10–18, NRSV)

How widespread is this defect and corruption of human nature? It is universal. "[A]ll have sinned and fall short of the glory of God." (Rom. 3:23, NKJV). "They have all gone astray, they are all alike perverse; there is no one who does good, no, not one" (Ps.14:3, NRSV).

However, we must point out the one and only exception to the otherwise universal corruption of human nature by sin: the Lord Jesus Christ. He and he alone is the only human being to be without sin (Heb. 4:15), for he always did what was pleasing to God the Father (Jn.8:29).

How deep does this corruption go into our human nature? It goes to the very core, the very heart, of our being. "The heart is devious above all else; it is perverse—who can understand it?" (Jer. 17:9, NRSV). "[T]he Lord saw that the wickedness of man was great in the earth, and that every intent of the thoughts of his heart was only evil continually" (Gen. 6:5). Jesus, God in human flesh, said:

> "For it is from within, from the human heart, that evil intentions come: fornication, theft, murder, adultery, avarice, wickedness, deceit, licentiousness, envy, slander, pride, folly. All these evil things come from within, and they defile a person."
>
> (Mk. 7:21–23, NRSV)

Jesus certainly believed in the truth we call "original sin." In the Sermon on the Mount, he said: "If *you* then, *who are evil,* know how to give good gifts to your children, how much more will your Father in heaven give good things to those who ask him!" (Mt. 7:11, NRSV, emphasis added. *See also,* Lk.11:13).

We only need to read the daily newspaper or watch the news on television to see the truth of the biblical picture of what fallen, sinful human nature looks like.

In the midst of this dark picture, we need to point out that human nature in its essence remains basically good, although corrupted by sin. The reason it remains basically and essentially good is that a good God has created it. God has not wavered from his love toward his sinful people. He remains merciful to us, even when we are in rebellious sin. Our human nature has become corrupted from its original innocence, but it is redeemable.

Without God's grace, we are helpless and hopeless, dead in transgressions and sins (Eph. 2:1). Only God can bring us out of our death into life (Ezek. chapter 37; Rom. 4:17).

And he has promised to do exactly that for those who believe in Jesus Christ, his only begotten Son.

D
GOD'S PROMISE OF SALVATION

Verse 15: God said to the serpent: *"And I will put enmity between you and the woman, and between your offspring and hers; he will crush your head, and you will strike his heel."*

God said this to the serpent, but for the benefit of Adam and Eve, to give them (and us) hope in the midst of distress.

This verse has a far deeper meaning than simply the truism that most women hate snakes, although it is generally true that women hate snakes and snakes are afraid of people. God put hatred between the woman Eve who is the "mother of all the living" and the serpent, the destroyer who would try to kill all of the children of Eve by his malignant, evil poison, if he could. And this enmity and lifelong struggle between the offspring (literally, *seed,* plural) of the serpent and the Offspring (literally, *Seed,* singular) of the woman would persist until the Day of Redemption.

Here in the midst of God's pronouncement of judgment on the serpent, the ground, and the human race, he gives a magnificent promise and prophecy of hope to fallen humanity. When God's time is right, he will send forth One who will be his Son and the Son of the Woman. The Church throughout the ages has seen this verse as a prophecy of the coming of Jesus Christ into the world, for he was the Offspring of the Virgin Mary, conceived by the Holy Spirit, with no participation by any male descended from sinful Adam.

"But when the fullness of the time had come, God sent forth his Son, born of a woman, born under the law" (Gal. 4:4, NKJV. *See also,* Rev. 12:13–17).

This Offspring of God and the woman will crush the serpent's head, although he will be bruised by the serpent striking his heel. In his life and ministry, Jesus defeated the devil in many skirmishes. But the decisive battle took place in Jesus' sufferings and death on the cross where the devil did indeed injure his heel when he was nailed to the cross. And the devil inflicted far more injuries upon Jesus, not only to his heel, but to his head with the crown of thorns, to his face and body by being beaten and flogged, by the nails in his hands, and by the spear wound in his side. But not one of Jesus' bones was broken.

And Jesus won the decisive victory over the devil by his death on the cross and his glorious Resurrection and opened the way for us fallen sons and daughters of Adam and Eve to be restored to a right relationship with God and with each other and to enjoy eternal life with God forever.

Long centuries before the cosmic victory was won, God gave humanity hope by the promise and prophecy in the 15th verse of the third chapter of Genesis. God himself would provide a way for men and women to be saved from their own sins as well as from the congenital sin they inherited from their original ancestors.

Introduction to Parts Three, Four, and Five
God Saving: Past, Present, and Future

As we consider the Scriptures dealing with salvation, we find that the New Testament speaks of salvation in terms of being Past, Present and Future: we have been saved, we are being saved, and we will be saved. Salvation in these three time dimensions is the subject of Parts Three, Four and Five of this book.

Salvation in the past: Our salvation is firmly based on historical facts that happened at a particular place and time in human history. The foundation of our salvation is what Jesus did for us in his life, ministry, death, resurrection, and ascension. It is basic to the Christian faith that Jesus lived a real life on this earth at a definite time and place in human history: born of the Virgin Mary; preaching, teaching, healing, working miracles, and training his followers; suffering and dying "under Pontius Pilate"; being raised from the dead; and then ascending back into the heavenly glory from which he had come to earth.

Although every aspect of Jesus' life and ministry is important, in the New Testament the focus is on Jesus' death on the cross for our salvation. It tells us over and over again that we have been saved by the "blood of Jesus Christ." That is what has accomplished our salvation.

Here are a few of the many references:

- "... having now been justified by his blood, we shall be saved from wrath through him. For if when we were enemies we were reconciled to God through the death of his Son ... we shall be saved by his life." (Rom. 5:9,10)
- "In him we have redemption through his blood, the forgiveness of sins ..." (Eph. 1:7)
- "... having made peace through the blood of his cross." (Col. 1:20)
- "... the blood of Jesus Christ his Son cleanses us from all sin." (1 Jn. 1:7)

The Book of Hebrews emphasizes the finished work of Christ on the cross by using a Greek word translated *"once for all,"* meaning that the death of Jesus on the cross took place in human history once for all time and never needs to be repeated, as it is forever effective to cleanse us from sin and bring us salvation (Heb. 7:27; 9:12; 10:10).

Just before Jesus died on the cross, he cried, "It is finished!" (Jn. 19:30). His great work of bearing the sins of mankind on the cross, making the one and only full, perfect, and eternally sufficient sacrifice for the forgiveness of sin, was done, accomplished, completed.

Once a bishop of the Orthodox Church was asked the question, "Have you been saved?" "'I have,' he replied. "'And when were you saved?' he was asked. The bishop replied immediately, 'On a Friday afternoon at three o'clock in the spring of the year 33 AD on a hill outside the City of Jerusalem.'"[109]

In a real sense, salvation is in the past tense because we have been saved by what Jesus did for us. However, the salvation that Jesus won must be applied to us individually in the present time, here and now. The thing that connects our lives here and now, in the present, with the salvation Jesus has won for us in the past is faith working in our hearts by the Holy Spirit. So salvation has a present tense, as well as a past tense

Salvation in the present: The Lord Jesus said that "he who hears My word and believes in him who sent Me has everlasting life," here and now. (Jn. 5:24). The Apostle Paul tells us that we "are being saved" (1 Cor.1:18; 2 Cor. 2:15); that "now is the day of salvation" (2 Cor. 6:2); that "having been justified by faith, we have peace with God through our Lord Jesus Christ" (Rom. 5:1). St. Luke tells us that "the Lord added to the church daily those who were being saved" (Acts 2:47).

Salvation in the present tense is when the forgiveness of sins accomplished for us by Jesus' death on the cross is applied to our lives here and now in the present through faith. But our salvation is not complete here in this life; its fullness will take place in the future. It is not until Jesus' Second Coming that our salvation will be consummated and perfected.

Salvation in the future: The Lord Jesus told us more than

once that "He who endures to the end will be saved" (Mt. 10:22, 24:13), and that if we are faithful unto death, he will give us a crown of life. (Rev. 2:10). The Apostle Peter said that our salvation will be revealed in the last time (1 Pet. 1:5). The Apostle James tells us that the believing Jews will be saved through the grace of the Lord Jesus, just as the believing Gentiles will (Acts 15:11). The Apostle Paul also speaks of salvation in the future, at the Last Day (Rom. 5:9–10. *See also,* 1 Cor. 5:5; 1 Thes. 5:8–9). The Book of Hebrews also speaks of salvation in future terms for "those who will inherit salvation" (Heb.1:14).

Accordingly, Part III of this book will deal with salvation in the past, centered in Jesus Christ and what he has done to save us, in his life, ministry, death, resurrection, and ascension. Part IV will deal with salvation in the present, that is, how the salvation Jesus won for us is applied to our lives here and now, centered in the work of the Holy Spirit. Part V will deal with our salvation which will be completed in the future at the Last Day, when the Lord Jesus returns to earth, raises the dead, and judges all people, concluding with their entering either hell or heaven.

Part Three:
God has Saved His People

Since human nature had become corrupted through sin in the Fall, in order for God to save us, it was necessary for God to enter into our human nature and come to earth as a human being. But he could not accomplish this through the conception of a child in the normal way, through the union of sperm from a human father with the egg (*ovum*) of a human mother, for a child conceived in the normal human manner would be subject to the corruption and defilement of inherited sin resulting from the sin of Adam and Eve. The way God worked it out to enter human life without the corruption and defilement of inherited (original) sin was by means of the Virgin Birth.

THE VIRGIN BIRTH OF JESUS CHRIST

St. Luke's Gospel tells us what happened to Mary (Lk. 1:26–38). God sent his messenger, the Angel Gabriel, to the little town of Nazareth, to a young woman, a virgin named Mary, who was betrothed to be married to a man named Joseph who was a carpenter. Joseph was a direct descendant of King David, and possibly Mary herself was also. Betrothal (engagement) in those days was a binding legal contract, as binding as marriage itself, and could only be ended by death of one of the parties or by divorce.

It is amazing how God works! Nazareth was a small village of about a dozen houses, archeologists tell us. Mary was probably a teenage girl, as women were quite young when they were married in Bible times. And Mary and Joseph were poor people, as we know from other references.

The Angel Gabriel appeared to Mary and greeted her. Naturally, she was upset and perplexed at this visit of a Messenger directly from heaven. The angel reassured her: "Do not be afraid, Mary, for you have found favor with God" (v. 30). Then Gabriel procceded to give her astounding news:

"And behold, you will conceive in your womb and bring forth a Son, and shall call his name *Jesus*. He will be great, and will be called the Son of the Highest; and the Lord God will give him the throne of his father David. And he will reign over the house of Jacob forever, and of his kingdom there will be no end."

(Lk. 1:31–33)

Mary was understandably perplexed. "How can this be," Mary asked, "since I do not know a man?" (v.34).

Gabriel explained that the Holy Spirit would come upon her, and the power of the Most High would overshadow her (just as the cloud of the Glory of God, the *Shekinah*, overshadowed the Tabernacle in the wilderness, filled the Temple of God in Jerusalem, and later overshadowed Jesus in the Transfiguration). Mary's womb would become the Tabernacle of the Most High God to contain God's only-begotten Son.

Therefore, the Angel explained, "… that Holy One who is to be born will be called the Son of God" (v.35). To strengthen her faith that nothing is impossible with God (v. 37), Gabriel reminded Mary of the miracle which was happening to her relative Elizabeth who in her old age had conceived her first child [John the Baptizer] (v.36).

Then in tremendous faith and obedience, Mary accepted God's will for her: "Behold the maidservant of the Lord! Let it be to me according to your word" (v.38).

By Mary's obedience to God and her belief in his message to her through the Angel Gabriel, God's plan for reversing the disobedience of Adam and Eve and for overcoming the effects of their rebellion was set in motion. God's work for the salvation and redemption of sinful fallen humanity began to take form and shape in the human flesh and body of Jesus as he began to develop and grow in Mary's womb.

St. Matthew tells us what happened to Joseph, betrothed to be Mary's husband (Mt. 1:18–25). When he found out that Mary was pregnant, at first he was shocked and decided to divorce her quietly, for he was a good-hearted man and did not want to disgrace Mary or endanger her life. Death by stoning was the penalty for adultery under the Law of Moses.

> "But while he thought about these things, behold, an angel of the Lord appeared to him in a dream, saying, 'Joseph, son of David, do not be afraid to take to you Mary your wife, for that which is conceived in her is of the Holy Spirit. And she will bring forth a Son, and you shall call his name *Jesus*, for he will save his people from their sins."
>
> (Mt. 1:20–21)

Joseph, too, had his part in fulfilling God's plan for the salvation and redemption of the human race by entering human life through the miraculous conception of the Child Jesus by a virgin, foretold long ago by the prophet Isaiah (Is. 7:14).

Like Mary, Joseph believed God's message from an angel and was obedient, for when he awoke from sleep, he did as the angel of the Lord had commanded him. He took Mary as his wife, and they began living together as husband and wife, but he "did not know her [have marital relations with her] till she had brought forth her firstborn Son. And he called his name *Jesus*" (Mt. 1:24–25).

It is amazing how God works! He chose an obscure, poor Jewish couple living in an obscure, small village in Galilee to begin his mighty work of saving and redeeming lost and fallen humanity. But he also works through the high and mighty rulers of this world to accomplish his purposes, such as Caesar Augustus, Emperor of Rome (ruled 44 BC to AD 14).

In God's plan and purpose, it was necessary for the Messiah, the Savior of the world, to be born in Bethlehem in order to fulfill the prophecy of Micah 5:2–5. Yet Mary and Joseph lived in Nazareth in Galilee. The circumstance that God used to get Mary and Joseph from Nazareth to Bethlehem for the birth of the Messiah was this: Caesar Augustus issued a decree that everyone living in the Roman Empire must be enrolled (for purposes of taxation) (Lk. 2:1). For purposes of this census, each Jewish family was required to return to the husband's family home to be registered. So Joseph and Mary traveled from Nazareth to Bethlehem, the ancestral home of Joseph's ancestor King David, and it was while they were there that Mary's child was born.

The biblical record gives us sparse but poignant details of Jesus' birth. The town was so full of visitors that the inn was full to overflowing. So Joseph and Mary stayed in a stable, probably a cave in the side of a hill, and it was there that Jesus was born. Mary wrapped him in strips of linen cloths according to the Jewish custom, and placed him in a manger, an animal food trough, for his cradle (Lk. 2:4–7).

The night of Jesus' birth, an amazing thing happened in a field outside Bethlehem where shepherds were tending their sheep. An angel of the Lord stood before them, and the glory of the Lord's presence shined around them. Naturally, they were terrified. Then the angel spoke to them, saying:

> "Do not be afraid, for behold, I bring you good tidings of great joy which will be to all people. For there is born to you this day in the city of David a Savior, who is Christ the Lord. And this will be the sign to you: You will find a Babe wrapped in swaddling cloths, lying in a manger."
>
> (Lk. 2:10–12)

This was absolutely amazing that a messenger directly from God would appear to these shepherds, for at that time in Judaism, shepherds were considered ritually unclean and could not even set foot in the Temple to worship God because they did not keep God's laws. Their work required their constant presence with the sheep in their charge and they could not go to the synagogue to worship God on the Sabbath. Furthermore, they were migrant workers and often accused of stealing as they went from place to place.

"And suddenly there was with the angel a multitude of the heavenly host praising God and saying:

"Glory to God in the highest,
And on earth peace,
Good will toward men!"

(Lk. 2:13–14)

When the angels had left them to return to heaven, the shepherds decided to go immediately to Bethlehem to see this amazing thing that had happened which the Lord had made known to them. So they hurried to Bethlehem, and found Mary and Joseph, and the Baby lying in the manger (Lk. 2:15–16).

These despised shepherds became in a sense the first evangelists, because everywhere they went they told everyone the news that God's messenger had told them about this Child, Whom they had seen with their own eyes (Lk. 2:17).

God had entered human life as a Person who was really, fully and truly human and at the same time was really, fully and truly God. This is the mystery we call "the Incarnation," (literally, the "enfleshment"). God himself had come to earth in human flesh to begin his rescue operation, to save and redeem lost, fallen, and sinful humanity.

"For God so loved the world that he gave his only begotten Son, that whoever believes in him should not perish but have everlasting life" (Jn. 3:16).

B
JESUS' HIDDEN YEARS

We know only a few facts about Jesus' life between his birth and age thirty when he began his public ministry, but what little we know is highly significant.

Evidently, the Holy Family stayed in Bethlehem for some time after Jesus was born. Before Jesus was two years old, Wise Men (*magi*, astrologers) came from the East to find the Child born to be King of the Jews, as they had determined from the rising of an extraordinary star which signified the birth of a child destined to be a great king.

They went first to Jerusalem to the court of King Herod and asked where the royal heir had been born. Their question threw Herod and his advisers into consternation. The Jewish scribes gave the Magi the information that the Messiah was to be born at Bethlehem (Micah 5:2). The Magi, following the star, then went to Bethlehem and found Mary and the Baby Jesus. They worshipped him and gave him gifts of gold, frankincense, and myrrh (Mt. 2:1–12). [The Holy Family was then living in a house (v. 11), whereas Jesus' birth had taken place in a stable. Lk. 2:7).]

In his jealous rage and fear of this rival king, Herod ordered all the male children in Bethlehem and its vicinity two years old and under to be killed. However, God warned Joseph in a dream, and Joseph took his wife Mary and the Child Jesus and fled in the nighttime to Egypt (Mt. 2:13–18), where they lived until King Herod died. Then in response to another angel visitation in a dream, Joseph took Mary and the Child Jesus back to the land of Israel to the little village of Nazareth, where Jesus grew up (Mt. 2:19–23).

In God's plan and purpose, it was necessary that the Savior, the Messiah, be born in Bethlehem but to grow up in Nazareth approximately seventy-five miles distant. The reason was to fulfill two ancient prophecies (Jer. 23:5 and Is.11:1) that use Hebrew words for the Messiah that sound like "Nazarene." "And he [Joseph] came and dwelt in a city called Nazareth, that it might be fulfilled which was spoken by the prophets, 'He shall be called a Nazarene'" (Mt. 2:23).

During his formative years, Jesus learned the Aramaic language commonly spoken in Palestine at that time. He also learned Hebrew, the ancient language of the Jewish people, and became extremely well versed in the Holy Scriptures of the Old Testament. He probably committed the entire Scriptures of the Old Covenant to memory, as many rabbis have done up to the present time. He may also have learned some Greek which was commonly spoken by many of the peoples living in the Mediterranean lands at that time.[10]

The townspeople of Nazareth had no inkling that Jesus was any special person; they thought that Joseph the carpenter was his father (Mt. 13:55; Lk. 3:23; Jn. 6:42). However, in the privacy of their home, Mary and Joseph must have told Jesus their family secret as to his miraculous conception and birth. As a boy growing up, Jesus must have spent many hours in prayer and meditation about his unique relationship with God the Father and what that meant for his life.

During those private years, Jesus learned the trade of carpentry from Joseph and worked at it until it was time for him to begin his public ministry (Mk. 6:3).

When he was twelve years old, Jesus went with his family from Nazareth to Jerusalem for the Passover celebration, and for his Bar Mitzvah. When the family started their journey home, Jesus stayed behind in the Temple, "sitting in the midst of the teachers, both listening to them and asking them questions. And all who heard him were astonished at his understanding and answers" (Lk. 2:46–47). When Mary and Joseph discovered Jesus was not with the group traveling home, they went back to Jerusalem, a three days' journey, and were astonished to find him in the Temple. Jesus asked them why they were looking for him: "Did you not know that I must be about My Father's business?" (Lk. 2:49: alternate translation: "Didn't you know that I must be in My Father's house?" RSV). They didn't understand. However, Jesus went back home with them to Nazareth and was obedient to them.

During his entire life, Jesus was an orthodox, fully observant Jew. He lived a life of complete obedience to the Law of God, in every respect. Here are some Scriptural references:

- When he was born, his mother Mary wrapped him in "swaddling cloths" according to Jewish custom (Lk. 2:7). These were strips of cloth like bandages four or five inches wide and five or six yards long, to bind the baby's arms and legs.[11] (*See* Ezekiel 16:4)

- Jesus was circumcised on the 8th day of his life as required by the Law of Moses, and given the name Jesus (Lk. 2:21). Thus, he became *B'nai Brith,* a "son of the Covenant."

- He was presented to the Lord in the Temple at Jerusalem when he was 33 days old, as required by the Jewish Law (Lk. 2:22,23; Leviticus ch.12)

- We know by implication that Jesus received a thorough education in the Jewish Scriptures (our Old Testament) and customs. He memorized large portions of those Scriptures and may have committed the entire Old Testament to memory.

- When he was twelve years old, his Bar Mitzvah was observed in the Temple at Jerusalem (Lk. 2:41–51). Here he became *Bar Mitzvoth,* a "son of the Law," whereby as an adult he bound himself to observe the Law of God.
- He habitually worshipped in the Synagogue on the Sabbath Day. (Lk. 4:16)
- He prayed frequently, as many Gospel references tell us.
- Jesus paid the Temple tax imposed on all adult Jewish men. (Mt. 17:24–27)
- He also worshipped and preached and taught in the Temple at Jerusalem, as many verses tell us.
- Jesus kept the Jewish festivals, such as Passover (Jn. 2:23; Lk. 22:7–13), Tabernacles (Jn. 7:1–14), and Dedication (now known as Hanukkah) (Jn.10:22), as well as other festivals (Jn. 4:45, 5:1).
- After his death on the cross, he was buried "according to the burial customs of the Jews" (Jn.19:40) by Nicodemus and Joseph of Arimathea.

From the New Testament record, there is no doubt that Jesus lived his entire life, from birth to death, as a fully observant Jew, obeying the Law of God in every detail. Thus, he totally and completely fulfilled the Law of God and was righteous before God in every respect, without any sin whatsoever. And for those who believe in him, God credits his righteousness to our account, thus totally nullifying the sins of us unrighteous violators of God's Holy Law. "For Christ is the end [the completion, the fulfillment] of the law for righteousness to everyone who believes" (Rom.10:4).

After his Bar Mitzvah, the next major event in his life, the Scriptures tell us, is when he stepped out of obscurity into the public arena when he was about thirty years of age and came to his cousin John the Baptizer to receive baptism and to begin his public ministry.

JESUS' BAPTISM AND TEMPTATION

The voice of the prophets had been silent for 400 years. For four centuries, no preacher in Israel had come forward bringing a message directly from God himself. Then as unexpectedly as a bolt of lightning out of a cloudless sky, the word of the Lord came to John in the wilderness. "And he went into all the region around the Jordan [River], preaching a baptism of repentance for the remission of sins" (Lk. 3:3).

Crowds flocked to hear his preaching and to be baptized. John the Baptizer told them that he baptized with water, but another was coming, more powerful than he, who would baptize with the Holy Spirit and with fire. Jesus, too, went to the Jordan River to receive the baptism by John. Jesus was without sin and had no need to repent and be baptized for himself, but he did it to identify himself with God's sinful people, receiving baptism on their behalf as he would later go to the cross on their behalf.

St. Luke tells us that after Jesus had been baptized and was praying, coming up out of the water, "the heaven was opened. And the Holy Spirit descended in bodily form like a dove upon him, and a voice came from heaven which said, 'You are My beloved Son; in You I am well pleased'" (Lk. 3:22).

Here Jesus was accepting the life-work for which he had been born, to be the Messiah to save God's people from their sins, to redeem them and set them free. Here the Holy Spirit of God was empowering Jesus for his ministry. Here God the Father was commissioning him for the mighty work he would do to accomplish salvation for mankind.

The voice of God from heaven gave Jesus the mandate to fulfill two different roles foretold for the Messiah by the prophets: (1) to be the King of Israel in the line of David ["You are My Son," Ps. 2:7 which was used in the coronation and enthronement of kings of Israel] and (2) to be the Suffering Servant of the Lord who would be humiliated, beaten, brutalized, and put to death on behalf of God's people so that they might have healing, freedom and life ["Behold! My Servant whom I uphold, My Elect One in whom My soul delights!" Is. 42:1; *See also*, Is. 52:13–53:12].

Immediately after he was baptized, the Holy Spirit drove Jesus into the wilderness where he was tempted by Satan (Mk.1:12–13). In his temptations, Jesus the Messiah was struggling and wrestling with the issue of what methods he would use to fulfill his God-given destiny, of *how h*e would carry out the task of saving the world, of what kind of Messiah he would be.

Jesus fasted forty days and nights, and afterwards he was famished (Mt. 4:2).

The First Temptation: The devil came and said: "If You are the Son of God, command that these stones become bread" (Mt. 4:3). Jesus' first temptation was to doubt God's word that he was indeed the Son of God and to disobey God his Father by using the super-human powers he possessed as God the Son to turn stones into bread. By working spectacular miracles he would attract an enormous following by meeting human needs in a grandiose worldly manner rather than by means of God's Word which would work in and among humanity in the quiet way that yeast leavens bread. In other words, to try to do God's work of salvation in a worldly, ungodly manner. Jesus overcame this temptation by resolving to do his work in God's way, by God's method, through God's Word: "It is written, 'Man shall not live by bread alone, but by every word that proceeds from the mouth of God,'" Jesus said quoting Deuteronomy 8:3.

The Second Temptation: Then the devil took Jesus to Jerusalem, the Holy City, and set him on the highest point of the Temple. The devil said: "If You are the Son of God, throw Yourself down," for the Bible says in Psalm 91 that God will send angels to protect you, so that you will not dash your foot against a stone. This second temptation was for Jesus to distrust God, to seek assurance now, in the present, that God could be trusted to give him the power he would need to have at the moment he would need it in the future; in other words, to seek a miraculous sign from God like Gideon in olden days who did not trust his calling until God worked three miracles with the wool fleece, needing proof before he believed what God had said. The specific form of this temptation was for Jesus to throw himself down from the pinnacle of the Temple to the rocks 400 feet below to see whether God would indeed send angels to save him from harm, as he had promised in Psalm 91. Jesus overcame this temptation by recalling and telling Satan that God had forbidden his people to put him to the test (Dt. 6:16). Jesus resolved that he would live by faith, by believing what God had said and trusting God to give him the power at the very time when he would need it in the future.

The Third Temptation: Now Satan took Jesus to a very high mountain and showed him all the kingdoms of the world and their glory. Jesus' third temptation was to carry out his task as Messiah by means of worldly power and glory, doing God's work but not in God's way, rather by worldly power; in other words, to be disloyal to God his Father. In this temptation, Satan showed Jesus all the kingdoms of the world and their splendor and offered them all to Jesus if he would fall down and worship him. This was no play-acting temptation to Jesus; it was very real. The whole world and all its glory was Satan's to give. True, God had created it, but Satan had usurped and stolen the world from God through the Fall of Man in the Garden of Eden. Satan had the wrongful but real power to give the whole world. Scripture tells us that "the whole world lies under the sway of the wicked one" (1 Jn. 5:19).

Wouldn't it be a tremendous advantage in bringing in God's Kingdom if all the power of the world were available to Jesus? This was a very real temptation to Jesus, for the common expectation of the Jewish people was that when the Messiah came, he would be a glorious king of David's line who would overthrow all their enemies and extend his rule over all the world, for the benefit of God's chosen people Israel. Here again Jesus overcame this temptation by resolving to do things God's way, to be the kind of Messiah that God his Father wanted him to be, namely, the spiritual King of Israel rather than an earthly king. Thus, his kingdom would be extended over all the world to all peoples by means of the Holy Spirit operating through God's word, and not by military might. Jesus told Satan: "Away with you, Satan! For it is written, 'You shall worship the Lord your God, and him only you shall serve'" (Mt. 4:10).

Jesus had won the victory over the tempter. Jesus had determined that he would be the Messiah in the way God his Father wanted him to be, and not in the way the people expected. Jesus had set his course.

D

THE EARTHLY MINISTRY OF JESUS

To cover Jesus' earthly ministry adequately, we would have to reprint all four Gospels. All we can do here is to give a brief summary of various aspects of Jesus' ministry, under these headings: (1) preaching; (2) teaching; (3) healing; (4) casting out evil spirits; (5) exercising power over nature; (6) raising the dead; and (7) training his disciples.

1. JESUS' PREACHING

After his private years of preparation, after he had been baptized by John the Baptizer, after he had faced the temptations in the wilderness in which he had determined that he would be the Messiah that God his Father wanted him to be, Jesus began his public ministry in Galilee, "preaching the gospel of the kingdom of God, and saying, 'The time is fulfilled, and the kingdom of God is at hand. Repent, and believe in the gospel'" (Mk.1:14–15).

Jesus preached that the time the Jewish people had long waited for, the time foretold by the prophets when God would send his Messiah to save his people, had come. The prophecies of the Messiah had been fulfilled. The Kingdom of God had come near. What response did God expect from his people? To repent of their sins, change their minds and hearts, and believe the Good News that God was about to save his people.

The theme of Jesus' preaching was the Kingdom of God.

The Gospels give us accounts of one sermon Jesus preached in the synagogue in his home town, Nazareth (Lk. 4:16–30), and two sermons he preached to the crowds, "The Sermon on the Mount" (Mt. chapters 5–7) and "The Sermon on the Plain" (Lk. 6:17–49).

His best known preaching is "The Sermon on the Mount." It opens with a poem we call "the Beatitudes," in two stanzas of four verses each, where Jesus paints a word portrait of the children of the Kingdom, showing the gracious gifts God wants to bestow upon them.

Then Jesus tells us how a child of the Kingdom will act in certain situations, first, toward his fellow human beings (Mt. 5:21–48), and second, toward God (chapter 6). Here Jesus is showing what it means to obey God's Commandments, to love God and to love others. Jesus explained that God's intentions in his Law go so deep, that keeping his Law requires not merely outward observance but godly motives and purity of heart, that it is impossible, on the human level, to fulfill God's Law. Yet we have no excuse for not doing so, for God requires perfection of his people, and Jesus requires the same of his followers. "Therefore, you shall be perfect, just as your Father in heaven is perfect" (Mt. 5:48).

But has anyone ever been perfect? Has anyone ever been that good and righteous, and can anyone be that good and righteous? Jesus answers no, illustrated by the facts that we humans all judge one another while we should not do so (God is the Judge), and we are all hypocrites who see other people's faults so clearly (the speck in their eye) while we are totally blind to our own faults (the log in our own eye) (Mt. 7:1–5).

Then how can we possibly be righteous in God's sight? The answer Jesus gives is that we cannot, in our own strength. The only way is by God's gracious gift to us, by his grace, his unmerited favor, which we must learn to seek from him in persevering prayer: "Ask [and keep on asking, *the verb forms indicate continuing action*], and it will be given to you; seek [and keep on seeking], and you will find; knock [and keep on knocking], and it will be opened to you" (Mt. 7:7–11).

Jesus concludes the Sermon with four illustrations setting the two ways before us, one way leading to life and blessedness and the other way leading to death and destruction: the narrow gate and the broad gate (Mt. 7:13,14), the good tree and the bad tree (v. 15–19), the true disciple and the self-deceived follower (v. 21–23), and the wise man who builds his house on rock (who hears and acts on the words of Jesus) and the foolish man who builds his house on sand (who hears the words of Jesus but does not act on them) (v. 24–27).

No wonder that when Jesus finished preaching, "the people were astonished at his teaching, for he taught them as one having authority, and not as the scribes (Mt. 7:28–29).

2. JESUS' TEACHING

Without doubt, Jesus was the greatest teacher in the history of the world. Two thousand years after his earthly ministry, every day millions of people throughout the world read, study, and meditate on his teachings. Every week many more millions of people study his teachings in Bible classes and hear sermons expounding and applying the lessons he taught. First, let us consider his method of teaching and then a summary of some aspects of the message he taught.

The Method of Jesus' Teaching

The primary method of Jesus' teaching was to tell parables, stories that demonstrated one or more truths, usually having one main point. Jesus was the absolute master of the narrative story parable. What a great loss it would be to the world's literature if he had not told parables like "The Good Samaritan" and "The

Prodigal Son." The sheer number of Jesus' parables is amazing, about thirty-eight. They deal with a tremendously wide range of human life and activity. Jesus' teaching was so fresh and powerful and memorable it is no wonder the crowds were astounded at his teaching (Mt. 7:28–29; Mk.1:22; Lk. 4:32).

Jesus instructed the crowds who followed him primarily by means of parables (Mt.13:34). Then with his disciples privately, away from the crowds, typically he would explain the parables in discourses, responding to their questions and making certain they understood the teaching (Mk. 4:10–12). The Gospels give us details of three of Jesus' explanations of parables, "The Sower," "The Dragnet," and "The Weeds in the Wheat" (also called "The Wheat and the Tares").

Jesus also taught his disciples in discourses not growing out of parables. The most extensive of these teachings was given on the night he was betrayed, when he was preparing the disciples for his death, found in the Gospel According to St. John, chapters 13–16.

The Message of Jesus' Teaching

Here we can only give a sketch of the content of some of Jesus' teachings. Such an attempt is bound to be woefully inadequate because Jesus' teachings are so broad and so deep.

Jesus' Use of The Old Testament

Jesus' teaching was based squarely and solidly on the Jewish Scriptures, our Old Testament from Genesis to Malachi. Jesus quotes from it verbatim at least forty times, clearly alludes to it another 60 times, and possibly alludes to it another one hundred times. For Jesus, the Holy Scriptures were God's Word and could not be broken nor annulled (Jn. 10:35). Everything written in the Scriptures must be fulfilled, even the dot on every *i* and the crossing of every *t* (Mt. 5:17–18).

Even many of the details of Jesus' earthly life happened "to fulfill the Scriptures," from start to finish, from his virginal conception and birth (Mt.1:22–23) to his Resurrection (Jn. 20:9). In God's plan and purpose, it was necessary that everything written about the Messiah in the entire Old Testament be fulfilled (Lk. 24:44–45). In particular, it was necessary that the Messiah be "The Suffering Servant of the Lord" as written in the prophet Isaiah, that he would be spit upon, mocked, flogged, and be condemned to death, and after three days rise from the dead (Mk. 10:33–34). This was contrary to the common expectation of the people that the Messiah would be a conquering hero who would defeat their enemies and restore the earthly kingdom to Israel with the glory and power it had had in the days of King David, and more than that, to put all the Gentile nations under subjection to Israel.

Jesus frequently quoted Old Testament texts and applied them to himself as being their fulfillment, especially the Messianic passages. Sometimes he applies to himself texts which are not specifically Messianic but which speak of God acting. For example, see Matthew 11:5 fulfilling Isaiah 35:5–6 as to the miracles of the Messiah; Luke 19:10 fulfilling Ezekiel 34:16–22 as to seeking out and saving the lost sheep; and Luke 22:20 ("This cup is the new covenant in My blood, which is shed for you") fulfilling Jeremiah's prophecy of the New Covenant (Jer. 31:31 ff).

Perhaps most surprising is that Jesus applied to himself historical passages from the Old Testament, which are not predictive prophecy at all. In Matthew 12:40–42 Jesus says that like the prophet Jonah was three days and nights in the belly of the great fish, so he will be three days and three nights in the heart of the earth. He also refers to the visit of the Queen of Sheba to King Solomon and says he is greater than Solomon. In his temptation (Mt. 4:1–11), Jesus quotes three texts from Deuteronomy (6:16,13; 8:3) in winning his victory over Satan's temptations. In Mark 12:10,11 Jesus applies Psalm 118:22–23 to himself, that he is the stone the builders rejected which has become the cornerstone of the building.

In Jesus' use of the Old Testament, he shows that he himself is the fulfillment of the prophecies about the Messiah, but more than that, in his very person, life, ministry, sufferings, death, and Resurrection, he is the fulfillment and completion of the entire pattern of God's dealings with his people. All of the Jewish Scriptures and the whole history of Israel come together and focus in Jesus Christ and find their fulfillment in him.

The Time of Fulfillment

Underlying all of Jesus' teachings is the concept that in him, the time of fulfillment has arrived. In him, the Day of the Lord has come. In him, the New Age has dawned. In him, God himself has come to earth in human flesh to be the Messiah, the King of David's line whose reign would last forever, the Shepherd of Israel who would gather together all the lost sheep of God. And not just to be the fulfillment of God's promises for Israel, but to be the Light to enlighten the Gentiles, the One who would call the Gentiles, all the peoples of the earth, into God's gracious kingdom.

Jesus himself announced this theme of fulfillment as the very foundational truth of his ministry: "Jesus came to Galilee, preaching the gospel of the kingdom of God, and saying, 'The time is fulfilled, and the kingdom of God is at hand. Repent, and believe in the gospel.'" (Mk.1:14–15). In Jesus' sermon in his hometown of Nazareth, he took his text from Isaiah 61:1–2a:

> "The Spirit of the Lord is upon Me,
> Because he has anointed Me to preach the gospel to the poor.
> He has sent Me to heal the brokenhearted,
> To preach deliverance to the captives
> And recovery of sight to the blind,
> To set at liberty those who are oppressed,
> To preach the acceptable year of the Lord."
>
> (Lk. 4:18–19)

Then he announced the startling news: "Today this Scripture is fulfilled in your hearing" (Lk. 4:21). He was the Anointed One, the prophet Isaiah had written of.

In Jesus a new era in God's dealings with mankind had begun. The Old Covenant, based on observance of the Law God had given by Moses, was now fulfilled and superseded by God's New Covenant foreseen by the prophet Jeremiah (31:31–34), based on the forgiveness of sins. The Old Passover was fulfilled and superseded in the New Passover inaugurated by Jesus at the Last Supper: "This cup is the new covenant in My blood, which is shed for you" (Lk. 22:20; 1 Cor.11:25).

In Jesus, the day of God's visitation had come, the time when God himself intervened in human life and history, directly and decisively. In Jesus, the old age was passing away and the new life of God's kingdom had begun.

The Overlap of the Ages

One aspect of Jesus' teaching is what we might call "The Overlap of the Ages." This refers to the relationship between the "present age" and the "age to come."

The common expectation of the Jewish people was that when the Messiah came, the present age would instantly pass away and immediately be replaced with the age to come in which all wrongs would be set right, all evil would be banished, and peace and prosperity would reign, the Kingdom of David would be restored, and the Jews would take their rightful place ruling the Gentile nations of the world.

However, in his coming to earth, Jesus the Messiah did fulfill the promises of God but not in the way the people had expected. The old world, the present age, did not immediately pass away.

It is certainly true that in Jesus' coming to earth, the new age had dawned, the kingdom of God had come near, and the "year of the Lord's favor" had begun. But it was not God's will that the old world, the present age, cease and terminate yet.

The Scriptures reveal God's purpose for this, namely, so

that in his gracious mercy he might give people time to repent, so that he might gather a people unto himself from both the Jews and the Gentiles (Rom. 11:25–26). As the Apostle Peter wrote: "The Lord ... is longsuffering toward us, not willing that any should perish but that all should come to repentance" (2 Pet. 3:9).

Several times in his teaching, Jesus spoke in the same sentence about this age and the age to come (Mk. 10:30; Mt. 12:32).

Perhaps the strongest evidence of this teaching of Jesus is the Lord's Prayer in which he taught his followers to pray "Thy kingdom come, Thy will be done, on earth as it is in heaven" (Mt. 6:10; Lk. 11:2). If God's kingdom had already fully come on earth, why would Jesus have taught us to pray for it to come?

The end of the present age (the end of this world) and the coming of the new age in its fullness and power remain in the future (Mt. 13:39–40,49; Mk. 9:1; Lk. 18:30) and will come to pass when Jesus returns to earth in his glory and all the holy angels with him (Mt. 25:31).

Until that glorious Day of the Lord comes, this present world continues with its sufferings (Rom. 8:18), sins (Gal. 1:4), trials, and tribulations (Jn. 16:33; Acts 14:22). Until then, Jesus' people must continue to struggle against the devil and his demons, "against the cosmic powers of this present darkness, against the spiritual forces of evil in the heavenly places" (Eph. 6:12, NRSV). Until then, even though the devil is a defeated enemy, he continues to afflict Jesus' people, to the extent that St. John says that "the whole world lies under the sway of the evil one" (1 Jn. 5:19).

And yet Christians are not left alone to struggle in their own strength. We have God's Holy Spirit, the Spirit of Jesus, within us to sustain and strengthen our faith in Jesus. And in that faith, we have increasing victory over the world, over the sin within us ("the flesh"), and over the devil. This God-given faith in Jesus is powerful and life-giving. Those who believe in Jesus have eternal life, here and now (Jn. 3:36; 5:24; 6:47). The gift of the Holy Spirit is a guarantee, a pledge, of our eventual complete redemption. (Eph.1:14). Through the Holy Spirit, God gives us here in the present time a taste of "the powers of the age to come" (Heb. 6:4–5).

Every time we have an answer to prayer, a healing, a restoration to health, a deliverance from addiction or from the devil's power, the forgiveness of sins, the restoration of a broken relationship, the renewal of a marriage, joy and peace in the midst of pain, suffering, and sorrow, God has given us a taste of the "heavenly gift," a taste of the "powers of the age to come" (Heb. 6:4–5).

This teaching of the overlap of the ages is not easy to grasp; it requires spiritual direction by the Holy Spirit who leads us into all truth. It was not easy for Jesus' original disciples to grasp. Even after spending three years with Jesus, near the end of his ministry, they did not understand. They "thought the kingdom of God would appear immediately" (Lk. 19:11). So Jesus explained by the parable of the nobleman who went away to a distant country to obtain royal power for himself and then return, who gave ten of his followers each one *mina* (3 months wages for a working man) to do business with until he returned (Lk. 19:11–27). The disciples still did not get the point. Even after Jesus' Resurrection, at his Ascension back into heaven, they were still asking him, "Lord, will You at this time restore the kingdom to Israel?" (Acts 1:6).

Later on, the disciples did get the point that God's kingdom has come with Jesus and in him the New Age has dawned, but the close of the present age will not come until Jesus returns to earth again to bring it to an end, to bring human history to its conclusion, and to bring God's kingdom in its full power and glory, forever and ever.

Jesus Christ is "the King of the Ages" (1 Tim.1:17; Rev. 15:3, NIV), past, present, and future!

3. JESUS' HEALING MIRACLES

Not only did Jesus preach and teach the Gospel of the Kingdom of God, he also worked miracles. "Then his fame went throughout all Syria; and they brought to him all sick people who were afflicted with various diseases and torments, and those who were demon-possessed, epileptics, and paralytics; and he healed them" (Mt. 4:24).

When God came to earth (God the Son in Jesus of Nazareth), it would be a natural expectation that extraordinary, supernatural things would happen. Indeed, the prophet Isaiah had foretold that these things would happen when the Messiah came to earth: "Then the eyes of the blind shall be opened, And the ears of the deaf shall be unstopped. Then the lame shall leap like a deer, And the tongue of the dumb sing" (Is. 35:5–6). In fact, these miracles did happen when God's Messiah came.

Jesus' miracles do not by themselves prove that Jesus is the Messiah. Many of the world's religions have miracle workers, but Jesus' miracles were quite different from those performed by non-Christian miracle workers, in his time and now.

What is different and distinctive about the miracles Jesus did?

1. Jesus did nothing out of a sense of exhibitionism. He had rejected the temptation to be a flamboyant Messiah when he rejected Satan's enticement to throw himself down from the pinnacle of the Temple.

2. Jesus did not usually work miracles to prove that he was the Messiah. (One exception was the healing of the paralytic man when Jesus told him to stand up, take up his mat and go home so "that you may know that the Son of Man has power on earth to forgive sins" Mk. 2:1–12). Jesus expressly rejected demands that he perform miracles to prove that he was the Messiah. Jesus was the King of God's Kingdom come to earth, and he did not need to prove anything to anybody.

3. Jesus worked miracles for individual suffering persons who presented themselves before him. "He laid

his hands on every one of them and healed them" (Lk. 4:40). He did not wave his hand over Palestine and heal everyone in the land all at once. That is not the way God's kingdom works.

4. Jesus worked miracles out of his great love and mercy toward suffering people. We read in the Gospels that Jesus had compassion on suffering people, such as the leper (Mk.1:41), the blind men (Mt. 20:34), and the crowd. (Mk. 6:34).

5. Jesus worked miracles by the power of God Almighty, not by the power of Satan or demonic forces.

We see the exact opposite of Jesus' spirit and attitude concerning miracles in Simon the Sorcerer. He practiced magic in Samaria by the power of Satan and amazed the people, saying that he was someone great. All the people listened to him eagerly, saying, "This man is the great power of God." Instead of love and compassion for hurting people, we see in Simon the motivation of self-aggrandizement, showing off his magic powers so the people would glorify him, so that he would become famous and make a lot of money (Acts 8:9–24).

The Gospels only tell us a few of the miracles of healing that Jesus worked, samples as it were (Jn. 20:30). But the range of human illnesses, sicknesses, and diseases which Jesus healed is simply astounding:

Leprosy (Mk.1:40–42; Lk.17:11–19)
Fever (Mt. 8:14,15)
Paralysis (Lk. 5:18–25)
Woman with hemorrhages for 12 years (Lk. 8:43–48)
Blindness (Mt. 9:27–31; 20:29–34; Mk. 8:22–26; Jn. 9:1–7).
Deafness (Mk. 7:31–37)
Dropsy (Lk.14:1–4)

The Gospels also tell us that on several occasions, great crowds came to Jesus for healing, and that he healed them all. However, he dealt with them each individually, not by magically waving hands over the crowd as we have discussed above. (*See* Lk.4:40).

Jesus never worked miracles on demand, to amaze a crowd or to meet some test (Lk.11:16; Mt. 16:1) or expectation such as King Herod had (Lk. 23:8).

In fact, when some of the scribes and Pharisees asked to see a sign (a miracle) to show whether or not he was the Messiah, Jesus told them:

> "An evil and adulterous generation seeks after a sign, and no sign will be given to it except the sign of the prophet Jonah. For as Jonah was three days and three nights in the belly of the great fish, so will the Son of Man be three days and three nights in the heart of the earth."
>
> (Mt. 12:39–40)

Thus, Jesus' Resurrection, coming alive again after being dead for three days, would be the final proof, the foremost and greatest sign, that he is indeed Who he said he was, the Son of God, the Savior, the Messiah.

Jesus himself pointed out that in the end times, false messiahs and false prophets would appear and produce great signs and wonders and omens (Mt. 24:24; Mk. 13:22). Christians must be alert and heed his teaching (Mk.13:23). We must have discernment to test the spirits to see whether they are from God or whether they are false (1 Jn. 4:1).

> "By this you know the Spirit of God: Every spirit that confesses that Jesus Christ has come in the flesh is of God, and every spirit that does not confess that Jesus Christ has come in the flesh is not of God. And this is the spirit of the Antichrist, which you have heard was coming, and is now already in the world."
>
> (1 Jn. 4:2–3)

One test that separates the true from the false miracle-worker is whether or not he or she gives all the credit and praise for the miracle to Jesus Christ, and whether or not he or she teaches plainly that believing in Jesus Christ is the only way to God.

4. JESUS CASTING OUT EVIL SPIRITS

A very important element in Jesus' earthly ministry was exorcism, the casting out of evil spirits.

As in the case of the healing miracles, Jesus performed exorcisms in response to human need, when he was confronted with specific individuals who were tormented and afflicted with demons, and he acted out of his great love and compassion toward suffering people.

The Gospels set forth in detail some examples of Jesus exercising this ministry:

- The man with the unclean spirit in the synagogue at Capernaum (Mk.1:21–28; Lk. 4:33–37)
- The Gadarene (Gerasene) demoniac who had superhuman strength and lived among the tombs, howling and bruising himself with stones; Jesus sent the legion of demons into a herd of 2,000 pigs which ran down a steep bank into the Sea of Galilee and drowned (Mt. 8:28–34; Mk.5:1–20; Lk. 8:26–39).
- The daughter of the Syro-Phoenician woman (Mt.15:21–28; Mk.7:24–30). [*Note*: Jesus performed this exorcism at a distance, not in the presence of the afflicted girl.]
- The boy with a demon that caused him to be mute and have convulsions (Mk. 9:14–29)
- The epileptic boy who suffered terribly, often falling into the fire and into the water (Mt.17:14–21; Lk. 9:37–43)

The Gospels also tell us of occasions when Jesus cast evil spirits out of many people (Mt. 4:24; Mk.1:32–34, 39).

Jesus' ministry of exorcism is highly significant. Some of the Old Testament prophets had worked miracles of healing, miracles over the natural world, and even raising the dead. But none of the Old Testament prophets had cast out evil spirits.

Jesus' power over the spiritual world of angels and demons is paramount and absolute, and the evil spirits recognized and acknowledged Jesus' power over them. "And the unclean spirits, whenever they saw him, fell down before him and cried out, saying, 'You are the Son of God.' But he sternly warned them that they should not make him known" (Mk. 3:11–12; *see also*, Lk. 4:34–35). It was not yet time for Jesus' true identity to be made known.

Jesus' power over the spiritual realm is evidence that Jesus is the King in God's Kingdom, and that when he is present, the Kingdom of God is there. Not only has it "come near," it is a present reality. As Jesus told his opponents: "But if I cast out demons with the finger of God, surely the kingdom of God has come upon you" (Lk.11:20). The phrase "finger of God" means God present in his sovereign power. It was by "the finger of God" that the Ten Commandments were written on the stone tablets and delivered by God to Moses on Mount Sinai. (Ex. 31:18; Dt. 9:10).

Jesus' casting out demons showed conclusively that he had defeated and bound "the strong man," that is, Satan, the devil. Otherwise, he could not have freed the devil's prisoners (Mt. 12:22–29; Mk. 3:22–27; Lk. 11:14–23).

Every time Jesus healed someone or cast evil spirits out of a person, he was raiding Satan's territory and setting the devil's captives free.

The exorcisms performed by Jesus demonstrate that he is the Lord of the spiritual realm, that he has defeated Satan and broken his power, indeed, that all authority and power in heaven and on earth has been given to him (Mt. 28:18), that he is "King of kings, and Lord of lords" (Rev. 19:16), not only of this visible earthly realm but also of the invisible spiritual realm.

5. JESUS EXERCISING HIS POWER OVER NATURE

Another group of miracles worked by Jesus shows his power over nature. Here again, in working these miracles, Jesus was responding to immediate human needs.

One of these took place shortly after the beginning of Jesus' public ministry. He and his disciples were in a boat crossing the Sea of Galilee when a great windstorm arose and the boat was being swamped by the waves. Jesus was asleep on a cushion in the stern of the boat, the perfect picture of calm, peace, and absolute trust in God in the midst of great danger. The disciples woke him up, saying, "Lord, save us! We are perishing!" Jesus asked them, "Why are you fearful, O you of little faith?" Then he rebuked the winds and the sea, and there was absolute calm. The disciples were amazed, saying, "Who can this be, that even the winds and the sea obey him?" (Mt. 8:23–27; Mk. 4:35–41; Lk. 8:22–25).

The miracle of Jesus' feeding the crowd of five thousand is of the utmost significance, as shown by the fact that it is the only miracle recorded in all four Gospels. Jesus was with his disciples in a deserted area across the Sea of Galilee. People heard he was there, and a crowd gathered. Jesus spoke to them about the Kingdom of God and healed the sick. Evening came and the disciples were concerned about the people being hungry out in the deserted place far from the towns. In all the crowd, the only food available was five barley loaves and two small fish. Jesus took the food, looked up to heaven, blessed it, broke it, and gave it to the disciples to distribute to the crowd. The food was multiplied miraculously so that everyone was fed and twelve baskets of pieces were left over. The crowd consisted of 5,000 men, not counting the women and children (Mt.14:15–21; Mk. 6:35–44; Lk. 9:12–17; Jn. 6:5–13).

On another occasion, in Gentile territory, Jesus worked the same miracle to feed a crowd of 4,000 men, not counting women and children, because he had compassion for the crowd who had been with him for three days and had nothing to eat (Mt.15:32–38; Mk. 8:1–9).

St. John in his Gospel tells us that the very first miracle Jesus worked was at the wedding in Cana in Galilee when a crisis arose because the host had run out of wine. Jesus turned six large stone jars of water into wine, something like 120 to 180 gallons of it. The Master of Ceremonies was amazed because this wine was much better quality than the first they had had, the exact opposite of what usually happened at weddings. St. John tells us the significance of this miracle: "This beginning of signs [miracles that show his supernatural power] Jesus did in Cana of Galilee, and manifested his glory; and his disciples believed in him" (Jn. 2:1–11).

Another miracle that Jesus performed twice, once near the start of his ministry and then again after his Resurrection, involved a miraculous catch of fish, again in response to human need in that the disciples had been fishing all night and caught nothing (Lk. 5:4–11; Jn. 21:1–11).

Other miracles showing Jesus' power over nature are his walking on water (Mt.14:25; Mk. 6:48–51), the coin in the fish's mouth (Mt.17:24–27), and the withered fig tree (Mt. 21:18–22; Mk.11:12–14, 20–25).

Skeptical people, including some Christians, have difficulty believing these nature miracles of Jesus. But for Christians who believe the Bible, they are the easiest of all to accept. This is because everything was created through Jesus Christ (Jn. 1:3). He created every molecule, every atom. It is his creation; He is its Lord and Master. He has absolute power over all created things. Therefore, he has the right and authority to order every created thing what to do, to multiply it at his touch as he did in feeding the multitudes. When he came into the world, he came to his own things (literal meaning of Jn. 1:11).

To scientifically-minded people, God's "natural laws" are unbreakable and unchangeable. To believers, the "natural laws" simply describe the way God normally and ordinarily operates his creation most of the time; but there is no reason why God cannot do something out of the ordinary on rare occasions, under extraordinary circumstances, for reasons which are good and sufficient to himself.

Jesus' miracles in which he exercised power and authority over nature, over created things, show that he is the Lord, Owner, and Master of all created things. He is Lord of all creation.

6. JESUS RAISING THE DEAD

During the course of his earthly ministry, Jesus raised three dead persons to life: Jairus' daughter, the son of the widow of Nain, and his friend Lazarus.

Early in Jesus' ministry, a man named Jairus, a leader of the synagogue, came to Jesus, fell at his feet, and begged him over and over to come to his house and heal his little twelve-year-old daughter who was at the point of death. Jesus went with him, and while they were on the way, word came from Jairus' house that his daughter was dead. Jesus told Jairus not to be afraid, only believe. When they got to the house, they found a commotion with people weeping and wailing loudly. Jesus put them all out of the house, and he took the child's parents, Peter, James, and John with him and went into the room where the little girl was lying. Jesus took her by the hand, and spoke to her in their native Aramaic language, "*Talitha, cumi,*" which is translated, "*Little girl, I say to you, arise*" and immediately she got up and began to walk about. At this, they were overcome with amazement. Jesus told them not to tell what had happened and to give the girl something to eat (Mk. 5:21–24, 35–43).

Later in his ministry, Jesus and his disciples and a large crowd with them were approaching the little town of Nain. The dead body of a man was being carried out to be buried. His mother was a widow, and he was her only son. Jesus had compassion on her and told her not to weep. Then he touched the death bed and said, "Young man, I say to you, arise." And the dead man sat up and began to talk, and Jesus presented him to his mother. Fear seized the people; they glorified God; and the news spread throughout Judea and the vicinity (Lk. 7:11–17).

Near the end of his earthly ministry, Jesus received word from his dear friends—Mary and Martha of Bethany—that their brother Lazarus was sick. After two days, Jesus left with his disciples to go to Bethany, and when they arrived, Jesus found that Lazarus had already been in the tomb four days. Jesus spoke these power-filled words to Martha: "I am the resurrection and the life. He who believes in Me, though he may die, he shall live. And whoever lives and believes in Me shall never die" (Jn.11:25–26). With Mary and Martha and his disciples and the crowd, Jesus went to Lazarus' tomb. Jesus was disturbed in spirit and deeply moved, so much so that he began to weep. The tomb was a cave, with a stone lying against the opening.

When Jesus told them to take the stone away, Martha protested, "Lord, by this time there is a stench, for he has been dead four days." Jesus told her, "Did I not say to you that if you would believe you would see the glory of God?" So they took away the stone, and Jesus looked upward and prayed: "Father, I thank You that You have heard Me. And I know that You always hear Me, but because of the people who are standing by I said this, that they may believe that You sent Me." Then Jesus cried with a loud voice, "Lazarus, come forth!" And the dead man came out of the tomb in his burial garments, his hands and feet bound with strips of cloth and his face wrapped in a cloth. Jesus told them, "Loose him, and let him go" (Jn. 11:1–53).

These miracles where Jesus raised the dead and restored them to life show that Jesus is the Lord of life, "the Prince of life" (Acts 3:15). They prove the truth of Jesus' saying that the time would come, and was already present in his ministry, when the dead would hear his voice and those who hear will live (Jn. 5:25).

In these miracles, the dead person was restored to life, but it was to the natural, normal human existence. They would have to die again, in the way of all flesh. They were restored to life in their natural bodies, not raised in the spiritual bodies of the Resurrection at the Last Day. The difference is shown in the fact that Lazarus came out of the grave bound in his graveclothes, but Jesus' body was raised from the dead into the new life of the age to come, leaving his grave clothes behind like an empty cocoon (Jn. 20:6–7).

Ironically, it was the raising of Lazarus that led the Jewish leaders and Caiaphas, the high priest, to the final decision that Jesus would have to be put to death (Jn.11:53). As far as they were concerned, this miracle showing Jesus' power over death itself was the straw that broke the camel's back. Life for Lazarus meant death for Jesus.

7. JESUS TRAINING HIS DISCIPLES

Another very important aspect of Jesus' earthly ministry was training his disciples. The Gospels tell us that early in his ministry, Jesus called seven men to follow him as his disciples: Simon (Peter) and Andrew, brothers; James and John, brothers; Philip and Nathanael (Bartholomew); and Matthew (Levi). Then after praying all night, out of the larger group of his followers, Jesus chose twelve of them to be his apostles (Lk. 6:12–16), to be those he sent out as his authorized spokesmen and representatives (which is the meaning of "apostle"). This group of twelve formed the nucleus of the New Israel, the Church that Jesus was establishing.

The Twelve were with Jesus during the entire three-year course of his earthly ministry, traveling with him. Jesus spent a great deal of time teaching and training them in private, apart from the crowds which followed him wherever he went. Also, they learned how to minister to people by observing what Jesus did and listening to what he said.

Jesus sent the Twelve out on a mission to "the lost sheep of the house of Israel." He gave them instructions and authority to proclaim the good news, heal the sick, raise the dead, cleanse the lepers, and cast out demons. (Matthew chapter 10). They found that they had been empowered to work the same miracles that Jesus had done. (Mk. 6:12–13).

Later in his ministry, Jesus appointed seventy others out of the larger group of his followers, and sent them out two-by-two to every town and place where he himself intended to go, to prepare the people to receive him and his ministry. The seventy were specifically instructed to proclaim that "The kingdom of God has come near to you," and to heal the sick. (Lk. 10:1–12).

The seventy returned from their mission rejoicing: "Lord, even the demons are subject to us in Your name." Jesus told them that he saw Satan fall from heaven like a flash of lightning, and said:

> "Behold, I give you the authority to trample on serpents and scorpions, and over all the power of the enemy, and nothing shall by any means hurt you. Nevertheless do not rejoice in this, that the spirits are subject to you, but rather rejoice because your names are written in heaven."
>
> (Lk.10:19,20)

Jesus' intensive training of the Twelve and his other disciples was of the utmost importance so that after he was physically absent from the earth (after his death, Resurrection, and Ascension into heaven), his ministry in the world would be carried on by his followers by the power of his Holy Spirit. Jesus told them: "Most assuredly, I say to you, he who believes in Me, the works that I do he will do also; and greater works than these he will do, because I go to My Father" (Jn. 14:12).

Jesus taught his disciples well. Although they were slow of heart to believe and to assimilate Jesus' teachings and instructions, nevertheless, in the Book of the Acts of the Apostles we find Jesus' followers, not only the Twelve but also other believers, continuing the same ministry Jesus had exercised on earth.

For example, Peter preached such a powerful sermon on Pentecost that 3,000 people were converted and baptized (Acts chapter 2). Peter and John healed a beggar crippled from birth at the Beautiful Gate of the Temple (Acts 3:1–10), and when they preached, another 2,000 men were converted (Acts 4:4). The apostles worked many signs and wonders, healing miracles, and exorcisms (Acts 5:12–16). Following the same pattern when Jesus had raised Jairus' 12-year old daughter from the dead, Peter raised Tabitha (Dorcas) from the dead in Joppa (Acts 9:36–43). The Apostle Paul worked many miracles in his ministry.

Of course, none of these miracles were done through the power of the individual Christian, but by the power of the Risen, Living Lord Jesus, through his Holy Spirit. As Peter explained, following the healing of the crippled beggar:

> "Men of Israel, why do you marvel at this? Or why look so intently at us, as though by our own power or godliness we had made this man walk?... And his [Jesus'] name, through faith in his name, has made this man strong, whom you see and know. Yes, the faith which comes through him has given him this perfect soundness in the presence of you all."
>
> (Acts 3:12,16)

This miracle-working, life-transforming work of Jesus Christ has been carried on through those who believe in him, by the power of his Holy Spirit, from the time of his Ascension continuously throughout history up to our own time and will continue to the end of the world.

THE TURNING POINT

As we read the Gospels' record of Jesus' earthly ministry, we come to a definite turning point. Up until this time, Jesus had been preaching, teaching, healing, casting out evil spirits, working miracles, even raising the dead. His ministry had had great success with multitudes of people following him wherever he went.

When Jesus and his disciples came into the area of Caesarea Philippi, following the great miracle in which he had fed the multitude, he asked his disciples, "Who do men say that I, the Son of Man, am?" (Mt. 16:13). They answered that some thought he was John the Baptizer come back from the dead; others said that he must be the Prophet Elijah (who was expected to return at the end of the age); and other people said he was Jeremiah or another one of the prophets.

Then Jesus asked his disciples directly: "But who do you say that I am?" (v.15). Simon Peter answered: "You are the Christ, the Son of the living God." And Jesus replied:

> "Blessed are you, Simon Bar-Jonah, for flesh and blood has not revealed this to you, but My Father who is in heaven. And

I also say to you that you are Peter *[Petros]*, and on this rock *[petra]* I will build My church, and the gates of Hades shall not prevail against it."

(Mt. 16:17–18)

Jesus sternly ordered his disciples not to tell the secret that he was the Messiah (Mt.16:20; Mk. 8:30; Lk. 9:21). It was not yet time for this greatest truth of all ages to be revealed to the world.

The truth of St. Peter's confession of faith (Mt. 16:16), which is the rock upon which Jesus founded his church, was corroborated and vindicated a few days later by God the Father himself in the event called the Transfiguration.

Jesus took his closest disciples, Peter, James and John, with him up on a high mountain. Then an absolutely unique, amazing thing happened: the glory of heaven focused on the Man, Jesus of Nazareth, and flowed out from his very body. He "was transfigured before them. His face shone like the sun, and his clothes became as white as the light" (Mt. 17:2).

Suddenly, two of the greatest men from Israel's history appeared in glory with Jesus: Moses, the Law-giver, and Elijah, the greatest prophet. They were talking with Jesus about his death, his departure, his Exodus, which in God's plan he was about to accomplish at Jerusalem (Lk. 9:31).

The cloud of God's heavenly glory came and overshadowed the three terrified disciples, and the voice of God the Father himself came from the cloud of glory (the *Shekinah)* and said: "This is My beloved Son. Hear him!" (Lk. 9:35).

As soon as the Voice had spoken, the disciples looked around, and Moses and Elijah had vanished, and "they saw no one anymore, but only Jesus with themselves" (Mk. 9:8). The Law and the Prophets (the old revelation of God), represented by Moses and Elijah, were fulfilled in Jesus, and he was the only One mankind needed for salvation for this life and the life to come.

From this point on, there was a new note of urgency in Jesus' words and actions. The time was drawing near for him to complete his mission, and "He steadfastly set his face to go to Jerusalem" to fulfill his destiny (Lk. 9:51, KJV). On three separate occasions, Jesus told his disciples what awaited him in Jerusalem: that he would have to "suffer many things from the elders and chief priests and scribes, and be killed, and be raised again the third day" (Mt.16:21).

From this turning point forward, Jesus' tone with his disciples became more stern, more severe, as he spoke of the necessity of commitment and self-sacrifice involved in following him. One example:

> "If anyone desires to come after Me, let him deny himself, and take up his cross, and follow Me. For whoever desires to save his life will lose it, and whoever loses his life for My sake will find it."
>
> (Mt. 16:24–25)

On his journey to Jerusalem with his disciples, Jesus continued his ministry of preaching, teaching, healing, working miracles, casting out evil spirits, and training his disciples.

F
JESUS AT JERUSALEM

When Jesus reached Jerusalem, the conflict between him and the Jewish leaders intensified.

As Jesus entered Jerusalem, riding on a donkey, the crowds exuberantly hailed him as the Messiah, according to their understanding that the Messiah would be a descendant of David who would be the King of Israel and bring back the glories of the ancient Jewish Kingdom. They spread garments in his path and cut palm branches and spread them on the road, as they "rolled out the red carpet" for him. The crowds shouted in praise:

> "Hosanna to the Son of David!
> Blessed is he who comes in the name of the Lord!
> Hosanna in the highest!"
>
> (Mt. 21:9)

The whole city of Jerusalem was in uproar and turmoil over him (v.10). It was widely expected that Jesus would go to the Temple and be proclaimed King of Israel.

Jesus did go to the Temple, but his actions were quite different from what the people expected. He did not proclaim himself King and take his place on the throne of David. Instead, he was angered by the sight of merchants buying and selling the animals for sacrifice, changing money into the Temple shekel for a fee, taking up space in the Court of the Gentiles reserved for them to worship the Lord God of Israel. Jesus was so angry that he made a whip and drove the moneychangers from the Temple, overturning their tables. Jesus quoted as his authority for such drastic actions the words of the prophets: "My house shall be called a house of prayer for all people" (Is. 56:7, NRSV), "but you have made it a den of robbers" (Jer. 7:11, NRSV).

In the next several days, there were confrontations between Jesus and the scribes, Pharisees, and Sadducees. There was scheming and plotting among the Jewish leaders as to how to arrest and kill Jesus. Meanwhile, Jesus continued his ministry of preaching, teaching, and healing in the Temple. As the controversy between Jesus and the Jewish leaders intensified, Jesus pronounced woes and doom upon them for their unbelief in rejecting him, the Messiah God had sent, and for their hypocrisy. Also, Jesus foretold the destruction of the Jerusalem Temple, that not one stone would be left standing.

The issue between Jesus and the Jewish leaders was whether he was the true Messiah. Was He, as he claimed to be, the Son of God?

Judas Iscariot, one of the Twelve Apostles, conspired with the Jewish leaders to betray Jesus to them. Judas is an enigmatic character in the events of Holy Week, but apparently he was a member of the revolutionary Zealot faction and was bitterly disappointed that Jesus did not seize political and military power to overthrow the Romans. Jesus had rejected this temptation at the beginning of his ministry because in God's plan, his Kingdom was not to be an earthly political kingdom of Israel, but a spiritual kingdom for all the peoples of the earth.

After Jesus had celebrated the Passover with his disciples at the Last Supper (thus establishing and ordaining the Lord's Supper), he opened his heart to the remaining disciples after Judas Iscariot had left on his mission of betrayal. Jesus spoke words to encourage and strengthen them and to prepare them for what was to come (John chapters 13–16).

Jesus prayed a heartfelt prayer for his disciples and for those who would later believe in him through their testimony (John chapter 17). Then after Jesus and his disciples had sung a psalm, they went out to the Mount of Olives to the Garden of Gethsemane.

There Jesus left the rest of the disciples and took Peter, James, and John deeper into the garden and asked them to remain there and stay awake with him. Then he went a little farther into the garden, threw himself on the ground and, deep in grief and agony, prayed, "O My Father, if it is possible, let this cup pass from Me; nevertheless, not as I will, but as You will" (Mt. 26:39). Then he returned to the three disciples, hoping for their support in his time of agony, but found them sleeping. He asked them to stay awake and pray. Jesus went away from them twice more and prayed, "O My Father, if this cup cannot pass away from Me unless I drink it, Your will be done" (v. 42–44). St. Luke the Physician tells us that Jesus' anguish was so severe that he sweated big drops of blood (Lk. 22:44). Then he returned and woke up his sleeping disciples.

Then Judas Iscariot appeared, leading a crowd of the Jewish leaders and Temple guards, and identified Jesus and betrayed him by kissing him. They arrested Jesus as a criminal and took him to the house of Caiaphas the High Priest for a hearing or trial before the scribes and elders gathered there. In an illegal nighttime session, the Jewish Council condemned Jesus for blasphemy in claiming to be the Son of God. Under Jewish law, death by stoning was the penalty for blasphemy.

However, at this time Judea was under Roman government and under Roman law. The Jews did not have the right to impose a death sentence, which was reserved to the Roman authority. Moreover, it was of utmost importance to the Jewish authorities that Jesus be put to death by the method of crucifixion (the Roman method of execution) rather than by stoning (the method prescribed by Jewish law). The reason was that the Law of Moses stated flatly that anyone "hung on a tree is under God's curse" (Deut. 21:23, NRSV). The Jewish leaders wanted Jesus to be killed by hanging on a tree (cross made of wood) in order to prove that he was under the curse of God and therefore could not possibly be the Messiah.

Ironically, God's plan agreed that it was necessary for Jesus to be put to death on "the tree" (the cross) so as to prove that in his death, Jesus was indeed under the curse of God. In God's plan and purpose it was necessary to show that in his sufferings and death, Jesus bore the curse of God against the sin of guilty humanity, for us, in our place, and on our behalf, so that we might be freed from the curse and receive God's blessing. As explained by St. Paul:

> "Christ redeemed us from the curse of the law by becoming a curse for us—for it it written, 'Cursed is everyone who hangs on a tree'—in order that in Christ Jesus the blessing of Abraham might come to the Gentiles, so that we might receive the promise of the Spirit through faith."
>
> (Gal. 3:13–14, NRSV)

Thus, "according to the definite plan and foreknowledge of God" (Acts 2:23, NRSV), Jesus was taken by the Jewish leaders before the Roman governor, Pontius Pilate. Pilate found no fault in Jesus deserving death, but the leaders and the crowd insisted otherwise, screaming, "Crucify him! Crucify him!"

When Pilate found out that Jesus was a Galilean, he sent Jesus to King Herod who happened to be in Jerusalem for Passover. Frustrated by Jesus' silence at the charges against him, Herod mocked him and with his soldiers treated Jesus contemptuously, put a royal purple robe on him, and sent him back to Pilate.

Pilate summarized the situation, that he had not found Jesus guilty of any charges against him, and neither had Herod, and thus Pilate proposed to have Jesus flogged and released. It was the custom that at Passover, the Roman governor would release a prisoner to show mercy. Pilate asked the crowd which prisoner they wanted released, whether Barabbas, in prison for sedition and murder (what we today would call "terrorism"), or Jesus called the Christ (Mt. 27:17). Apparently, Pilate thought that the crowd would choose Jesus to be released. But the crowd, now an angry mob, shouted more loudly and insistently that Barabbas be released and that Jesus be crucified. The crowd kept shouting for Jesus to be crucified: "Crucify, crucify him!"

So Pilate gave his judgment that Barabbas be released and that Jesus of Nazareth be crucified. Jesus' crime against Roman law was officially stated to be sedition, specifically in claiming to be the King of Israel, thus committing treason against Rome. Pilate ordered that the headboard on Jesus' cross (which stated the prisoner's crime) read "King of the Jews" in letters of Hebrew, Greek, and Latin (Jn.19:19).

The Roman soldiers took Jesus along with two other convicted criminals to the place of execution on a hillside near Jerusalem called Golgotha ("Place of the Skull") and there they crucified Jesus and the other two, with Jesus in the middle and one criminal on his right and one on his left.

Execution by crucifixion was barbaric, cruel, and exceedingly painful. First, the condemned prisoner was beaten by the soldiers, then flogged with a *fragellum*, a whip made of strips of leather with small bits of bone and metal tied into the ends of the strips which had the effect of cutting the flesh off the bone, even down to the spine. Then the soldiers led the weakened, bleeding prisoner outside the city, forcing him to carry the cross-beam of the wooden cross on his shoulders. Jesus was too weak to carry his cross, so the soldiers commandeered Simon of Cyrene to carry Jesus' cross for him.

Once they had arrived at the place of execution, the soldiers stripped the clothes from the prisoner, assembled the wooden cross on the ground, laid the prisoner on it, and nailed him to it. One large nail was put through the wrists of each of his outstretched arms between the armbones (the ulna and the radius).

[The wrist was considered part of the hand in the medicine of that time.] Then they nailed his feet to the upright post of the cross with one iron spike through both heels. Then the cross was lifted up and set in place and the prisoner hung there until he died.

Every breath caused excruciating pain and required tremendous exertion, as the prisoner had to force his body upward, pushing against the spike in his heels, in order to exhale. Death was finally caused by suffocation with the lungs filling with fluid. If it took too long for the prisoner to die, the soldiers would break his legs to hasten his death. This was not done in Jesus' case because when the soldiers came to him, they found that he had already died. Not one of his bones was broken.

The Bible does not go into great detail as to Jesus' suffering and agony, but rather stresses the eternal, cosmic significance of his death.

In the words of a well-known hymn:

"We may not know, we cannot tell,
What pains he had to bear.
But we believe it was for us
He hung and suffered there."

C.F. Alexander (1848)

THE MEANING OF JESUS' CRUCIFIXION

Jesus' death on the cross for our salvation is absolutely central to the Christian faith. On the cross, Jesus made atonement for the sins of the world and opened the way for fallen, sinful, rebellious mankind to be brought back into a right relationship with God. "Atonement" is the theological term for this. We can see the meaning of this significant word when it is broken down into syllables: at-one-ment. Through Jesus' Crucifixion mankind, separated from God by sin, is re-united with God and they are made one again.

The truth of the atonement is so profound that human words are inadequate to express it. Through the ages, Christians have tried to express something of its truth and meaning in various word-pictures. None of them by itself contains the full meaning of the atonement. Its profound mystery remains hidden within the depths of God's being.

However, in the Holy Scriptures God has revealed something of its meaning. He has not revealed all that we would like to know, but he has revealed all that we need to know.

The atonement is like a magnificent cut diamond with many facets. Each facet sparkles with some of the divine truth, but no one facet contains the entire truth as to what Jesus' death on the cross means and what it accomplished.

To enter more deeply into some understanding of this central teaching of the Christian faith, although our understanding will of necessity be very limited, let us examine some of the word-pictures that Jesus and his Apostles gave us to reveal some of God's truth about this profound mystery.

1. SACRIFICE FOR SINS

Perhaps the way the New Testament most often speaks of the atonement is in terms of it being a sacrifice for sins. In his summary of the Gospel, St. Paul says that we sinners "are now justified by [God's] grace as a gift, through the redemption that is in Christ Jesus, whom God put forward as a sacrifice of atonement by his blood, effective through faith" (Rom.3:24–25, NRSV).

We citizens of the 21st century have difficulty with the concept of animal blood sacrifices as part of the worship of God. We find even the thought primitive and repugnant. Yet in the ancient world the sacrifice of animals was the primary way people worshipped. Not only the Jews with the elaborate system of sacrifices required by the Law of Moses, but all the peoples around the Mediterranean Sea and elsewhere worshipped with animal sacrifices, not only primitive peoples but also the cultured and sophisticated ones like the Greeks and Romans. This practice still exists in parts of the modern world, such as among the Hindus and some Muslims.

The truth of Hebrews 9:22 seems to be embedded deep in the primitive psyche of human beings: "Without the shedding of blood there is no forgiveness of sins" (RSV). To understand anything of religion, we have to have some knowledge of the concept of sacrifice.

In the Jewish religion animal blood sacrifices were the primary way God was worshipped in the Old Testament, under the

Law God gave through Moses, from the very beginning. This continued until AD 70 when the Romans conquered Jerusalem and destroyed the city and the Jewish Temple, thus bringing the Jewish animal sacrifices to an end.

The Jewish religious law provided several different types of sacrifice for different purposes, such as whole burnt offering ("holocaust"), sin offering, peace offering, guilt offering, Passover, and so on. Each type of sacrifice had its own particular rules which were quite detailed. Various sacrifices used different subjects: bulls, rams, goats, lambs, birds, grain, oil, wine, etc., but the most common was the sacrifice of a lamb.

Despite the varied and diverse types of sacrifices under the Law of Moses, one principle underlaid them all: *"the best for God."* Sacrificial lambs were required to be males, mature (between one and two years old), physically perfect ("without spot or blemish"), and valuable ("precious").

Jesus Christ is "the Lamb of God who takes away the sin of the world!" (Jn.1:29). He fulfills the requirements for the sacrificial lamb: He was a male; He was mature (around 33 years of age); He was without spot or blemish, being sinless; and he was the most valuable, being God the Son ("the precious blood of Christ, like that of a lamb without defect or blemish," 1 Pet. 1:19, NRSV).

The ritual prescribed by the Jewish law of sacrifices was fulfilled by the sacrificial death of Jesus on the cross.[12]

1. The gift to be sacrificed was brought to the priest and voluntarily offered. [Jesus said: "I lay down my life for the sheep (His followers)....No one takes it from Me, but I lay it down of myself." Jn.10:15,18.]

2. The worshipper laid hands on the sacrificial victim, symbolizing the transfer of his sins to the victim. [The New Testament points out over and over that Jesus' death on the cross was substitutionary, that he died "for us," "in our place," "on our behalf." For example, "He...Himself bore our sins in his own body on the tree" (I Pet. 2:24).

The Scriptures see Jesus' death as the fulfillment of the "Suffering Servant of the Lord" passages in the prophet Isaiah (52:13–53:12) such as this verse: "He was wounded for our transgressions, he was bruised for our iniquities; The chastisement for our peace was upon him, And by his stripes we are healed" (Is. 53:5).]

3. The sacrificial animal was slaughtered. [Jesus "was handed over to death for our trespasses." Rom. 4:25, NRSV]

4. The priest caught the blood in a basin and sprinkled some on the four corners of the altar, and poured out the remainder at the foot of the altar. [Of course, this was not fulfilled literally in Jesus' case, but the Book of Hebrews in chapters 8–10 develops the meaning of this aspect most fully, picturing Christ as the Great High Priest entering the Most Holy Place, heaven itself, bringing with him not the blood of an animal, but his own blood which he offered to God for the purification of our sins.]

5. The portion of the sacrifice that belonged to God was burned, ascending to God in the smoke. (In some sacrifices only the fat was burned and the rest of the animal was roasted and shared by the worshippers; in the "holocaust" (the whole burnt offering) the entire animal was consumed by fire). [Jesus' death does not literally fit this description because his body was not burned; but his death symbolically was a 'holocaust,' because he offered his entire being to God in his death. This picture of the smoke ascending to God lies behind St. Paul's statement that "Christ also has loved us and given himself for us, an offering and a sacrifice to God for a sweet-smelling aroma" Eph. 5:2]

6. In the "peace offering," the fat of the kidneys, liver, and intestines was burned, and the rest of the animal was

roasted and eaten in a sacrificial meal by the worshippers and the priest. [Of course, this was not literally fulfilled in Jesus' death, but the shared sacrificial meal is the symbolism underlying the sharing of Christ's body and blood in the holy feast of the Christian Church, the Lord's Supper. (Mt. 26:26–29; Mk. 14:22–25; Lk. 22:17–20; Jn. 6:25–59). As St. Paul wrote: "The cup of blessing that we bless, is it not a sharing in the blood of Christ? The bread that we break, is it not a sharing in the body of Christ?" (1 Cor.10:16, NRSV)]

Jesus' sacrifice of himself on the cross not only fulfilled the meaning of the sacrifices under the Old Covenant, but it was also far superior to them. They were but shadows of the reality which is Jesus' atoning death for the sins of the whole world. Now that the reality has come, the shadows have disappeared.

Here are some reasons that Jesus' sacrifice of himself is infinitely superior to the Old Testament sacrifices:

(1) There was a glaring defect and deficiency in the Old Testament sacrifices: they provided no way of atoning for willful, deliberate, intentional, rebellious, "high-handed," "presumptuous" sins (Nu.15:30–31). For some "presumptuous" offenses, the Law of Moses provided that the guilty person was to be "cut off from the people," that is, excommunicated, banished, exiled, shunned. For more serious offenses, the Law required the death penalty by stoning. For such willful, intentional, deliberate offenses no sacrifice could take away the guilt. The person who committed such a presumptuous sin had to bear his own guilt and take the punishment.

How wonderful are God's grace and mercy under the New Covenant made through the blood of Jesus! As St. Paul proclaimed in his sermon in the synagogue at Antioch of Pisidia:

> "Let it be known to you therefore, my brothers, that through this man [Jesus] forgiveness of sins is proclaimed to you; by this Jesus everyone who believes is set free from all those sins from which you could not be freed by the Law of Moses."
>
> (Acts 13:38–39, NRSV)

Under the New Covenant in Jesus' blood, God gives us forgiveness for all our trespasses (Col. 2:13) and our sins. (1 Jn. 1:7). Thank God that under the New Covenant, we have forgiveness of all our sins: the big ones, the little ones; the deliberate and willful ones as well as the accidental ones; the intentional ones, the careless ones; the one-time sins, the besetting sins; the ones everybody knows about, and the ones only God knows about.

In the ancient statement of faith known as "The Apostles' Creed," Christians confess that "we believe ... in the forgiveness of sins"—all of them.

(2) The sacrifices under the Old Covenant effected only outward, ritual cleansing; they did not cleanse the sinful heart of mankind; they did not "perfect the conscience of the worshipper" (Heb. 9:9, NRSV).

By contrast, under the New Covenant made by the blood of Jesus Christ, the consciences (Heb. 9:13) and hearts (Acts 15:9) of believers are cleansed and purified. Therefore, sinners though we are, we can approach God through Jesus our High Priest with "a true heart in full assurance of faith, having our hearts sprinkled from an evil conscience and our bodies washed with pure water" (Heb.10:22).

(3) Furthermore, the sacrifices under the Old Covenant had to be repeated. If they had really been effective and the worshippers had been truly cleansed, they would no longer have had any consciousness of sin, but instead the very repetition of the sacrifices had the effect of continually reminding the worshippers of sin (Heb.10:1–3).

Moreover, they never were truly effective to remove sin, "For it is not possible that the blood of bulls and goats could take away sins" (Heb.10:4).

The offering of Jesus' blood for the sins of the world was truly effective to atone for sins once for all time. His sacrifice of himself once offered would never need to be repeated, but would be operative completely forever. One of the key words the New Testament uses in connection with Jesus' sacrifice is the Greek word *apax* and its cognate *ephapax*, both of which mean "once" or "once for all [time]," that is, something that happens one time and never needs to be repeated, being fully effective thereafter forever (Rom. 6:10; Heb. 7:27, 9:12, 9:26, 10:10; 1 Pet. 3:18).

(4) Also, the sacrifices under the Old Covenant were temporary and God never intended them to continue forever (Heb. 8:7). They would last only until God established the New Covenant (Jer. 31:31–34) through the death of Jesus Christ when God would "set things right" (Heb. 9:10, NRSV).

The New Covenant in Jesus' blood lasts forever and is eternally effective to cleanse God's people from their sins—"for all time" (Heb. 7:25; 10:10,12,14, NRSV). By his one sacrifice of himself on the cross, Jesus has brought us "eternal salvation" (Heb. 5:9), "eternal redemption" (Heb. 9:12), an "eternal inheritance" (Heb. 9:15), and established with us an "everlasting covenant" (Heb.13:20).

As a historical fact, the Jewish sacrifices ceased forever in AD 70 when the Roman General Titus (later Emperor of Rome) conquered Jerusalem, killed thousands of Jews, defiled and completely destroyed the Temple. Roman law prohibited Jews from even setting foot in Jerusalem, upon pain of death. This utterly traumatic event in Jewish history was foretold by Jesus (Mt. chapter 25; Mk. chapter 13) and by the author of Hebrews who wrote that the Old Covenant was obsolete, growing old, and would soon disappear (Heb. 8:13).

Throughout the centuries, Christians have seen the events of AD 70 in this light: God gave the Jewish nation forty years to repent and accept Jesus' one sacrifice as all-sufficient for the forgiveness of sins, and when the Jewish nation did not repent (although thousands of individual Jews became Christians, even some of the Temple priests), God's judgment and wrath were poured out on the nation. There was no nation of Israel from AD 70 until the modern nation of Israel was established in 1948.

The Jewish sacrifices under the Old Covenant came to a

sudden, unexpected, and traumatic end in the year AD 70 and have never been resumed. The death of Jesus Christ on the cross fulfilled the Old Testament sacrifices, superseded them, and made them obsolete. Jesus Christ's sacrifice of himself for the sins of the world remains fully effective and powerful to save God's people, for all time and for all eternity.

2. PASSOVER LAMB

One word picture that is particularly significant in helping us understand more deeply the meaning of Jesus' death on the cross is this: Jesus' death is the New Covenant fulfillment of the sacrifice of the Passover lamb under the Old Covenant.

Chapter 12 of Exodus sets out the origin of the Jewish Passover. God had poured out nine plagues upon the land of Egypt to induce Pharaoh to free the Hebrew people, but Pharaoh had adamantly refused for nine times to let God's people go. Then God through Moses warned Pharaoh that if he did not free the children of Israel from slavery and let them go, God would let loose the most horrible plague upon Egypt: the first-born of every Egyptian family, from the royal family down to the lowliest slave, and the firstborn of every animal, would die.

However, God provided a way for his people to be protected and saved from the destruction. God instructed Moses and Aaron to have the Hebrew people sacrifice a lamb or a goat, a year-old male without blemish, and to take some of the blood and sprinkle it on the two doorposts and the lintel of the houses where the families gathered to eat the lamb. They were to roast the lamb and take care not to break any of its bones (Ex. 12:46), and eat it hurriedly, with their traveling clothes on. Then when God passed through the land of Egypt that night to strike down the firstborn of the Egyptian people and animals, the blood of the Passover lamb on the doorposts and lintels of the Hebrews' houses would be a sign, and when he saw the blood, God would pass over them and the death plague would not touch them.

That did indeed happen. God passed through Egypt and

the firstborn of the Egyptian people and animals were stricken dead, but he passed over his people, and they were protected and safe. Pharaoh changed his mind, summoned Moses and Aaron in the nighttime, and told them to get out of Egypt as soon as possible and take their people out with their flocks and herds

In connection with the Passover, God commanded the people to cleanse their houses of all yeast and to eat unleavened bread (made without yeast) for seven days. Thus, the Feast of Unleavened Bread and the Passover were inseparably linked together.

From the earliest New Testament times, Christians have made the connection between the Passover and Jesus' sacrificial death. Within about twenty years of Jesus' death, St. Paul wrote: "For indeed Christ, our Passover, was sacrificed for us. Therefore let us keep the feast…" (1 Cor. 5:7–8). Even today, most Christians use unleavened bread when they celebrate the Lord's Supper

St. John makes the same point by stressing that when Jesus died on the cross, the Roman soldiers did not break Jesus' legs like they did the other two men crucified with him. "For these things were done that the Scripture should be fulfilled, 'Not one of his bones shall be broken'" (Jn. 19:36). This is an unmistakable identification of Jesus with the Passover lamb, because the Passover sacrifice was the only type of sacrifice under the Law of Moses that specifically prohibited any bone of the victim to be broken (Ex.12:46).

Furthermore, the Gospel accounts make it clear that the Last Supper of Jesus with his disciples was a Passover meal (Mt. 26:17 ff; Mk.14:12; Lk. 22:7–13; John chapter 13).

Through the centuries Christian preachers have proclaimed that Jesus' death corresponds with the sacrifice of the Passover lamb and fulfills it. Just as the Hebrews were delivered from slavery in Egypt on the night of the Passover, so we Christians are set free from the bondage and slavery of sin by the sacrificial blood of Jesus. Those whose hearts have been sprinkled with the blood of Jesus (Heb.10:22, 12:24; 1 Pet. 1:2), whose lives are "under the blood of Jesus," will be protected and safe when Jesus returns to earth and the wrath of God is poured out on unbelievers.

Furthermore, the Lord's Supper is our Christian Passover, the sacramental meal we share in which the Lord Jesus is present with us, in, through, and with the consecrated bread and wine. After his Resurrection from the dead, the Risen Lord Jesus appeared to his followers and made himself present and known to them three times in the context of a meal: (1) to the two disciples on the road to Emmaus in the breaking of the bread (Lk. 24:13–35); (2) to the Eleven Apostles and those with them in eating a piece of broiled fish (Lk. 24:36–42); and (3) to seven of his disciples in the breakfast of bread and broiled fish Jesus himself prepared for them beside the Sea of Tiberias (the Sea of Galilee) (Jn. 21:1–14).

The symbolism of the Passover goes a long way in helping us better understand the meaning of Jesus' atoning death on the cross and his presence among us when we celebrate the Supper of the Lord. "For indeed, Christ our Passover was sacrificed for us. Therefore let us keep the feast, not with old leaven, nor with the leaven of malice and wickedness, but with the unleavened bread of sincerity and truth" (1 Cor. 5:7–8).

3. PROPITIATION FOR SIN

Mankind's biggest problem is not that we are ignorant and need education, not that we are weak and need strength, not that we are poor and need money, but that we are sinful and need forgiveness. It is our sin that has separated us from God (Is. 59:2). God's diagnosis of our sickness is that all our symptoms of bad behavior (sins) are but the outward manifestations of our underlying illness, namely, sin.

God is the living God, not a dispassionate, unemotional being. And he has a very strong reaction to human sin. It makes him angry. The Bible calls this "the wrath of God." God is pure; He is holy; He is love. Thus, his love is a holy love. God would be untrue to his own nature if he paid sin no attention, if he ignored it, if he overlooked it. He is the God of Truth; He would be lying if he said our sin doesn't matter. When we sin, when we do something God has commanded us not to do or when we fail to do something he has commanded us to do, God reacts with anger, and his anger is a just anger, a righteous anger, a holy anger.

Many people have difficulty accepting the concept of "the wrath of God." They say God is love, which is true, but they draw the false conclusion that therefore he can never be angry.

Perhaps an illustration will help us see the falseness of that conclusion. Here is a father who loves his teenage son dearly. An evil blasphemous movie is coming to a theater in town, and the father tells his son not to see that film. The son willfully disobeys his father and goes to see the forbidden film. The father finds out about it. What will be his reaction? He will be angry with the son he loves because of the son's deliberate, rebellious disobedience. And the father will hurt because he knows that in the long run his son will be injured in his soul for subjecting his mind and soul to such pollution. The father still loves his son dearly, but the son's sin rightly angers the father deeply.

God's wrath is the reaction of his holy love against the rebellion of sinful man.[13] Because God's wrath is a reaction, it is not intrinsic to his nature like his love is, for "God is love" (1 Jn. 4:8). Therefore, his wrath can cease (and will cease when sin ceases), but God's steadfast love never ends; it endures forever, as Psalm 136 tells us twenty-six times.

But something must happen to remove God's wrath, to propitiate his anger, so that a right relationship between God and mankind can be restored. God's wrath must be propitiated by a sufficient offering. Because our sin is so deep and our rebellion against God so fierce, it requires an offering of infinite value to propitiate God's anger. We human beings are not able to provide such a valuable offering. Even the best we can do is woefully inadequate. Even "all our righteousnesses are like filthy (literally, *menstruous*) rags" (Is. 64:6). The sin debt we owe to God is so overwhelming that we are bankrupt; we have no way to make the payment.

But wonder of wonders! God himself provides the offering that is sufficiently valuable to propitiate his wrath: He did this through the death of his only-begotten, well beloved Son, Jesus Christ. St. Paul explains it this way:

> "[F]or all have sinned and fall short of the glory of God, being justified freely by his grace through the redemption that is in Christ Jesus, whom God set forth to be a propitiation by his blood…"
>
> (Rom. 3:23–25)

In order to make propitiation for us, on behalf of us sinful people, Jesus had to become fully human; He had to become one of us (Heb. 2:17). Therefore, the propitiation Jesus made is effective not only for us, but for the whole world (1 Jn. 2:2). But it is operative only for those who have faith in Jesus.

And the reason Jesus offered himself for us—gave his very life for us—is because of his great love for us. "In this is love, not that we loved God, but that he loved us and sent his Son to be the propitiation for our sins" (1 Jn. 4:10).

The result of the propitiation of God's wrath brought about by the death of Jesus Christ is that if our lives are united through faith with the life of Jesus, we will be saved from the wrath of God. In the Last Day when Jesus returns to judge the living and the dead, those who are in Christ, whose lives are united with his by faith, will be saved and protected from God's wrath. But those who are outside Christ, "those who do not know God…those who do not obey the gospel of our Lord Jesus Christ" will have no protection against God's wrath against sin, and therefore "shall be punished with everlasting destruction from the presence of the Lord and from the glory of his power" (2 Thes.1:5–12).

At the Final Judgment, those who belong to Christ will receive God's mercy rather than the strict justice in the form of punishment they deserve. But those who do not belong to Christ will receive the strict justice they deserve without mercy, because they have not acknowledged their sin and repented of it and sought God's mercy and forgiveness.

In and through Jesus Christ and his propitiating death on the cross, God himself has provided the way for us to be saved from his own wrath.

The question for each of us is this: "[H]ow shall we escape if we ignore such a great salvation?" (Heb. 2:3, NIV).

4. RECONCILIATION

Another way the New Testament pictures the atonement accomplished by Jesus' death on the cross is that it brought about reconciliation between God and mankind. Reconciliation means doing away with enmity or hatred between two parties who were previously hostile.

The Bible pulls no punches: it tells us bluntly that sinful man is an enemy of God (Rom. 5:10; Col. 1:21; James 4:4). For two hostile parties to be truly reconciled, the root problem between them must be dealt with. Sin is the root problem between God and mankind; it is mankind's sin that has caused the problem.

Jesus' death on the Cross dealt with mankind's sin problem, removed sin, and took it out of the way, bringing about reconciliation between God and mankind (Rom. 5:6–11; 2 Cor. 5:17–21).

The reconciliation brought about through Jesus' death on the cross also made it possible for the deep divisions and hatred between races, nations, and ethnic groups to be removed and done away with, and peace to be established between them. This reconciliation is exemplified in the chasm between Jews and Gentiles being bridged in the cross (Eph. 2:11–22). This is an amazing thing and was a reality in the early Christian congregations containing both Jews and Gentiles, such as the church at Antioch.

Moreover, the reconciliation through the cross is of cosmic significance, as stated by the Apostle Paul:

> "For it pleased the Father that in him [Jesus] all the fullness should dwell, and by him to reconcile all things to himself, by him, whether things on earth or things in heaven, having made peace through the blood of his cross."
>
> (Col. 1:19,20)

Jesus' atoning death on the cross reconciled the holy God and sinful mankind and opened the way for a right relationship to be re-established between us and God, and for right relationships to be established between individuals and between peoples.

5. REDEMPTION

Redemption or ransom is another picture the Scriptures use to express the meaning and significance of Jesus' atoning death. Jesus himself explained his mission in these terms: He came from heaven to earth "to give his life a ransom for many" (Mt. 20:28; Mk.10:45).

Redemption means to pay a price to obtain deliverance from imprisonment or bondage. For example, a prisoner of war or a kidnapped person might be released upon payment of a sum of money called the "ransom." In Greek the same word is used for ransom and redemption, while in English we have two different words, but they express the same idea, that is, payment of money to obtain freedom.

Release from slavery upon payment of money is the primary situation the New Testament writers have in mind when they use the term "redemption" to describe what Jesus accomplished for us by his death on the cross. The picture is this: When Adam and Eve sinned, they and all their descendents became slaves to sin and lost their freedom. As the Lord Jesus himself taught: "Most assuredly, I say to you, whoever commits sin is a slave of sin" (Jn. 8:34). St. Paul said the same thing: "I am ... sold into slavery under sin" (Rom. 7:14, NRSV *see also;* 6:17).

However, when God the Son came to earth in Jesus Christ, one aspect of his mission as Messiah was "to proclaim liberty to the captives, and release to the prisoners" (Is. 61:1). The price he had to pay to obtain our freedom was his very life. His blood shed on the Cross was the price of our redemption, of our ransom, of our freedom. St. Paul makes this clear:

> "For there is no difference [between people]; for all have sinned and fall short of the glory of God, being justified freely by his grace through the redemption that is in Christ Jesus, whom God set forth to be a propitiation by his blood, through faith ... "
>
> (Rom. 3:22–25)

Therefore, since Jesus has paid the ransom price for our freedom with his own blood—with his very life—He has redeemed us from our sin (Tit. 2:14), and we have forgiveness of sins (Col. 1:14; Eph. 1:7) and freedom from "the curse of the Law" (Gal. 3:13).

It seems that behind some of the New Testament statements about redemption lies the legal procedure by which a slave was freed in the Roman world. Typically, when a Roman slave was redeemed and set free, the price of the slave was paid into the treasury of a pagan temple, and in a legal fiction, the slave was purchased by the pagan god and sold to the god. As far as the former owner and people in general were concerned, the slave was now free. But because the slave had technically been purchased by the pagan god who held the legal title to him, the slave now had certain obligations to the pagan god. This legal procedure seems to lie behind St. Paul's statement to the Christians at Corinth, a pagan city: " ... do you not know that your body is the temple of the Holy Spirit who is in you, whom you have from God, and you are not your own? For you were bought at a price; therefore glorify God in your body and in your spirit, which are God's" (1 Cor. 6:19–20).

Notice in the New Testament epistles how often the writer

describes himself as being a "servant (literally, *slave*) of Jesus Christ:"

- Paul in Rom.1:1, Phil.1:1; Titus 1:1
- Peter in 2 Peter 1:1
- James in James 1:1
- Jude in Jude v.1:

Although God certainly would have the right to treat us as his slaves, he does not do so, but instead adopts us into his family as his beloved children, with Jesus as our Elder Brother. God redeems us from under captivity to the Law

> "...so that we might receive adoption as children. And because you are children, God has sent the Spirit of his Son into our hearts, crying, 'Abba! Father!' So you are no longer a slave but a child, and if a child then also an heir, through God."
>
> (Gal. 4:5–7, NRSV)

Through Jesus' redeeming death on the Cross, God frees us from slavery to sin and death and gives us "the glorious liberty of the children of God" (Rom. 8:21). And in heaven we will join with the four living creatures and the twenty-four elders and all the saints in singing a new song to Jesus the Lamb:

> "For You were slain,
> And have redeemed us to God by Your blood
> Out of every tribe and tongue and people and nation,
> And have made us kings and priests to our God;
> And we shall reign on the earth."
>
> (Rev. 5:9–10)

Amazing grace! By Jesus' death on the cross, he has redeemed and ransomed us from slavery, he adopts us as members of his family, and he will make us into kings and priests serving our God!

6. PAYMENT OF OUR SIN DEBT

Perhaps one of the New Testament word pictures of the meaning of Jesus' death on the cross that is easier for us to grasp than some others is this: Jesus' death on the cross paid our sin debt to Almighty God in full.

Although we moderns may have some difficulty understanding the meaning of the Atonement in terms of sacrifice, Passover lamb, propitiation, reconciliation, or redemption because those are not concepts we commonly use in modern life, we certainly should have no problem grasping the idea of the Atonement in terms of money: sin is a debt we owe to God, a debt so large that we sinners cannot pay it, and God forgives that indebtedness by accepting Jesus' death in satisfaction of that debt as payment in full.

Jesus knew that we humans understood money, indebtedness, and the forgiveness of indebtedness, so in his ministry he taught that sin, the breaking of God's Holy Law, is like owing money to God.[14] This teaching of Jesus was not original with him. The Old Testament contained this concept, and the rabbis of Jesus' time taught it.[15]

This same concept applies in modern life. Under the criminal law, a violation usually carries the penalty of so much time in prison and so many dollars' fine, plus court costs, and often requires making restitution to the victim of the crime.

Two examples of Jesus' teaching that sin puts mankind under obligation to God, like owing him a debt, are these: (1) The Lord's Prayer in St. Matthew's Gospel: "And forgive us our debts, as we forgive our debtors" (Mt. 6:12); and (2) the incident where the sinful woman anointed Jesus' feet with the expensive ointment in an alabaster jar, leading to Jesus' Parable of the Two Debtors, one who owed 500 denarii (one denarius was a days' wages for a day laborer) and the other who owed only fifty denarii; the creditor cancelled the debt of both of them; the one who owed the greater sum will naturally love the creditor more (Lk. 7:36–50).

Jesus' teaching on this point is also set forth in the Parable of the Unforgiving Servant (Mt. 18:23–35). In Jesus' story one servant owed his king 10,000 talents. This is an unimaginably enormous sum of money, since one talent equaled approximately nineteen years' earnings for a day laborer, meaning it was so much money that an ordinary working man would have to work 190,000 years to pay the debt. Jesus' point is that we humans owe God an enormous debt because of our violation of his Holy Laws, such a gigantic amount that it is impossible to pay it or work it off.

However, God in his mercy accepts Jesus' death on the cross as payment in full of our unimaginably enormous sin debt. The reason God considers Jesus' blood shed on the cross as satisfaction (payment in full) of our enormous sin debt is that the life of Jesus is immeasurably valuable ("precious") in the sight of God (1 Pet. 2:7). As the Apostle Peter wrote: "[Y]ou...were redeemed...with the precious blood of Christ, as of a lamb without blemish and without spot" (1 Pet. 1:18–19). Even in today's business world a creditor will sometimes accept payment of a debt in full by the debtor transferring property to the creditor, rather than paying money, property which the creditor considers to be sufficiently valuable.

The Apostle Paul gives us this picture of what Jesus accomplished for us in his death on the cross: "...God...cancelled the bond [the handwritten certificate of indebtedness] which stood against us with its legal demands [to pay God the debt or penalty we owed for breaking his Holy Laws]; this he set aside, nailing it to the cross" (Col. 2:14, RSV).

The picture is that in Jesus' crucifixion, God took the bond representing the debt we owed to God because of our sins, marked it "paid in full," and nailed it to the cross.

7. TRIUMPH OVER THE DEVIL

Another picture the New Testament gives us to help us better understand the meaning of the cross is that in his death,

Jesus triumphed and won the victory over the devil and all his demonic powers.

St. Paul tells us that in the cross, "Having disarmed principalities and powers, he made a public spectacle of them, triumphing over them in it" (Col. 2:15).

The background that underlies this concept is that of a Roman general's triumph. When a general had won a war and returned to Rome, a great triumphal parade would be held in his honor. There would be the general riding in his chariot, resplendent in his finest uniform, his armor gleaming in the sunlight, with his children beside him. There would be his proud soldiers marching along, so happy to be home safe and sound after being gone away to war for so long. There would be exotic animals from the conquered territory. And last of all, there would be the miserable, pathetic slaves and prisoners captured from the conquered territory, weighed down with chains.

St. Paul is telling us that in his death on the cross, despite all the outward appearances of abject failure, of a criminal's bloody execution, Jesus is really the Conquering Hero! Jesus is the Victor! In his death, Jesus disarmed the devil and all his evil soldiers and made them prisoners, and in the Triumphal Parade Jesus made a public spectacle of them, dragging them along in chains, their power broken, Jesus triumphing gloriously over them in his death on the cross.

The writer of Hebrews tells us::

> "Inasmuch then as the children have partaken of flesh and blood, he himself likewise shared in the same, that through death he might destroy him who had the power of death, that is, the devil, and release those who through fear of death were all their lifetime subject to bondage."
>
> (Heb. 2:14–15)

The fear of death afflicts all human beings to some extent, and with some people it is a paralyzing dread. The fear of death gives the devil power over us and makes us his slaves. What is the most terrifying thing the devil can say to us? *"If you don't do what I want you to do, I'll torture you and then I'll kill you!"* To free us from this bondage, Jesus not only had to take upon himself our human flesh and blood, but also to go through death itself and then be raised from the dead.

Jesus' death on the cross was not only a sacrifice for sin, not only the sacrifice of the true Passover lamb, not only the propitiation of God's wrath against sin, not only the reconciliation between God and mankind, not only the redemption and ransom from the slavery of sin, not only payment in full of our sin debt to Almighty God, it was also the victory over the devil and all his demonic powers.

Jesus' word from the cross, "It is finished!" was a shout of victory (Jn. 19:30). In the words of one of the great Easter hymns of the Church:

> "The strife is o'er, the battle done;
> The victory of life is won;
> The song of triumph has begun. Allelluia!
> "The powers of death have done their worst,
> But Christ their legions hath dispersed.
> Let shout of holy joy outburst. Allelluia!"
>
> (Latin hymn[16])

H
THE BURIAL OF JESUS

Jesus died on the cross on Friday afternoon. It was the Day of Preparation for the Sabbath, which was a high holy day that year. The Jewish authorities did not want the three dead bodies left hanging on the crosses on the Sabbath, so they asked Pilate to order the soldiers to break the legs of the three prisoners to end their lives, then remove the bodies from the crosses.

So the soldiers took sledge hammers and crushed the legs of the other two crucified men, but when they came to Jesus, they saw that he was already dead, so they did not break his legs. One of the soldiers thrust a spear in Jesus' side from down below his body, and apparently it ruptured his lungs (filled with fluid) and his heart, for both water and blood gushed out (Jn.19:31–37). This fulfilled the Scriptures which said that none of his bones would be broken (Ps. 34:20) [for he was the true Passover lamb (*See*, Ex. 12:46; Nu. 9:12)] and that they would look on the One whom they had pierced (Zech. 12:10).

Joseph of Arimathea was a wealthy and prominent Jewish leader who was a member of the Council (the Sanhedrin). However, he had not consented to Jesus' death for he was a secret disciple of Jesus. He went to Pilate and obtained permission to remove the body of Jesus. Joseph along with Nicodemus, another Jewish leader, took Jesus' body and prepared it for burial, binding it "in strips of linen with the spices, as the custom of the Jews is to bury" (Jn.19:40).

The Jews did not embalm bodies as the Egyptians did. The Jewish burial custom was to cover the body in spices [in Jesus' case about a hundred pounds of myrrh and aloes] and in paste, which were bound to the body by strips of white linen cloth wrapped around the corpse like a roller bandage. "The paste hardened and impregnated the bandages until a hard preservative mould or cocoon was formed about the body. A cap was put on the head…"[17] The corpse's neck was left exposed.

Joseph of Arimathea owned an expensive tomb near the place where Jesus was crucified, a tomb which had never been used. He and Nicodemus laid Jesus' body there (Mt. 27:57–61; Jn.19:38–42). A large heavy stone was rolled over the opening to the tomb to seal it shut. Mary Magdalene and the other Mary sat outside the tomb, observing what happened. Pilate ordered the tomb to be sealed and the Roman soldiers to guard the tomb (Mt. 27:62–66).

From sundown Friday through sundown Saturday, Jesus' followers rested as required by the Jewish Sabbath laws.

THE RESURRECTION OF JESUS CHRIST

1. THE DIRECT EVIDENCE

Early on Sunday morning, the first day of the week, while it was still dark, Mary Magdalene, Mary the mother of James, Joanna, and some other women came to Jesus' tomb. They first noticed that the large stone over the tomb opening had been rolled back. They ventured cautiously into the tomb and saw that Jesus' body was not there! Suddenly two angels in dazzling garments stood beside them and said: "Why do you seek the living among the dead? He is not here, but is risen! Remember how he spoke to you when he was still in Galilee, saying, 'The Son of Man must be delivered into the hands of sinful men, and be crucified, and the third day rise again'" (Lk. 24:5–7).

They remembered Jesus' words, and fearfully yet joyfully, they hurried back to the place where the Apostles and Jesus' other followers were gathered and told them the news. But "... this story of theirs seemed pure nonsense, and they did not believe them" (Lk. 24:11, Jerusalem Bible).

But Peter and John went running to the tomb. John, the younger man, outran Peter and got to the tomb first. John bent down to look into the tomb, but he did not go inside until Peter had entered the tomb first. Then John went in and saw the linen burial wrappings lying there, and he believed that Jesus was indeed risen from the dead.

What did John see that caused him to believe immediately? The body of Jesus was not there although the linen burial wrappings were lying there like an empty cocoon. John noticed particularly the detail that the cloth which had been on Jesus' head was lying apart from the linen body wrappings, separated by the space where Jesus' neck had been, and the head covering was collapsed lying apart by itself (Jn. 20:6–7). The body of Jesus was gone but the grave clothes, the burial wrappings, were still there! What had happened?

The only conclusion was that Jesus' body had somehow been changed so that it had passed through the burial wrappings and the head covering, leaving them lying like an empty cocoon.

Jesus' physical body had been changed into a resurrection body that had passed right through physical matter! Jesus had been raised from the dead!

This conclusion was confirmed and verified by Jesus' resurrection appearances to his disciples. Jesus, risen from the dead, appeared to his disciples on at least eleven occasions. There may have been others not mentioned in the New Testament (Jn. 21:25; Acts 1:3), but it tells us explicitly of these:

1. To Mary Magdalene (Jn. 20:14–18; Mk.16:9–11) and "the other Mary" (Mt.28:1–10)

2. To Simon Peter, whose original Aramaic name was Cephas (Lk. 24:34; 1 Cor.15:5)

3. To Cleopas and another disciple on the road to Emmaus (Lk. 24:13–35)

4. To the Apostles that first Easter Sunday evening [Thomas was absent] (Jn. 20:19-24; Lk. 24:36)

5. To the Apostles a week later with Thomas present (Jn. 20:26–29)

6. To seven of the Apostles by the Sea of Tiberias (Sea of Galilee) when Jesus prepared breakfast for them, namely, Simon Peter, Thomas, Nathanael, "the sons of Zebedee" (James and John) and two others (Jn. 21:1–14)

7. To the Eleven Apostles on a mountain in Galilee Jesus had appointed, where he gave them "The Great Commission" (Mt. 28:16–20)

8. To over five hundred disciples at one time, most of whom were still alive when St. Paul was writing about 20 years after the event, though some had died ("fallen asleep") (1 Cor.15:6)

9. To James (probably James, the brother of Jesus) (1 Cor.15:7)

10. To the Apostles when Jesus ascended into heaven (Acts 1:1–11)

11. To Saul of Tarsus (the Apostle Paul) on the road to Damascus (Acts 9:1–19; 22:1–16; 26:12–18)

The Apostles have an important and absolutely indispensable role in salvation history. They are the official eyewitnesses to Jesus' Resurrection. They had been with him for three years, through all of his public ministry, beginning with his baptism by John the Baptizer up through his Ascension into heaven, and they are the eyewitnesses of Jesus' Resurrection (Acts 1:21–22).

The Apostles are absolutely unique in history. They are the persons specially appointed by God to bring their eyewitness testimony concerning the life, death, and resurrection of Jesus Christ to the world, including us today. They are the ones who could say from first-hand knowledge:

> I know Jesus came back from the dead. I saw him with my own eyes. I heard him speaking with my own ears. He was no ghost: I saw him eat a piece of fish. I was there in the

Upper Room when he appeared suddenly in our midst after passing through the locked doors. I saw the marks on his hands and feet where the nails had been. I saw the marks from the spear wound in his side. He ate and drank with us. I saw him lifted off the earth in a cloud of heavenly glory. Jesus is alive!

The various books of the New Testament were either written by an Apostle, or based on the testimony and teaching of an Apostle, and the climactic point in their testimony is that Jesus is alive. He has been raised from the dead.

The factual, historical basis for our belief that Jesus was put to death and then three days later was raised to life again is the eyewitness testimony of the Apostles.

2. THE INDIRECT EVIDENCE

In courts of law, there are two types of evidence: direct evidence and indirect evidence, also called circumstantial evidence.

The direct evidence of the fact that Jesus was brought back to life again after his death and burial is the evidence of the eyewitnesses, the Apostles and his other followers to whom he appeared.

The indirect or circumstantial evidence of Jesus' Resurrection is those things which have happened after the event which would not have happened if the primary fact, the Resurrection of Jesus, were not true. There are six items of indirect evidence of Jesus' Resurrection to consider here:

a. The drastic change in the disciples. The night Jesus was betrayed, his disciples all deserted him and ran away (Mk.14:50). At the Crucifixion at Calvary (Golgotha), John is the only one of the Twelve mentioned as being present, but the women who followed Jesus, including Mary his mother, were there. Apparently, the men were afraid of being arrested themselves and put to death, for when they met, it was in secret with the doors locked "for fear of the Jews" (Jn. 20:19).

Then three chapters later in the Bible, we find Peter and the other Apostles boldly appearing in public, preaching Jesus and his Resurrection with such power that on the day of Pentecost about 3,000 were converted (Acts chapter 2). We see Peter and John going boldly into the Temple in Jerusalem, healing a lame man in public, preaching in Solomon's Porch with the result that hundreds more were converted (Acts 3:1–4:4).

What had happened to change the apostles from hiding and cowering in fear to preaching in public with great boldness? Jesus had been raised from the dead and had appeared to them, and they had been empowered by the life-giving Spirit of the Risen Lord Jesus.

The Apostles were so completely convinced of the truth of Jesus' Resurrection that they left their homes and traveled far and wide carrying on the work of Jesus, preaching, teaching, working miracles, healing the sick, casting out evil spirits, and even raising the dead.

A fact that shouts with significance is that all of the apostles, except John, died the death of martyrs rather than deny their belief in Jesus and his Resurrection. The blood of the martyrs from the 1st century to the 21st century cries out the truth that Jesus is God and that he is not dead but alive now and forevermore.

b. The change of worship from Saturday to Sunday. For many centuries the Jews had worshipped God on the seventh day of the week, Saturday ("Sabbath" means 7th). It seems that at first, the Jewish Christians continued to observe the Jewish laws and customs, including Sabbath worship, but they also gathered to celebrate the Lord's Supper ("the breaking of the bread") on Sunday, the first day of the week (Acts 20:7). Sunday became known as "the Lord's Day," that is, the special day to worship Jesus the Lord. St. John was "in the Spirit on the Lord's Day" in exile on the Island of Patmos when he received the Revelation (Rev. 1:9–10).

It seems that as the Jewish religion and the Christian faith separated, the Christians ceased the Sabbath observance and began worshipping only on Sunday, the special Day of the Lord Jesus. Something drastic had happened to change such a deeply held, centuries-old custom: Jesus had been raised from the dead on the first day of the week.

The fact that the vast majority of Christians worship God through Jesus Christ on Sunday, the first day of the week, rather than on Saturday, the seventh day of the week ("the Sabbath"), is strong indirect evidence of Jesus' Resurrection from the dead. Indeed, every Sunday is a celebration of Jesus' Resurrection. Every Sunday is an Easter.

c. The very existence of the New Testament writings. The New Testament is an extraordinary collection of writings. There are twenty-seven different books written by eight or nine different persons. The writings are of different literary types: Gospels, history (Acts), letters ("Epistles"), and a book of Apocalypse (Revelation).

But despite their diversity and variety, the New Testament writings agree on the central fact that Jesus died and came back from the dead and is now alive.

The New Testament was written either by those who were eyewitnesses to the events (such as the Gospels of Matthew and John) or by those who based their accounts on the testimony of the eyewitnesses (such as Mark and Luke and Paul). If the Resurrection were not true, the very existence of the New Testament would make no sense.

d. *The existence of the Christian Church.* The Church of Jesus Christ is an astounding thing: here is a multitude of people all over the world, speaking many different languages, of many cultures, of many different racial and ethnic groups, of all social classes, of all levels of education, from the desperately poor to the incredibly rich, who despite their tremendous differences are united in one spiritual body, in one great family, brothers and sisters to each other, agreed on two basic beliefs: that the man Jesus is Lord (God) and that after being put to death, he came back to life again (Rom.10:9).

Despite its diversity and divisions, its many differing forms and styles of worship, its various doctrines and practices, its many churches, denominations and organizations, the people that constitute the church are united in believing that Jesus is God and that he rose from the dead.

The existence of such a group of people through 2,000 years of human history, and the spread of this people throughout the world, is absolutely astounding. The existence of the Church would not make any sense if the Resurrection of Jesus were not true.

e. *Baptism.* The practice of baptism is a strong indirect evidence of the Resurrection of Jesus Christ. In Christian baptism, we are united with the burial and resurrection of Jesus. As St. Paul wrote:

> "[D]o you not know that as many of us as were baptized into Christ Jesus were baptized into his death? Therefore we were buried with him through baptism into death, that just as Christ was raised from the dead by the glory of the Father, even so we also should walk in newness of life. For if we have been united together in the likeness of his death, certainly we also shall be in the likeness of his resurrection."
>
> (Rom. 6:3–5)

Various issues concerning baptism divide Christian groups. But the Lord Jesus himself commanded that his followers baptize disciples with water "in the name of the Father and of the Son and of the Holy Spirit" (The "Great Commission," Mt. 28:19).

The Risen Lord Jesus himself said: "He who believes and is baptized will be saved; but he who does not believe will be condemned" (Mk.16:16).

If it were not for Jesus' Resurrection, baptism would not make sense. Throughout the ages since Jesus walked on this earth, Christians have found by their own experience that baptism joins their lives to the death and resurrection of Christ and enables them to live in newness of life.

f. *The Lord's Supper.* On the first Easter Sunday afternoon, Cleopas and another disciple were walking from Jerusalem to a village named Emmaus about seven miles away, discussing the extraordinary events which had just taken place. The man they hoped was the Messiah had been put to death on a cross three days earlier, but amazingly, some of the disciples had gone to the tomb and found it empty and an angel had told them Jesus was alive.

As they were talking, a Stranger joined them and asked them what they were discussing as they walked along. They told him the things that had happened. The Stranger said that they were so foolish and slow of heart to believe what the prophets had written. Then he explained to them from the Old Testament Scriptures how it was necessary for the Messiah to suffer such things and then enter into his glory.

When they reached Emmaus, the two disciples urged the Stranger to come inside and stay with them that night. During supper, the Stranger took bread, blessed it, broke it, and gave it to them, the same way he had done when he fed the multitude of 5,000, when he had fed the Gentile crowd of 4,000, and when he had celebrated the Passover with his disciples in the Upper Room on the night he had been betrayed.

It was only "[t]hen their eyes were opened and they knew him; and he vanished from their sight."

They hurried back to Jerusalem in the nighttime and found the Apostles and the others gathered together, and told them what had happened to them on the road and how Jesus had made himself known to them in the breaking of the bread (Lk. 24:13–35).

From that day to this, hundreds of millions of Christians have had this same experience, that the Risen Lord Jesus Christ is present and makes himself known in the breaking of the bread, whether it is called the Lord's Supper, the Holy Communion, the Mass, the Divine Liturgy; whether it is called an ordinance or a sacrament or a mystery; whether it is celebrated very simply in a mud hut or with exalted ritual in a magnificent cathedral. In this worship, the Risen Lord Jesus Christ shares his very life, his body and his blood, with his people, renewing and refreshing and strengthening them with his presence.

This experience could not happen if Jesus had not been raised from the dead to life and were not now alive, ruling and reigning over heaven and earth

Summary

The Christian faith is founded on the fact of Jesus' Resurrection: that after he died on the cross for the sins of the world, and he was buried on Friday, on Sunday he was brought back to glorious life in his Resurrection body. There is ample evidence of the fact. There is the direct, eyewitness testimony of the Apostles to the empty tomb and the Resurrection appearances where Jesus met with them, spoke with them, and ate and drank with them. Furthermore, there is the indirect evidence of uncontroverted facts that would not have happened and would not make any sense if Jesus had not been raised from the dead.

The bodily resurrection of Jesus Christ is the best proved fact in the history of mankind, said the British educator Thomas Arnold; it is a "fact beyond dispute," said Lord Caldecote, a Lord Chief Justice of England. "…there is no single historic incident better or more variously supported than the resurrection of Christ," said B. F. Westcott.[18]

Because Jesus has been raised from the dead, we can have confidence as his followers, that we, too, shall be raised from the dead and come to the glorious resurrection. We have Jesus' word on it: "I am the resurrection and the life. He who believes in Me, though he may die, he shall live. And whoever lives and believes in Me shall never die" (Jn. 11:25–26).

And, wonder of wonders, even today in this world of troubles, trials, and tribulations, in the midst of our suffering and sorrow and pain, by the power of Jesus' Resurrection coming to us through faith, we can live here and now in newness of life, and even now we can experience something of "the powers of the age to come" (Heb. 6:5).

THE ASCENSION OF JESUS

For forty days after his Resurrection from the dead, Jesus made at least ten bodily appearances to his followers, sometimes to only one person as to Mary Magdalene and James, more often to a group of his followers, to the Apostles, to a wider group of disciples, once to as many as 500 people at one time.

During these forty days, the Risen Jesus seemed to pass back and forth between the natural, physical realm of existence and the supernatural, spiritual realm. He could pass through physical matter, first through his grave clothes, then through locked doors. He walked and talked. He could appear suddenly and vanish just as quickly. He ate food and drank, but there is no indication that eating and drinking were necessary for him. He showed the disciples the marks from the nails in his hands and his feet and the spear wound in his side, so there would be no doubt that it was he himself, that the same person who had been put to death on the cross had risen from the dead.

Then after the forty-day period was over, his bodily appearances here on earth ceased and Jesus left this earth in bodily form to return to heaven. This event is called his Ascension into heaven. He ascended—that is, went up—from earth to heaven.

St. Luke gives us the most details of that event, at the end of his Gospel and also at the beginning of the Acts of the Apostles. At the end of his Gospel, St. Luke writes:

> "And he [Jesus] led them out as far as Bethany, and he lifted up his hands and blessed them. Now it came to pass, while he blessed them, that he was parted from them and carried up into heaven. And they worshiped him, and returned to Jerusalem with great joy; and were continually in the temple praising and blessing God."
>
> (Lk. 24:50–53)

While Jesus was in the very act of blessing them with his hands uplifted, he was taken up from them. What a blessed memory the disciples must have carried with them the rest of their lives: the last glimpse they had of Jesus was of him with arms uplifted, bestowing his blessing upon them.

In Acts 1:1–11 St. Luke gives us more details of the event, including the fact that Jesus was lifted up off the earth in a cloud which took him out of their sight. This was not an ordinary rain cloud, but was the cloud of the glory of God's presence (the *Shekinah*). It is on the cloud of God's glory that Jesus will return from heaven (Acts 1:11; Rev.14:14).

The truth of the event called "The Ascension" is further shown by the many references in the New Testament to Jesus sitting at the right hand of God and awaiting his return to earth in his Second Coming. In his sermon on the Day of Pentecost, St. Peter said that Jesus the Messiah "must remain in heaven until the time of universal restoration that God announced long ago through his holy prophets" (Acts 3:21, NRSV). Some other references are Jn. 6:62, Eph. 4:8–10, 1 Thes.1:10, Heb. 4:14 and 9:24, 1 Pet. 3:22 and Rev. 5:6.

It is significant that in heaven, Jesus is seated at the right of God the Father. The priests in the Temple in Jerusalem had to stand up while offering sacrifices over and over, but Jesus is sitting down in heaven because his work on earth is done. He has made the one final, all-sufficient sacrifice for the sins of the whole world, once and for all time (Heb.10:11–14). When Jesus died on the cross, his work of making atonement for sin was finished, completed, totally accomplished. That is why from the cross just before he died, he cried out, "It is finished!" (Jn.19:30).

No wonder that in heaven the "myriads of myriads and thousands of thousands" of angels, the beasts, and the elders sing with loud voice:

> "Worthy is the Lamb that was slain to receive power, and riches, and wisdom, and strength, and honor, and glory, and blessing."
>
> (Rev. 5:12, KJV)

and that all creatures everywhere in the universe respond, "Blessing, and honor, and glory, and power, be unto him that sitteth upon the throne, and unto the Lamb for ever and ever" (Rev. 5:13, KJV).

Now that Jesus has ascended back into heaven and is seated at the right hand of God the Father, we might ask, "What is he doing now?"

(1) *He is ruling and reigning over heaven and earth.* The Ascension is the Enthronement of Jesus as King ruling over all things. All power and authority has been given unto him, both in heaven and on earth (Mt. 28:18). He is the King above all earthly kings, the Lord over all earthly lords, and the Governor over all the world's governments (Rev. 1:5). This rule and reign of Christ fulfills the role of the Messiah foretold by the prophets as the One who will sit on the throne of David and reign over all nations forever. That is why the New Testament stresses the fact that Jesus was descended from the line of David (2 Tim. 2:8). King David died and his tomb is in Jerusalem to this day, but David's Lord, Jesus, is alive and will rule as King forever.

(2) *He is preparing a place for us.* To comfort his disciples on the night in which he was betrayed, Jesus told them something he had not told them before: "In my Father's house there are many dwelling places. If it were not so, would I have told you

that I go to prepare a place for you? And if I go and prepare a place for you, I will come again and will take you to myself, so that where I am, there you may be also" (Jn.14:2–3, NRSV).

(3) *Jesus is praying and interceding for us, his people.* That Jesus who is God is praying to his Father who is God is a spiritual mystery. But it is true. "He ever lives to make intercession for [us]" (Heb 7:25). St. Paul writes: "... Christ Jesus ... indeed intercedes for us" (Rom. 8:34, NRSV). God the Father always hears and answers the prayers of his Beloved Son (Jn. 11:41, 42). Therefore, since Jesus is praying, interceding, and pleading for us, there is no doubt that God the Father hears and answers Jesus' prayers for us. Until we get to heaven, we will never understand how we have been protected and blessed through Jesus' prayers for us, what dangers we were not even aware of God has protected us from, what strength and blessings God has given us.

(4) *Jesus is waiting for the time when he will return to earth.* "But when Christ had offered for all time a single sacrifice for sins, 'he sat down at the right hand of God,' and since then has been waiting 'until his enemies would be made a footstool for his feet'" (Heb.10:12–13, NRSV). In his sermon on the Day of Pentecost, St. Peter said that Jesus "must remain in heaven until the time of universal restoration that God announced long ago through his holy prophets" (Acts 3:21, NRSV).

The return of Jesus back into heaven that we call the Ascension is an indispensable element of the Gospel. During the forty-day period of his Resurrection appearances, it seems that Jesus was bound by the limitations of space and time. He could only be in one place at a time. However, with his Ascension from earth to heaven, he has gone back to the spiritual realm of heaven, seated at the right hand of God the Father, where he is no longer limited by space and time. Therefore, people all over the world can pray to him, and he hears them. His presence can be with people all over the world no matter where they are. He can be present with people throughout all time, through the centuries, now and forever. The Ascension has made it possible for Jesus to fulfill his parting word to his disciples: "And remember, I am with you always, to the end of the age"(Mt. 28:20, NRSV).

God has made this possible through the gift of the Holy Spirit which we will consider next.

Part Four:
God Is Saving His People

A PENTECOST

Before he ascended back into heaven, Jesus "ordered his apostles not to leave Jerusalem, but to wait there for the promise of the Father" for they would soon be baptized by the Holy Spirit (Acts 1:4–5, NRSV).

They did what Jesus had told them to do and returned to Jerusalem from Mount Olivet and went to the upstairs room where they were staying. All eleven Apostles were there [Judas had committed suicide], as well as Mary, the mother of Jesus, his brothers, and some other women. The group of about 120 believers devoted themselves to prayer and waited for God to act.

On the day of Pentecost, fifty days after Jesus' Resurrection, they were all together in one place when an amazing thing happened:

> "And suddenly there came a sound from heaven, as of a rushing mighty wind, and it filled the whole house where they were sitting. Then there appeared to them divided tongues, as of fire, and one sat upon each of them. And they were all filled with the Holy Spirit and began to speak with other tongues, as the Spirit gave them utterance."
>
> (Acts 2:2–4)

At the Feast of Pentecost, Jerusalem was filled with Jews and proselytes from all around the Mediterranean, from North Africa to Rome. "…[A]t this sound the crowd gathered and was bewildered, because each one heard them speaking in the native language of each," telling of the wonderful, powerful acts of God. They were amazed, bewildered and perplexed because the Apostles speaking in other languages were Galileans, yet each one of the gathering crowd heard them in his own mother tongue. The crowd was asking, 'What does this mean?' but others sneered and said, 'They are filled with new wine'" (Acts 2:6, 12–13, NRSV).

Peter, standing with the other Apostles, explained that they were not drunk (it was only 9 o'clock in the morning) but what was happening was a mighty thing: God was fulfilling his promise through the prophet Joel (2:28–31) that in the last days, he would pour out his Spirit upon all people, young and old, slave and free, men and women, so that "whoever calls on the name of the Lord shall be saved" (Acts 2:21).

Then Peter preached of the ministry of Jesus, his death, and Resurrection from the dead of which the Apostles were eyewitnesses, his exaltation at the right hand of God as Lord and Messiah, and that the people of Israel had murdered God's Messiah by handing him over to the Romans to be crucified. Jesus had said that when the Holy Spirit came, he would convict the world of sin (Jn. 16:8-9), and that was what happened—the people were convicted of the sin of murdering the Messiah (Acts 2:37). They asked the Apostles what they must do to be forgiven and saved. Peter responded:

> "'Repent, and let every one of you be baptized in the name of Jesus Christ for the remission of sins; and you shall receive the gift of the Holy Spirit. For the promise is to you and to your children, and to all who are afar off, as many as the Lord our God will call.'"
>
> (Acts 2:38–39)

So those who received Peter's message about Jesus were

baptized that day, about 3,000 people. The believers "devoted themselves to the apostles' teaching and fellowship, to the breaking of bread [the Lord's Supper, which they celebrated in their homes, Acts 2:46)] and the prayers" [the Jewish worship in the Temple] (Acts 2:42, NRSV).

The Church of Jesus Christ had been born into the world and, like a newborn healthy child, had begun its vigorous and vital life, breathing in the Holy Spirit and crying out praises to God.

WHO IS THE HOLY SPIRIT?

Many people have a confused, vague, and unclear idea of the Holy Spirit. It helps us to clarify and focus our understanding of the Holy Spirit to realize that the Holy Spirit is the Spirit of Jesus (2 Cor. 3:17).

The Holy Spirit was not given to the disciples until Jesus was ascended into heaven. Then at the day of Pentecost the risen, ascended Lord Jesus poured out his Spirit (Acts 2:33). The results were that the Apostles spoke in other tongues; the crowd heard them glorifying God in their own languages; and they were "cut to the heart;" and 3,000 of them were brought to repentance, faith, and baptism through the work of the Holy Spirit.

This was the same Holy Spirit who filled Jesus in his life on earth. He was conceived by the power of the Holy Spirit. At his baptism, the Holy Spirit descended upon him like a dove to empower him for his ministry. It was by the power of the same Holy Spirit that Jesus worked mighty signs and wonders and miracles. It was by the power of the same Holy Spirit that the Word of God went forth from the mouth of Jesus with powerful, life-giving effectiveness, even raising the dead.

Some Scriptural references which teach us that the Holy Spirit is the Spirit of Jesus are John 20:22 where the Holy Spirit is given to the Apostles through the breath of the Risen Lord Jesus. *See also,* Acts 16:7, Rom. 8:9, Gal. 4:6, 1 Cor. 15:45, and Phil. 1:19.

The Holy Spirit is a Person with his own personality. The Scriptures refer to the Holy Spirit as "He," not "It." The Holy Spirit has the attributes of personhood. For example,

- He speaks (Acts 1:16, 4:25, 21:11; 1 Tim. 4:1).
- He prays (Rom. 8:26–27).
- He thinks and makes decisions (Acts 15:28, 16:7).
- He has desires (James 4:5).
- He can be outraged (Heb.10:29).
- He can be grieved (Eph. 4:30).

The Holy Spirit is God; God the Father is God; Jesus Christ is God. There are not three Gods, but only One God (Deut. 6:4) who reveals himself to us in three different ways, as the Father, as the Son (Jesus Christ), and as the Holy Spirit, One God in three Persons, blessed Trinity.

HOW DOES SALVATION COME TO US?

Thus far in this book, all that God has done for our salvation has been accomplished apart from us, in the past. How does the great salvation which God has prepared for us become connected with our lives here and now? The mighty deeds of God in creation and in the life, death, resurrection, and ascension of Jesus took place centuries ago, and we live now. How is the time-gap bridged? God is in heaven and Jesus sits at the right hand of God in heaven, and we are on earth. How is the spiritual space-gap between us and God overcome?

In short, how is the salvation which God has provided through the life, death, resurrection, and ascension of his Son, Jesus Christ, applied to our lives here and now? How do we come into union with the Living God?

The answer is that the Holy Spirit, the Spirit of Jesus Christ, bridges the 2,000 year time-gap between the earthly life of Jesus and our lives now and bridges the space-gap between God in heaven and us on earth. It is the Holy Spirit that applies God's salvation to us here and now.

The Holy Spirit cannot be seen any more than God the Father can be seen. "No one has seen God at any time" (Jn.1:18). Although we cannot see the Holy Spirit any more than we can see the wind, we can see the effects of the Spirit's activity, just as we can hear the sound of the wind (Jn. 3:8) and see the leaves rustling on the trees.

Apart from Christ, we are "dead in trespasses and sins" (Eph. 2:1). Dead people cannot make a decision for Christ; they cannot make any decisions. Dead people cannot give their lives to Jesus Christ; they cannot give anything to anybody. Dead people cannot receive the salvation God has brought in Jesus Christ; they cannot lift up their hands and receive anything. So, in order for us to receive the salvation God has brought us through Jesus Christ, first the Holy Spirit must give us life. And this is exactly what he does:

> "But God, who is rich in mercy, because of his great love with which he loved us, even when we were dead in trespasses, made us alive together with Christ (by grace you have been saved) and raised us up together..."
>
> (Eph. 2:4–6)

The Lord Jesus himself taught that we cannot be saved without having the new life from God, indeed, that we cannot even see the Kingdom of God without being born again from above (Jn. 3:3). We have natural life now, the life of flesh, but we cannot enter God's Kingdom without being born into spiritual life, without being born of water and the Spirit. It is the Holy Spirit that gives us this re-birth, this new spiritual life (Jn. 3:1–8).

Thus, the first thing the Holy Spirit does within us is to regenerate us. Regeneration is the word theologians use to describe this work of the Holy Spirit in giving life to sinners who are spiritually dead in trespasses and sins, giving them new life like being born again, bringing them from the natural life of the flesh into the abundant life of the Spirit.

In bringing about our regeneration, the Holy Spirit works

not by himself, but through the Word of God. Of course, God is sovereign and he can do whatever he pleases (Ps. 115:3), by any method he chooses, sometimes by intervening directly in a person's life. But most of the time he works through means, not directly but through agents and instruments. Usually, when a person is converted and brought to new life, the Holy Spirit works through the Word of God.

The "Word of God" written is the Holy Bible, both the Old Testament and the New Testament. The "Word of God" incarnate is Jesus himself, for he is the Word of God and the Wisdom of God in human flesh. Jesus is God's final word to us. After Jesus ascended back up into heaven and the Holy Spirit was given, "the Word of God" is the message about Jesus Christ; that is, preaching and teaching that tells Who Jesus is and what he has done to accomplish salvation. This message about Jesus has been put into written form in the New Testament. The Holy Spirit works through the Word, the message about Jesus whether in spoken form or in written form, to convict us of sin, to make the message of the salvation God offers to guilty sinners alive in our hearts and minds, and to give us the desire to turn from our sin to Jesus and to receive the great salvation and new life he offers.

Peter's sermon on the day of Pentecost and the results that followed show us in a powerful way the Holy Spirit working through the Word of God to accomplish the purposes of God (Acts 2:14–42). Peter proclaimed that the Messiah Whom God had sent, Jesus Christ, had been wrongfully put to death by the people of Israel who were hearing his sermon, but that God had raised Jesus from the dead, that Jesus had ascended into heaven, and that God had now poured out his Holy Spirit as they had seen and heard. Then in the climax of his sermon, Peter proclaimed: "Therefore let all the house of Israel know assuredly that God has made this Jesus, whom you crucified, both Lord and Christ" (Acts 2:36).

The response of the people: "Now when they heard this,

they were cut to the heart, and said to Peter and the rest of the apostles, 'Men and brethren, what shall we do [to be saved]?'" (Acts 2:37).

Peter's answer: "Repent, and let every one of you be baptized in the name of Jesus Christ for the remission of sins; and you shall receive the gift of the Holy Spirit" (Acts 2:38).

How can we receive the gift of the Holy Spirit? Simply by asking God for it. The Lord Jesus himself said, "If you, then, bad as you are, know how to give your children what is good for them, how much more will the heavenly Father give the Holy Spirit to those who ask him!" (Lk.11:13, NEB).

D
HUMAN RESPONSE TO THE MESSAGE OF SALVATION

When the message of salvation is presented to us, what response is called for on our part?

Twice in the Book of Acts, the Apostles are directly faced with the question: "What must I do to be saved?" At Pentecost, Peter answered the question: "Repent, and let every one of you be baptized in the name of Jesus Christ for the remission of sins" (Acts 2:38). At Philippi, when Paul and Silas were in prison, the jailer, after being stopped from committing suicide, fell down trembling and asked: "Sirs, what must I do to be saved?" (Acts 16:30) and Paul answered: "Believe on the Lord Jesus Christ, and you will be saved, you and your household" (Acts 16:31). [At Pentecost, faith in Jesus as Messiah is implicit in repentance, for rejecting Jesus as the Messiah and having him put to death was the specific sin that "cut them to the heart."]

Thus, we see that normally when the Gospel is preached, a three-fold response is called for on the part of those who hear the message: (1) repent, (2) believe on the Lord Jesus Christ, and (3) be baptized. Let us consider these in order.

1. REPENTANCE

The root meaning of the word translated "repent" is "to change one's mind." Repentance involves changing our minds about who we are and who Jesus is.

Perhaps before the Gospel came through to us, we had thought we were pretty good people and had not done anything really seriously wrong. Certainly we were a lot better than many other people. But now we see that we have broken God's Law. We have not done things we should have done but rather have done things we should not have done. Now we begin to see that we have sinned and are sinners. Instead of being the good people we thought we were, we have deceived ourselves and the truth is that we are selfish to the core. Our motivations have been directed toward our own pleasure and comfort, with little thought for anyone else. We are corrupt in our hearts. We are separated from God, and have made a mess of our lives. When we repent, we come to see more of the truth about ourselves, that we are sinners deserving nothing but God's punishment.

Repentance also involves changing our minds about who Jesus is. Whereas before, we had paid him no attention, not acknowledged his claims upon us, perhaps even positively hated and scorned him. We had thought he was just another human being whom we could ignore, but now we see that he is God from heaven in human flesh. He has created us and all the whole creation, and we have been dependent upon him for every breath we have taken. Furthermore, now we come to see that he loves us and has always loved us with an everlasting love, that he has taken our sins upon himself in his death on the cross, and that he was raised from the dead and now rules over everything in heaven and on earth, so we need to get down on our knees and get right with him.

Often, however, the Holy Spirit as "the finger of God" convicts us in regard to a particular sin in our life. He puts his finger on our sore spot, perhaps a specific sin we have committed or a particular sinful, harmful personality trait we have which the Bible calls a "besetting sin." he puts pressure on us at that vulnerable point until the pain becomes unbearable, and we cry out to God for forgiveness and relief.

Repentance thus goes far beyond simply changing our thinking about ourselves and about Jesus Christ. It goes much deeper than simply being sorry for what we have done, regretting it, feeling remorse about it. To repent is to be converted, to turn from self to God, not just confessing our sins but forsaking them (Prov. 28:13), to change the direction of our lives from sin and self toward God, from being headed toward death and destruction to begin to move toward life and a productive life-style.

The Bible contrasts false and true repentance as "worldly grief" as opposed to "godly grief" (2 Cor. 7:10). A person can be sorry for a sin they have committed, regret it deeply, and feel great remorse over it. But without turning to Jesus for forgiveness, such a "worldly grief" can lead to hopelessness and overwhelming guilt resulting in deep depression and even suicide. In "godly grief" over sin, the person feels sorrow, regret and remorse, but also has the hope that God will have mercy upon him and forgive him of his sin, renew him, and lead him into a new life, so he turns to Jesus Christ for salvation and prays for God to have mercy upon him.

The lives of two of the Twelve Apostles give us a powerful illustration of the difference between worldly grief and godly grief over sin. Both Peter and Judas Iscariot sinned grievously against Jesus, Judas by betraying Jesus to his enemies, Peter by denying three times that he even knew him. Both Peter and Judas repented (Mt. 26:75, 27:3). But Judas' repentance was a worldly grief that led him to commit suicide; he did not turn to Jesus for forgiveness. Peter's repentance was a godly grief that led him to receive Jesus' forgiveness and new life. Judas' life ended in destruction; Peter's life was tremendously productive for God's Kingdom.

"Repent, and believe the Good News!" (Mk.1:15, NRSV).

2. FAITH

"Believe on the Lord Jesus Christ, and you will be saved, you and your household," the Apostle Paul said to the jailer at Philippi (Acts 16:31). What does it mean to believe on the Lord Jesus Christ?

Faith has many aspects to it; it is a word rich with meaning. With regard to faith in Jesus Christ, there are two things in particular that we must believe about him to be saved: "...if you confess with your lips that Jesus is Lord [that is, God] and believe in your heart that God raised him from the dead, you will be saved" (Rom.10:9, NRSV). True faith means believing (1) that Jesus is Lord, that is, that this man Jesus is God from heaven in human flesh, and (2) that after he was put to death on the cross, God raised him from the dead. This confession of faith is the heart and foundation of the Christian faith.

And yet saving faith is not simply believing in our minds that these propositions about Jesus are true, but believing sincerely, with all our hearts, that Jesus is God and that he is alive, ruling and reigning over heaven and earth. Faith is not merely a matter of the intellect but is a relationship between two persons: Jesus and ourselves. Faith is a vital, life-giving relationship by which our lives, our whole beings, are united with the living Lord Jesus. It is a relationship like the branch of a grapevine is related to the vine: the branch is part of the vine, it is attached to the vine, and it is totally dependent upon the vine to give it life and nourishment and make it fruitful (Jn.15:1–11). The branch has no life apart from the vine.

The primary indication that we are in this personal, vital, life-giving relationship with Jesus Christ is prayer. By the very act of praying to him, or to God the Father through him, we are acknowledging our faith. Because Jesus is fully human, as Man he himself has been tempted and tested just as we are (but without sinning), and because Jesus is fully God, he has all power in heaven and on earth and therefore has the power and ability to give us what we need (Heb. 4:14–15). "Let us therefore come boldly to the throne of grace, that we may obtain mercy and find grace to help in time of need" (Heb. 4:16).

Prayer may be expressed by our actions as well as by our words. Several times in the Gospel of Luke, we find people coming to Jesus and not expressing any verbal confession of faith in him, but showing by their actions that they believed that Jesus had power to help them, and Jesus said to them: "Your faith has saved you" (Lk. 7:50, 8:48, 17:19, 18:42). These people would not have come to Jesus to receive help with their problems if they had not believed that Jesus had power to help them and, in fact, would help them and answer their prayer. "And without faith it is impossible to please God, for whoever would approach him must believe that he exists and that he rewards those who seek him" (Heb. 11:6, NRSV).

Believe in the Lord Jesus Christ and you will be saved, because God promises that "whoever calls upon the name of the Lord shall be saved" (Rom.10:13).

3. BAPTISM

Jesus himself commanded that his followers be baptized. When he gave his Apostles their final instructions, his order was that they should "Go therefore and make disciples of all the nations, baptizing them in the name of the Father and of the Son and of the Holy Spirit, teaching them to observe all things" he had commanded them. (Mt. 28:19, "The Great Commission"). This is not a suggestion, but an imperative order from Jesus as the Commander of his army of believers.

In the Acts of the Apostles, we find Christians acting in obedience to Jesus' command to baptize those who became disciples:

- In Jerusalem on the day of Pentecost those who received Peter's message were baptized, about 3,000 people (Acts 2:41).
- In Damascus, when Saul was converted, he was baptized (Acts 9:18).

- In Caesarea when Gentiles were converted in Cornelius' house, they were baptized (Acts 10:47–48).

- In Philippi, when the Lord opened the heart of Lydia, a businesswoman, to the Gospel, she and her household were baptized (Acts 16:14–15).

- In Philippi, when the jailer was converted, "immediately he and all his family were baptized" (Acts 16:33).

- In Corinth, many of those who heard Paul preach became believers and were baptized (Acts 18:8).

Through the centuries, the Church of Jesus Christ has baptized its members with water in the name of the Father and of the Son and of the Holy Spirit.

Why should a follower of Jesus Christ be baptized with water in the name of God the Father and the Son and the Holy Spirit? The simplest answer is "because Jesus said so."

What is the meaning and significance of baptism?

First, baptism is the way Jesus Christ has prescribed for entering the community of those who believe in him. It is the procedure by which we enter into membership in his organization, the Church. It is the means by which we are made members of his Body here on earth, by which we are joined into union with him and his people.

Within the membership of the community of Jesus' people, there is a God-given equality. All have equal standing regardless of their earthly rank, class, caste, race, ethnic group, attainments, intelligence, age, gender, abilities, poverty or riches, or any other human factor. As St. Paul said:

> "For as many of you as were baptized into Christ have put on Christ.
> There is neither Jew nor Greek,
> there is neither slave nor free,
> there is neither male nor female;
> for you are all one in Christ Jesus."
>
> (Gal. 3:27–28)

As far as God is concerned, even the Apostles have no greater standing than a newly baptized member (Acts 10:47), because we are all members of the Body of Jesus Christ: "For by one Spirit we were all baptized into one body—whether Jews or Greeks, whether slaves or free—and have all been made to drink into one Spirit" (1 Cor.12:13).

Of course, we do not all have the same function to perform within the Body. Only the Apostles can be apostles. God does not call all of us to be evangelists or pastors, for example. But each one of us has our own place of service within Christ's Body (*See*, 1 Corinthians chapter 12). And one is not superior to another because his or her service to God is different from that of another.

God has no second-class citizens in his Kingdom. When the church values one person or group more highly than another on the basis of worldly distinctions, such as favoring the rich over the poor, or one race or ethnic group over another, it is sinning grievously, because it is violating the royal law, given by Jesus Christ the King, to love our neighbors as we love ourselves (James 2:1–13).

Being baptized into the Body of Christ, we are all equal before God, for we are all sinners saved only by his grace.

Second, baptism cleanses us from sin. At Pentecost, when the people asked Peter what they should do to be saved, he replied: "Repent, and let every one of you be baptized in the name of Jesus Christ for the remission of sins; and you shall receive the gift of the Holy Spirit" (Acts 2:38). When Saul of Tarsus was converted, Ananias said to him: "Arise and be baptized, and wash away your sins, calling on the name of the Lord" (Acts 22:16). St. Paul speaks of Christians being cleansed "with the washing of water by the word" (Eph. 5:26. *See also,* 1 Cor. 6:11).

Third, baptism unites us with the death, burial, and resurrection of Jesus Christ. We can see this best represented in the form of baptism by immersion: going all the way down into the water of baptism ("buried with him in baptism"), then being brought up from the water ("risen to walk in newness of life"). As the Apostle Paul wrote:

> "...[D]o you not know that as many of us as were baptized into Christ Jesus were baptized into his death? Therefore we were buried with him through baptism into death, that just as Christ was raised from the dead by the glory of the Father, even so we also should walk in newness of life."
>
> (Rom. 6:3–4; *see also*, Col. 2:12)

Fourth, baptism marks a far-reaching turning point in the direction of our lives. We are baptized "into the name" of God the Father, Jesus Christ the Son, and the Holy Spirit (Rom. 6:3). "This expression ("into the name of Jesus") is probably based on a principle of accounting and bookkeeping in the 1st century "where 'in/into the name of' meant 'to the account of.' That is, baptism was seen as a deed of transfer, an act whereby [the person baptized] handed himself over to be the property or disciple of the one named."[19]

Thus, baptism represents a transfer of control over our lives. Before baptism, we were under the power of Satan, "according to the course of this world, according to the prince of the power of the air, the spirit who now works in the sons of disobedience," as St. Paul says (Eph. 2:2). Then in baptism, God "delivered us from the power of darkness and translated us into the kingdom of the Son of his love, in whom we have redemption through his blood, the forgiveness of sins" (Col. 1:13–14).

Baptism marks a change in our allegiance and loyalty: from Satan to God. It is like a change of citizenship, like a naturalization ceremony whereby our nationality is changed from one country to another. From baptism onwards, "our citizenship is in heaven" (Phil. 3:20). Our ultimate allegiance is no longer to this world and its Satanic ruler, but to God, the Father, the Son Jesus Christ, and the Holy Spirit. After baptism, we no longer feel at home in this world, for it is not our native homeland any longer. Our true native homeland has become the Kingdom of our Lord and Savior Jesus Christ.

Summary

Baptism is of tremendous importance in the life of a Christian. If it were not so important, the Lord Jesus would not have commanded it. He himself said: "He who believes and is baptized will be saved; but he who does not believe will be condemned" (Mk.16:16).

When we consider how important baptism was to the Lord Jesus, being baptized by his cousin John the Baptizer in the Jordan River, commanding it to be observed by his followers, and when we consider the tremendous significance it has in the life of a Christian, it is no wonder that the Apostles speak of baptism in the most exalted terms:

> St. Peter: "And baptism ... now saves you—not as a removal of dirt from the body, but as an appeal to God for a good conscience, through the resurrection of Jesus Christ ..."
>
> (1 Pet. 3:21, NRSV).

> St. Paul: "But when the kindness and the love of God our Savior toward man appeared, not by works of righteousness which we have done, but according to his mercy he saved us, through the washing of regeneration and renewing of the Holy Spirit."
>
> (Tit. 3:4–5)

What response is called for on our part when we are presented with the good news of the salvation God has brought about through the life, death, and resurrection of his Son Jesus Christ? Repent, believe in the Lord Jesus Christ, and be baptized.

Is there an invariable order of events when a person responds to the Gospel? Must he or she first repent, then believe, then be baptized?

God has not commanded that these steps be followed in

any specific order. God can work as he sees best, and he is not bound by any rigid order of steps as to how his Holy Spirit works within people to apply the Gospel to their lives. "Where the Spirit of the Lord is, there is liberty" (2 Cor. 3:17). Like the wind, the Spirit blows where it wishes (Jn. 3:8). God freely works by his Holy Spirit to reach persons depending on their individual needs and circumstances.

Some may indeed repent of their sins first, being overwhelmed with their guilt and turning in faith to Jesus and the atonement he has made on the cross as the remedy for their sins, and then be baptized.

Others may believe in Jesus as Lord and Savior before they see their own sins and their need for cleansing and forgiveness. Some people do not come to an awareness of their sins and the wrongs they have done to other people and the hurts they have given others until they themselves have been overwhelmed with a sense of the astounding love of God toward them in Jesus Christ, and then are brought to repentance.

Many are baptized first, perhaps as infants or as children, before they had any conscious knowledge of sin or of Jesus, and then later in life be brought by the Holy Spirit into a committed relationship to Jesus Christ.

The important thing is not the order in which a person responds to the Gospel, but that he or she *does* respond in repentance, faith, and baptism, whichever comes first.

We must not allow our preconceived notions and ideas to blind us to the astonishing reality of the variety of ways in which God's amazing grace operates. Even in our own day, we are constantly amazed at the surprising diversity of the people Jesus Christ calls unto himself, and the many different ways he uses to bring them to faith.

The Individual Christian and the Local Church

Since New Testament times, there have been Christians who attempted to live their lives as Christians apart by themselves, without active participation in a local congregation of believers. This was a problem in the early church, for why else would the New Testament say, "Let us not hold aloof from our church meetings, as some do" (Heb.10:25, J. B. Phillips).

In our time, this problem seems to be more widespread than ever, to judge by recent articles in Christian publications.

And yet, most of the New Testament pictures of the church are metaphors of a group of people, not individuals. For example:

- "a flock" (Jn. 10:14–16; Acts 20:28; 1 Pet. 5:3)
- "God's household" (1 Tim. 3:15)
- "a commonwealth" (Eph. 2:12)
- "the company of those who believed" (Acts 4:32, RSV)
- "the brotherhood" (1 Peter 2:17).

The word translated "church" is the Greek word *ekklesia* which simply means an assembly.

One of the predominant New Testament pictures of the church, however, is "the body of Christ." The Apostle Paul writes: "Now you are the body of Christ, and members individually" (I Cor.12:27). The passage in 1 Corinthians 12:12–31 is an extended metaphor spelling out how individual Christians are members of the one body of Christ but with different functions. Of course, Jesus Christ is "the head of the church" (Eph. 5:23).

Why is it a necessity for Christians to be active in a local fellowship of believers?

Some reasons are:

1. It is the way we stay connected to Christ, for he is the vine and we are the branches. (John chapter 15). Apart from him, we can do nothing but if we abide in him, we will be fruitful for him and his kingdom (Jn. 15:5).

2. The local fellowship of believers, with all its faults and failings, is our support group, and if we do not gather regularly with God's people, we are depriving ourselves

of a great deal of help and encouragement. In this life we need all the help we can get, because our enemies—the world, our self-centered flesh, and the devil—seek every way possible to drag us down, sap our strength, and make our lives ineffectual.

3. The church is where we receive the life and strength of Jesus Christ through the Lord's Supper.

4. It is in the assembly of believers that we offer God our worship and praise and thanksgiving and receive his life-giving strength, renewal and refreshment.

5. It is there that the Gospel is read and preached and taught and passed on from generation to generation.

It may be theoretically possible to live a Christian life all by yourself, without being active in a local fellowship of believers, but it is not possible as a practical matter.

To try to do so is to disobey Jesus Christ and to separate yourself from him.

THE CHRISTIAN AT WAR

When a person comes to faith in Jesus Christ, repents of sin, believes the good news that in Jesus Christ God has come to save him, and is baptized, it seems that almost immediately he is attacked from every side, from outside himself and from inside himself. This is what happened to Jesus. As soon as he was baptized, immediately the Holy Spirit led him out into the wilderness where he was tempted, spiritually assaulted and attacked by the devil.

According to the Bible and traditional Christian teaching, the attacks upon us come not from one source, but from three directions: the world, the flesh, and the devil. To have victory in the warfare against us, we need to know our enemies and their tactics.

1. THE DEVIL

We may think of the devil as evil coming from beyond ourselves, indeed from beyond this earthly realm. Scripture tells us that the devil was originally an angel of light, but he rebelled against God and persuaded a third of the angels to join him in rebellion. (*See* Rev. 12:4). Michael the Archangel and the angels which remained loyal to God fought against the devil and his angels, defeated them, and cast them out of heaven down upon the earth.

The devil and his demonic soldiers fight fiercely against God's people here on earth. They cannot get at God, so they focus their malicious, malignant, destructive hatred and anger on God's people, trying to take as many of them as possible down with themselves to the eternal torment which awaits them in Hell, and in the meantime to cause God's people as much difficulty as possible. The fallen angels are the demons, the unclean, evil spirits which bedevil the human race. They function in a military type of organization under the devil's command.

The devil is a spiritual being who is more powerful than we are. He has various names which point to different aspects of his activity:

"Devil" means "divider" who separates and divides God and mankind by tempting mankind to hate God, and by causing hatred between human beings who should be united. He divides and causes tremendous hatred between races and ethnic groups, between one religious group and another, between husband and wife, between children and parents, between nations, between friends. The devil works through lies, deceit, fear, and murder. Can anyone deny that the devil is at work in the world today?

"Satan" means "the adversary, the accuser, the tempter." He is the enemy of God's people, accusing us of sins that God has forgiven and tempting us to think and do things which are wrong, which are against God's law and commandments.

"Beelzebub" means "lord of the flies." This name comes from a Canaanite god and points to the work of the devil as commander of the army ("hosts") of demons that seem to swarm around us like flies or bees when they attack, tormenting, afflicting, and oppressing us.

"The dragon" is pictured in Scripture as a gigantic fiery creature thrashing around with his powerful tail, struggling to overthrow the order of God's good creation and to bring disorder and chaos in its place.

The power of the devil is great, greater than human beings, for he is a spiritual being. He exercises his power and control over multitudes of people. No wonder the apostles refer to him as "the god of this age" (2 Cor. 4:4) and tell us that "the whole world lies under the sway of the evil one" (1 Jn. 5:19).

However, the devil and his followers are created beings. Their power is as nothing compared to God, for he is God Almighty. And they are defeated enemies. In his life, temptation, sufferings, death and resurrection, Jesus has defeated Satan. Jesus is Lord of all, of everything and every being in heaven, on the earth, and under the earth. And the devil's time on earth is short, for at the Final Judgment he will be thrown into the lake of fire in hell, to be tormented forever, along with his demons.

To have victory against the devil, our lives must be based solidly on God's truth. God's Word, empowered by the Holy Spirit, is the strongest weapon we have. We must saturate ourselves in the Scriptures. It was through his knowledge of the Scriptures and his unshakable trust in God that Jesus gained the victory over Satan in his temptations.

And right here and now, in this life, in this world filled with demons and under the devil's influence, Christians can have victory over Satan and the evil spirits, through the power of Jesus Christ. St. Paul tells us how:

> "Finally, my brethren, be strong in the Lord and in the power of his might. Put on the whole armor of God, that you may be able to stand against the wiles of the devil. For we do not wrestle against flesh and blood, but against principalities, against powers, against the rulers of the darkness of this age, against spiritual hosts of wickedness in the heavenly places. Therefore, take up the whole armor of God, that you may be able to withstand in the evil day, and having done all, to stand. Stand, therefore, having girded your waist with truth, having put on the breastplate of righteousness, and having shod your feet with the preparation of the gospel of peace;

above all, taking the shield of faith with which you will be able to quench all the fiery darts of the wicked one. And take the helmet of salvation, and the sword of the Spirit, which is the word of God; praying always with all prayer and supplication in the Spirit, being watchful to this end with all perseverance and supplication for all the saints..."

(Eph. 6:10–18)

However, it is a great mistake to think that the devil is the only enemy we have. If we think the devil is our only enemy, we fall into error and become subject to his deceptions, because then (1) we would be overestimating his power, for it is as nothing compared with God's, and (2) in Jesus' life and ministry, his death on the cross, and his Resurrection from the dead, Jesus has decisively defeated the devil, and (3) the devil's time on earth is short, and (4) we have other enemies besides the devil, just as strong, insidious, and potentially destructive.

2. THE WORLD

We may think of "the world" as evil around us, as the devil and his demons are evil beyond us. In the Bible, "world" sometimes means the created universe; and sometimes it means the world of mankind, the inhabited world. But "the world" as our enemy means "the spirit of this age" which is in rebellion against God, its Creator and rightful ruler. "The world" means everything on the human level that opposes God and his rule.

The things that the world values and prizes are quite different from what God values. The world values money, power, pleasure, position, and prestige. What God values most is loving him with all our strength, which includes obeying him, and loving others as much as we love ourselves.

To see most clearly the difference in the world's value-system and God's value system consider the difference in the lives of the persons the world honors as celebrities and the lives of those whom the Christian community honors as "saints." The world lavishly rewards movie stars, celebrities of the entertainment world, sports figures, the richest people, and "very important people," such as political figures. Often their lives are characterized by self-centeredness, self-aggrandizement, self-importance. Compare those whom the church honors most highly: those who give their lives in love to God and humble service to others such as Mother Theresa, Francis of Assisi, Albert Schweitzer, Father Damien, Billy Graham.

The world around us exerts a lot of pressure upon Christians to force us into its mold. The world cannot abide people whose values are so different from its values, people who consider what the world prizes as unimportant. The world hated Jesus and put him to death, and Christians should not be surprised that the world hates them. The world hates the Spirit of Jesus who lives within Christians. Indeed, it is as if Christians exude a fragrance which smells wonderful to fellow Christians but stinks to unbelievers (2 Cor. 2:15–16).

Christians are subject to powerful peer pressure from worldly people which attempts to make us ignore the claims of Jesus Christ upon our lives, or at least to keep our mouths shut about him. It is a difficult task that we have, to live in the world but not be of the world. It is hard to keep from being influenced by the values of the world when we are bombarded from every side by the world's propaganda.

What can we do to have victory over our enemy, the world? We must keep our attention focused on Jesus Christ, and be reminded continuously that this world is only temporary and is passing away, with all of its power and pomp and glory, while the unseen Kingdom of God is eternal and will last forever. To keep a proper perspective, we must give high priority to reading and studying the Word of God, the Holy Bible, and to praying. If we watch worldly programs on television three hours a day and do not read, study, and meditate on God's Word daily, or perhaps only fifteen minutes a day, it should be no surprise that our lives are influenced much more by the world's value system than by God's.

The Apostle Paul tells us how to have victory over the world, our enemy: "...[D]o not be conformed to this world, but be transformed by the renewing of your mind, so that you may prove what is that good and acceptable and perfect will of God" (Rom. 12:2).

For our minds to be transformed and changed from the world's value system to God's value system, we must make use of "the means of grace"; that is, the ways that God provides for his Spirit within us to be strengthened, such as:

- Bible study
- prayer
- worshipping God with his people regularly
- fellowship with Christian believers
- receiving the Lord's Supper which nourishes God's Holy Spirit within us
- making use of the opportunities for Christian education available to us
- engaging in practical loving service to people in need as we are able
- giving money for the spread of God's Kingdom as he directs us by his Holy Spirit

If we do not neglect the means of grace, we will find that we have increasing victory over our spiritual enemies and will grow in the grace and knowledge of our Lord and Savior Jesus Christ.

3. THE FLESH

"The flesh" as one of our enemies means evil within us, as "the devil" means evil beyond us, and "the world" means evil around us. Before God, we cannot excuse ourselves by blaming our sin on the devil, as Eve did ("the serpent gave it to me") nor by blaming it on the world (influence of other people around us) as Adam did ("the woman gave it to me"). Remember that the

Apostle John is writing to Christians when he says, "If we say we that we have no sin, we deceive ourselves, and the truth is not in us" (I Jn. 1:8).

To say that "the flesh" is our enemy does *not* mean that our physical bodies are evil. God created our bodies and breathed into them the breath of life. He created our physical bodies, male and female he created us, and pronounced them "very good" (Gen.1:31). Our physical bodies, including sexuality, are intrinsically good, because God, who is good, created them.

However, when our ancestors, Adam and Eve, flagrantly and rebelliously disobeyed God's command, they fell into sin, which substantially corrupted God's good creation. This corruption, the inclination toward sin and self and away from God, has been transmitted like a congenital disorder to every human being who has ever lived and who will ever live with one exception: Jesus of Nazareth.

Thus, to say that "the flesh" is our enemy means that we have inherited this inborn characteristic which makes us desire to sin and inclines us toward sin and away from God (called "original sin"). This sinful tendency or inclination is then actualized in our lives by actions which are in violation of God's Law, summarized in the Ten Commandments ("actual sins"). When a person is saved, his sins are forgiven, but his sin nature ("the flesh") is not obliterated. God views him as totally righteous because he belongs to Jesus (he is "in Christ"), but he remains "in the flesh" as long as he lives. As Luther said, the Christian is at one and the same time a righteous person and a sinner.

When salvation comes to us, God has put his Holy Spirit within us. Our self-centered, pleasure-seeking, comfort-seeking selves ("the flesh") then react against the Holy Spirit. Our old fallen sinful nature perceives the Holy Spirit to be an alien spiritual invader, and marshals all its forces to fight against God's Spirit, just as the body's immune system mobilizes all its strength to surround, isolate, and eliminate invading disease germs.

Thus, when we become Christians, a terrific spiritual battle begins to take place inside the very core of our being. The Apostle Peter describes this struggle as "the desires of the flesh" waging war against the soul (1 Pet. 2:11). The Apostle Paul writes from personal experience of this war raging inside the Christian:

> "I do not understand my own actions. For I do not do what I want, but I do the very thing I hate ... [I]t is no longer I that do it, but sin that dwells within me. For I know that nothing good dwells within me, that is, in my flesh. I can will what is right, but I cannot do it. For I do not do the good I want, but the evil I do not want is what I do. Now if I do what I do not want, it is no longer I that do it, but sin that dwells within me. So I find it to be a law that when I want to do what is good, evil lies close at hand. For I delight in the law of God in my inmost self, but I see in my members another law at work with the law of my mind, making me captive to the law of sin that dwells in my members."
>
> (Rom. 7:15–23, NRSV)

The Apostle Paul, writing as one who has been a Christian believer for many years, exclaims in anguish: "O wretched man that I am! Who will deliver me from this body of death?" (Rom. 7:24). Paul knows that he cannot deliver himself from this battle, for in himself he is too weak. But he exclaims: "I thank God—through Jesus Christ our Lord!" (7:25). By his death on the cross and glorious resurrection Jesus has won the victory over sin, the world, the flesh, the devil, and death. He will empower his people now in this life to persevere in the war, and he will give them complete victory over their enemies in the Day of Resurrection at his Second Coming, when he "will transform our lowly body that it may be conformed to his glorious body, according to the working by which he is able even to subdue all things to himself" (Phil. 3:21).

In the meantime, our marching orders as soldiers of Jesus Christ are to struggle, fight, and persevere against our spiritual enemies and not give ground to the devil, the world, and the sin within us. Jesus promised: "[H]e who endures to the end shall be saved" (Mt. 10:22; Mk. 13:13).

God has given us his own Holy Spirit to strengthen us and help us in our Christian warfare, but we must cooperate with the Holy Spirit and not fight against him. We must do all we can, using every means of grace and every weapon and every ounce of strength we have, to fight against our spiritual enemies. In his Holy Word, God has given us some directions for fighting against "the flesh" (that is, the sin remaining within us):

1. We are to be ruled and governed by the Holy Spirit and live by his directions, and not allow our sinful, self-centered flesh to rule and control and direct our lives (Rom. 6:12; 8:13–14; Gal. 6:7,8).

2. We are to set our minds on the things of the Holy Spirit, not on things of "the flesh" (Rom. 8:5; Col. 3:1–2; Phil. 4:8–9). We must saturate ourselves in the Scriptures; we must surround ourselves with Christian influences; we must spend time in Bible study and prayer rather than spending time watching worldly television and movies and viewing websites which exalt sin.

3. We are not to gratify the sinful desires of the flesh, but rather abstain from them. We must cut off the enemy's supply lines and deprive him of support, rather than supplying him. We are to starve him rather than feeding and nourishing him. We must deprive him of ammunition he will use against us (Gal. 5:16; Rom. 13:14; 1 Pet. 2:11).

4. We must keep our objective in mind and remember that living by the flesh leads to misery, destruction, and ultimate death, while living by the Holy Spirit leads to life and peace (Rom. 8:6). St. Paul gives us vivid descriptions of what living by the flesh looks like (Gal. 5:19–21, "the works of the flesh") and what living by the Holy Spirit looks like (Gal. 5:22–23, "the fruit of the Spirit").

5. We are to view matters from a long-range perspective and remember that this world with all its lusts is passing away but those who do the will of God live forever (1 Jn. 2:15–17).

6. We are to endeavor to see matters from God's perspective, and "consider [ourselves] dead to sin and alive to God in Christ Jesus" (Rom. 6:11, NRSV).

7. We must remember that the victory over sin, the world, the flesh, the devil, death, and all our enemies has already been won by Jesus Christ in his death on the cross and resurrection, and that we will fully and completely enjoy the fruits of his victory if we endure, if we persevere, if we are faithful to the end. If we die with Jesus, we shall also live with him; if we suffer with him, we shall also reign with him (2 Tim. 2:11–13).

Even now in the midst of our struggles, trials, and tribulations, Jesus graciously grants us the privilege of having a foretaste, a preview, of His victory through participating in his Supper, his victory banquet, and by making use of the other means of grace by which he communicates his love and joy and peace to us, and renews, refreshes, and strengthens us for the warfare in which we are engaged.

F
GOD'S WORK BEHIND THE SCENES

When a person responds to the good news of the salvation God has brought in Jesus Christ, he or she may express what has happened to them by saying that they have accepted Christ or have made a decision to follow Jesus. They may even think and feel that their own decision has somehow contributed to their salvation because they accepted God's invitation.

However, after the new baby Christian has matured enough to outgrow a milk diet and to eat the solid food of God's Word (Heb. 5:12–14), if you ask him or her the question, "Who gets the credit for your being saved, you or God?" he or she will probably answer something like this: "It is God who gets all the credit and all the glory for the wonderful things he has done in my life. Thank you, Jesus. Glory, glory to God! Praise his Holy name! If he had not saved me and helped me, I would still be in the miserable mess I had made of my life."

As Christians mature and grow in Christ, they come to see more and more how gracious God has been to them throughout the course of their lives. They come to see that they would not love God if he had not first loved them (1 Jn. 4:19). The old Gospel chorus becomes their song: "Oh, how I love Jesus, because he first loved me." As Christians grow in Christ, they are continually astounded at the amazing grace God has shown in so many ways in their lives.

As they grow in grace and in the knowledge of their Lord and Savior Jesus Christ, they come to see the truth that they would never have come to believe in Jesus as Lord and Savior if God's Holy Spirit had not first worked within their hearts and lives to bring them to receive the gift of faith [for "no one can say that Jesus is Lord except by the Holy Spirit" (1 Cor. 12:3)], the gift of repentance unto life (Acts 11:18), and the gift of baptism by water and the Holy Spirit. They come to see that they have been saved by God's grace, love, and mercy toward them, and that even the faith they have is not their own doing, but has been given to them as a gift from God. "For by grace you have been saved through faith, and that not of yourselves; it is the gift of God, not of works, lest anyone should boast" (Eph. 2:8–9).

God revealed to the Apostle Paul the way he has been working under cover, behind the scenes, to bring his salvation to his people. St. Paul writes these God-inspired words that give us a glimpse into the mystery of God's working which had been hidden for many ages and generations but which he has now brought to light through the Gospel:

> "For whom he foreknew, he also predestined to be conformed to the image of his Son, that he might be the firstborn among many brethren. Moreover, whom he predestined, these he also called; whom he called, these he also justified; and whom he justified, these he also glorified."
>
> (Rom. 8:29–30)

Thus, God has revealed the secret of his hidden work behind the scenes which he has done to bring his people to salvation: (1) he foreknew them; (2) he predestined them; (3) he called them; (4) he justified them; and (5) he glorified them.

Let's consider what each of these elements mean.

1. GOD FOREKNEW HIS PEOPLE

God's foreknowledge means that he knows ahead of time. He knows all things, from the beginning to the end. He knows everything that is going to happen before it happens, for he is the Sovereign Lord.

To the Greeks, the idea of "knowledge" was a cool and rational perception of a static, unchanging reality; it was a "head knowledge" of facts. To the Hebrews, however, although "knowledge" included intellectual perception, it was much more of a warm and personal thing; it was the "heart knowledge" of a person-to-person relationship. Thus, in the Bible, for a person to "know God" was not simply to know the facts about God, but much more, to have a personal relationship with him.

The depth of the Biblical meaning of knowing another person is shown by the fact that the Bible uses the word "to know" to include the deepest and most personal intimacy possible between a man and a woman—the act of sexual union. Thus, "Adam knew Eve his wife, and she conceived and bore Cain" (Gen. 4:1). "And Cain knew his wife, and she conceived and bore Enoch" (Gen. 4:17). "And Elkanah knew Hannah his wife, and … it came to pass in the process of time that Hannah conceived and bore a son" (1 Sam. 1:19,20).

Therefore, to say that God *knows* a person means that he has a special and personal relationship with that person, that he loves that person with a special, warm and close love, and thus that he wills the best for that person and has a plan and purpose for his or her life. God told Jeremiah: "'Before I formed you in the womb I knew you; Before you were born I sanctified you; And I ordained you a prophet to the nations'" (Jer. 1:5).

It is an overwhelming and humbling thing to realize that God foreknew us and loved us even before we were born, that he marvelously and wondrously formed us in our mother's womb. It sounds like David is speaking of the DNA chain which determines all of our individual genetic characteristics such as the color of our eyes and hair and skin, our height, the shape of our noses, all of our physical individualities, even the degree and type of our intelligence, when he wrote:

> "For it was You who formed my inward parts;
> You knit me together in my mother's womb.
> I praise You, for I am fearfully and wonderfully made.
> Wonderful are Your works; that I know very well.
> My frame was not hidden from You,
> When I was being made in secret,
> Intricately woven in the depths of the earth.
> Your eyes beheld my unformed substance.
> In Your book were written all the days that were formed for me;
> When none of them as yet existed."
>
> (Ps. 139:13–16, NRSV)

A beautiful example of the way our lives can be changed when we realize that God foreknew us is Jesus' calling of Nathanael (same person as Bartholomew). After Jesus called Philip to follow him, Philip went and found his friend Nathanael and told him: "We have found him of whom Moses in the law, and also the prophets, wrote—Jesus of Nazareth." Nathanael's reply was skeptical, almost contemptuous, quoting a common saying of the day: "Can anything good come out of Nazareth?" for Nazareth was an insignificant little village of about a dozen houses, not even mentioned in the Old Testament Scriptures. Philip said simply, "Come and see."

When Jesus first saw Nathanael coming toward him, he said of him: "Behold, an Israelite indeed, in whom is no guile!" Nathanael responded to the effect that Jesus had never met him before, and asked, "How do You know me?" Jesus answered: "Before Philip called you, when you were under the fig tree, I saw you." ["Under the fig tree" probably meant that Nathanael was a theological student, for the rabbis commonly held classes under the shade of fig trees.] Nathanael was so overwhelmed that Jesus knew him before they had ever met that he had an immediate change of heart and acknowledged Jesus as the Savior: "Rabbi, You are the Son of God! You are the King of Israel!" (Jn. 1:43–51).

2. GOD PREDESTINED HIS PEOPLE

"For whom he foreknew, he also predestined to be conformed to the image of his Son" (Rom. 8:29).

What does it mean that God predestined those whom he foreknew? [Later, under the heading "Fruit of the Holy Spirit," we will consider what it means "to be conformed to the image of his Son."]

Literally, the word "predestine" means to determine beforehand, to preordain. In considering this matter, we must be careful not to engage in philosophical speculation about determinism vs. freedom, but we must hold to what God has revealed in his Holy Word. We are not to attempt to pry into the secret, hidden things of God, but must hold fast to "those things which are revealed" (Deut. 29:29).

Many people have a strong, negative, emotional reaction to the very word "predestination." They feel that if God chooses and predestines those who are saved, their personhood is diminished and devalued and their dignity as human beings is violated.

They cannot bear the thought of God invading their free will and forcing them to do something they may not want to do. This view, however, is a great misunderstanding of the way God works in peoples' lives.

When a man and a woman experience the wonder and excitement of falling in love, it is a marvelous thing. They feel like the world has been made new. They feel that they have been given new life. They have hope for the future which replaces the fear and emptiness of facing a lonely single life. Often, they will express the amazement and blessing of finding their life's partner by saying, "We were meant for each other," or "We were destined for each other." They have no sense of having been forced into a relationship they did not want. Rather, they experience the freedom and joy of having their heart-felt desires fulfilled.

It is like that when a person comes to faith in Jesus Christ and experiences the newness of life he brings.

One common misconception about predestination is to think it means that God forces a person from outside of himself to turn to Jesus. But God does not knock us around by external force like a cue stick knocks billiard balls around on a pool table. Rather, God works from within ourselves by his Holy Spirit to draw us to himself.

When we begin to see salvation from God's perspective as revealed in Holy Scripture, we begin to see God's great love working within us, drawing us to Jesus Christ. Then we begin to be overwhelmed at the amazing love and grace of God. Then we begin to understand what Jesus said: "No one can come to Me unless the Father who sent Me draws him" (Jn. 6:44). Then we begin to see that God drew us to himself through Jesus Christ not by brute force, but "with gentle cords, with bands of love" (Hosea 11:4). Then we begin to understand Jesus' word to his followers: "You did not choose Me, but I chose you" (Jn. 15:16).

As we mature in the Christian life and come to a deeper knowledge of our own sins and our own sinful natures, we come to see more and more how God's hand has been at work behind the scenes in our lives, preparing our hearts to turn to him and his Son Jesus Christ. We begin to see how marvelous God's hidden work has been all along: that we could never have prepared our own hearts to turn to Jesus, but it is God who has prepared our hearts (Prov. 16:1, KJV).

Indeed, as we grow in Christ, we come to see that if we had been left to our own sinful desires and devices, we would never have turned to God. But God has worked within all the circumstances of our lives to bring us to himself. He has used not only good things that have happened to us, but especially bad things that have happened to us. such as our failures in financial matters, in morals, in love, in relationships, to draw us and bring us to himself. His love has gone before us behind the scenes. He has been with us all the way even though we were unaware of it. "God demonstrates his own love toward us, in that while we were still sinners, Christ died for us" (Rom. 5:8). "We love him because he first loved us" (1 Jn. 4:19).

As we mature further in Christ and are able to accept it, God reveals to us an even more astounding truth. God has loved us with an everlasting love that reaches back not only before our conception and birth, but back before time began, back into eternity. "He chose us in him [Christ] before the foundation of the world..." (Eph. 1:4). God not only foreknew us, he predestined us for salvation in Jesus Christ: "...we were destined for this, by the One who works out all his purposes according to the design of his own will" (Eph.1:11, J. B. Phillips).

And since God has decided even before the creation of the world to set his love upon us, and since he is sovereign and his plans and decisions will be accomplished, it gives us great strength and comfort to know that he will complete the good work he has begun in us (Phil.1:6), that he gives us eternal life and we will never perish and no one can snatch us out of God's hand (Jn. 10:28–29), and that no earthly power nor any spiritual power is strong enough to separate us from the love of God in Christ Jesus our Lord (Rom. 8:31–39).

The Gospel truth that God has foreknown us and predestined us in Jesus Christ is meant to comfort and strengthen and empower us for God's service, not to make us afraid, doubtful, or despairing.

If you believe in Jesus Christ, rejoice and give God thanks and praise, knowing that you would not have faith if God had not loved you and given you the gift of faith and chosen you for salvation, long before you were aware of it, even before the foundation of the world. You cannot save yourself; only God can save you. Therefore, having faith, being a Christian, does not make you better than anybody else, so there is no place for superiority and pride. Rather, give thanks and praise to God through Jesus Christ, and seek to live a life that pleases him, loving him with all your heart and with all your mind and with all your strength, and loving your neighbor as yourself.

If you have doubts whether God loves you and has chosen you for salvation, know that if you have any desire toward God, if you want to have his help, to have salvation, to have newness of life, such desires come from God. They show that God is at work within you, drawing you to himself. So turn from yourself and from your own doubts to God who promises that everyone who calls upon the name of the Lord will be saved. You have this promise from the heart of the Lord Jesus himself, that all that the Father gives him will come to him, and that anyone who comes to him, he will never reject (Jn. 6:37).

Responding to a Question about Election And Predestination

When some people are presented with the biblical doctrines of election and predestination, sometimes they respond by saying, "I thought God was going to save everybody!"

The Scriptures that raise this issue are:

> "The Lord ... is longsuffering toward us, not willing that any should perish but that all should come to repentance."
>
> (2 Pet. 3:9)

> "[God] desires all men to be saved and to come to the knowledge of the truth."
>
> (1 Tim. 2:4)

"If God is not willing that any should be lost but desires everyone to be saved, then how can it be that not everyone will be saved but only those God elects and predestines for salvation?" they ask.

The Lord Jesus himself was faced with this issue in a slightly different form when he was asked, "'Lord, are there few who are saved?'" (Lk. 13:23). This is a question which was much debated in Judaism at the time of Jesus, whether all the Jews would be saved or only the few the prophets spoke of as "the remnant."

Jesus did not answer the question directly, but turned it back on the one who asked it by saying, "[*You*, understood subject of verb] Strive to enter through the narrow gate, for many, I say to you, will seek to enter and will not be able" (Lk.13:24).

In effect, Jesus is saying that the answer to this question is a mystery hidden in the mind of God, and that rather than wasting time with speculation about how God is going to deal with other people, you had better be concerned about yourself and your salvation.

Jesus goes on to explain that right now the kingdom of God is open to those who repent and seek to enter it whether Jews or Gentiles, but the time is coming when the door will be shut and then people will not be able to enter God's kingdom, no matter how much they implore him (Lk.13:25–30).

We are not to speculate as to how God might work in the lives of others. Rather, as the Apostle Peter reminds us, we should "...be even more diligent to make [our] calling and election sure..." (2 Pet. 1:10).

To a person who feels that God has not elected him or her for salvation, I would point them to the Scriptures which state that Jesus will not reject anyone who comes to him (Jn. 6:37) and the promise that "everyone who calls on the name of the Lord shall be saved" (Joel 2:32; Acts 2:21; Rom.10:13 NASV).

There are several instances in the Bible where God had made a firm decision to execute judgment on a person or a city or a nation, but when someone prayed and asked God to have mercy, he changed his mind and lifted the sentence. Throughout the Bible when God changes his mind, it is always in the direction of mercy. (*See* the Book of Jonah, for example).

It is a deep mystery why some people refuse to repent of their sins and accept Jesus Christ as their Lord and Savior when they are presented with the Gospel.

A similar thing happens on the worldly level whenever a hurricane is approaching the coast. The governor puts out an appeal for everyone living in the flood plain to evacuate. Law enforcement personnel come to the door and tell people to get out because the storm surge is expected to be 24 feet, for example, and their house is only ten feet above sea level. And yet some people stubbornly refuse to evacuate and suffer the consequences, sometimes losing their lives. Why would they not go to safety when faced with such a terrible, unavoidable danger? It is a mystery.

3. GOD CALLED HIS PEOPLE

"Moreover whom he predestined, these he also called" (Rom. 8:30).

What does God's "calling" mean? Here we are not speaking about God calling individuals to a particular occupation or vocation, such as to be an evangelist, a pastor, a teacher, a secretary, a farmer, a doctor, a welder, a laborer, etc. We are talking about God inviting people to come to himself through Jesus Christ, to come and enjoy his blessings and the wonderful gifts he wants to give us in and through Christ.

The 43rd and 44th chapters of Isaiah help us to understand what God's call involves. God created Israel to be his special people; He calls them by name; they belong to him (43:1). They are precious to him and honored, and he loves them (43:4). They have a special task to do for him on earth: to be his witnesses (43:10–12; 44:8) and to praise (43:21) and glorify him (43:7). And he promises to forgive their sins (43:25) and to protect them from harm (43:2).

However, both Scripture and history tell us that not all Israel responded to God's gracious calling, but only a minority, "a remnant," responded to him in faith, love, hope and obedience (Joel 2:32).

So it is with God's call to people through the preaching of the Good News of his Kingdom. In the Gospel he invites everyone to enter through Jesus Christ Who himself is the door, the road, the gate, the entrance into life. But not everyone accepts his gracious offer. Jesus himself said: 'For many are called, but few are chosen" (Mt. 22:14); that is, the gracious invitation of God goes out to everyone, but not everyone accepts his invitation. (*See* Parable of the Wedding Banquet, Mt. 22:1–14).

God's plan and purpose to draw to himself a people who love and honor and obey him will not be thwarted. The wedding banquet of the King's Son will be filled with guests (Mt. 22:10). When God's Word goes forth, when the seed of the Gospel is planted, even though some of the seed falls on hard soil, some falls on thin soil, some falls on soil full of thorns; nevertheless, some of the precious seed does fall on good, fertile soil, and it will bring forth a great harvest (Parable of the Sower, Mk. 4:1–20).

Through the centuries, God's Word through the prophet Isaiah has been a tremendous encouragement to those who preach the Gospel and witness:

> "For as the rain comes down, and the snow from heaven,
> And do not return there,
> But water the earth,
> And make it bring forth and bud,
> That it may give seed to the sower
> And bread to the eater,
> So shall My word be that goes forth from My mouth;
> It shall not return to Me void,
> But it shall accomplish what I please,
> And it shall prosper in the thing for which I sent it."
>
> (Is. 55:10,11)

Some theologians distinguish between the "general calling" of the Gospel which goes out to everyone and the "effectual calling" of those who respond by believing the Gospel and turning to Jesus Christ.

Consider a crude illustration: a young girl is walking home from school one day and is downcast and sad. It is Valentine's Day, and all of the other children in the class are going to parties that afternoon, but no one invited her. All of a sudden, there is a shower not of rain, but of beautiful, lacy envelopes falling all around her. She picks up one of the envelopes from the ground, but it is addressed to someone else. Sad and lonely, she looks at several more envelopes, but they are all the same; they are addressed to other children. Then, amazingly one of the beautiful envelopes falls right into her hand! This one is different: it is addressed to her! It has her name on it! She is trembling as she opens it and is astonished to find her own name written on the valentine card inside the envelope, and the hand-written message: "I love you. Please come to My party," signed "God."

We must not take God's invitation for granted. When God sends you a personal invitation, like a valentine with your own personal name on it, telling you he loves you and invites you to his party, by all means accept his invitation. There is no guarantee you will receive another one.

4. GOD JUSTIFIED HIS PEOPLE

"…whom he called, these he also justified" (Rom. 8:30). "Justify" is a legal term meaning to be acquitted and declared to be not guilty, rather than being found guilty and condemned.

Imagine this scene:

God, "the Judge of all the earth" (Gen. 18:25), is presiding at his heavenly court, assisted by his Son Jesus Christ. God, the Presiding Judge, summons a person to appear before his court and answer charges of having violated his Holy Law. Then the charges are read listing the prisoner's specific sins and violations of God's Holy Commandments and they are very serious charges, deserving the death penalty.

Then God says, "How do you plead? Guilty or not guilty?" The prisoner before the Bar of Justice is trembling and shaking terribly, and is so frightened he is having difficulty in speaking because he knows that each and every offense charged against him is true.

However, before the prisoner can answer the charges and enter his plea, an amazing thing happens: Jesus stands up, and he leaves the Bench where he had been sitting as Judge beside

God the Father. Jesus comes down from the Bench and stands beside the trembling prisoner, puts his arm around him, and begins to speak for him. Instead of being the man's Judge, Jesus has become his defense attorney! There is a shocked silence in the courtroom.

Then Jesus speaks: "My Father, You are the Judge of the whole earth. You know all the facts concerning My brother standing here beside Me. You even know the innermost thoughts of his heart. On behalf of My brother, I point out to Your Honor that this matter has been completely taken care of. His sin debt has been paid in full. I respectfully call to Your remembrance that Friday in the month Nisan in the year 33 AD and the event that took place that day in the land of Israel outside the city of Jerusalem, when Pontius Pilate was the Governor. Three men were crucified as criminals that day. I was the One in the middle. In My death on that cross, I took upon Myself the sins of the whole world, including the sins of this prisoner now standing before the Court. In My suffering and death on that cross, I made the one full, perfect, and completely sufficient sacrifice for all the sins of mankind. On that cross, I paid the full price for the sins of the whole world, including the sins of My brother here.

"This brother of Mine has believed in Me, that I am Your Son, that My death paid the price for his sins in full. Consequently, this man belongs to Me and is one of Mine."

Jesus continues: "I most respectfully request Your Honor to consider that I have paid the full price for his sins, and the full extreme penalty of death for his sins has already been executed upon Me. Therefore, the charges against this man have been fully dealt with, and it would be most unjust for him to have to suffer any further, and I most respectfully ask that he be discharged from custody and be set free!"

Then God the Father spoke: "I remember well the event You have spoken of. It is always in My mind. When You hung on the cross, it was such a horrible sight to Me that I could not bear to look upon it, and so I had to blot out the light of the sun that afternoon. You, My Beloved Son, had never done any wrong, and You have always obeyed Me even to the smallest detail. When You became sin on that cross, You became a horrible, ugly sight to My eyes. I could not look upon You, for I cannot bear to look upon any iniquity; I cannot have any fellowship with impurity and sin. Therefore, it was necessary for Me to separate Myself from You, and to leave You all alone and abandon You for a time while You hung on the cross, making atonement for the sin of the whole world.

"As to Your petition on behalf of this prisoner, there is legal precedent, the case of My friend Abraham, who believed My promise to him, and I credited it to his account as being the equivalent of righteousness. Since the prisoner at the Bar has faith in You, My Beloved Son, he is counted as righteous in My sight. He is part of Your own Body. Your death has been credited to his account and the price for his sins has already been paid in full.

"Therefore, I hereby decree that the penalty for his sins has been fully satisfied, that the just and lawful death sentence upon him has already been carried out, and therefore the prisoner at the Bar is hereby declared, 'Not guilty.' Let him be released from custody and set free!"

5. GOD GLORIFIED HIS PEOPLE

"… and whom he justified, these he also glorified" (Rom .8:30). What does this mean, that God glorified his people, those whom he foreknew, predestined, called, and justified?

"Glory" in the New Testament means brightness, splendor, radiance, magnificence, honor, worthiness. The Bible speaks often of "the glory of God," which means all of these things.

One amazing thing about the Gospel is that the God of Glory who is Spirit and cannot be seen or touched, "dwelling in unapproachable light" (1 Tim. 6:16), became a human being in Jesus of Nazareth, human flesh and blood who could be seen and approached and touched.

Thus, Jesus Christ is the visible human manifestation of the glory of God. God's glory shone forth when he was born as the bright light shining on the shepherds in the field, when he worked miracles as at the wedding feast at Cana of Galilee, and when he was transfigured before Peter, James and John with his body and clothing shining with the radiant glory of heaven at the Transfiguration. We see the "light of the knowledge of the glory of God in the face of Jesus Christ," (2 Cor. 4:6), for he is "the Lord of Glory" (James 2:1; 1 Cor. 2:8).

But, paradoxically, Jesus was primarily glorified in his sufferings and death on the cross (Jn. 12:16–23; 13:31-33). Jesus went to the cross "not as a helpless martyr to his agony, but as a victorious king to his crowning."[20]

The glory of God is reflected in the lives of Christians, not as their own glory but as the moon reflects the light of the sun (2 Cor. 3:18). God's work of glorifying us begins here in this life, and sometimes it can be seen physically in the glow on the face of a person who is experiencing something of the presence of God, a preacher speaking earnestly of God's truth, a person newly converted, a person returning to his place in church after receiving the consecrated bread and wine in the Lord's Supper.

God's work of glorifying us continues in this life, changing and transforming us more and more into the image of Christ (1 Cor.15:49; Col. 3:10), from one degree of glory to another (2 Cor. 3:18).

Just as the culmination of Jesus' glorification on earth was his sufferings and death on the cross, so God's work in glorifying Christians on earth is focused in their sufferings (Rom. 5:3–5). As St. Peter wrote:

> "Beloved, do not be surprised at the fiery ordeal that is taking place among you to test you, as though something strange were happening to you. But rejoice insofar as you are sharing Christ's sufferings, so that you may also be glad and shout for

joy when his glory is revealed. If you are reviled for the name of Christ, you are blessed, because the spirit of glory, which is the Spirit of God, is resting on you."

(1 Pet. 4:12–14, NRSV)

We must suffer with Christ to be glorified with him (Rom. 8:17). No cross, no crown. "If we suffer, we shall also reign with him" (2 Tim. 2:12, KJV). God is working to bring us to the point in our lives that we can even rejoice in our sufferings, knowing that "suffering produces endurance, and endurance produces character, and character produces hope, and hope does not disappoint us, because God's love has been poured into our hearts through the Holy Spirit that has been given to us" (Rom. 5:3–5, NRSV).

Our lives glorify God when they are characterized by faith in Jesus Christ, obedience to him, and loving service to others (2 Cor. 9:13), regardless of our circumstances.

God has glorified us, and he is in the process of glorifying us now, at the present time. But we will not be fully glorified until Jesus comes again, raises us from the dead, and "will transform our lowly body that it may be conformed to his glorious body, according to the working by which he is able even to subdue all things to himself" (Phil. 3:21). Then we shall "shine forth as the sun in the kingdom of [our] Father" (Mt.13:43).

Since the New Testament references to God glorifying Christians are past (we have been glorified), present (we are being glorified), and future (we shall be glorified completely at the Last Day), why does St. Paul use the past tense in Romans 8:30 ("and whom he justified, these he also glorified") since it has not yet fully happened? Because if God has purposed something, he is certain to do it; if he has promised something, we can consider it accomplished. His will shall be done.

We can be sure that God who has begun a good work in us, having foreknown us, predestined us, called us, and justified us, "will complete it until the day of Jesus Christ" (Phil.1:6), when Jesus returns and glorifies us fully and completely.

THE GOAL OF THE CHRISTIAN LIFE: BECOMING LIKE JESUS

As we try to live the Christian life, oftentimes we are confused and baffled as to what is going on in our lives. In the midst of the conflicts, turmoil, troubles, trials and tribulations, we cannot help asking: What is God doing in my life? Where is he taking me? What is the purpose of all this?

In the Holy Scripture, God gives us the answer: in all the circumstances of life, in all of our joys and sorrows, pain and pleasure, sickness and health, work and rest, good times and bad times, God is working to change us and transform us to be like Jesus Christ. To be like him is our destiny. "For whom he foreknew, he also predestined"—For what purpose? To what end?—"to be conformed to the image of his Son, that he might be the firstborn among many brethren..." (Rom. 8:29). God's purpose in everything that happens in the lives of Christians is that we be changed to be more like Jesus, to help form a large family of God's people with Jesus as our Elder Brother.

What does "the image of Christ" look like in a human life? St. Paul gives a word picture of the character of Jesus, that character which God is working to form in the lives of his people.

He terms these nine characteristics "fruit of the Spirit." These are love, joy, peace, patience, kindness, goodness, faithfulness, gentleness, and self-control (Gal. 5:22–23).

Before considering them, we need to note an important point. Salvation is entirely the work of God. We do nothing to contribute to our salvation. All we do is to receive it as the most wonderful gift possible that God could give us. But in this matter of becoming like Jesus, of our lives bringing forth the fruit of the Holy Spirit, of the process theologians call "sanctification," which means being made holy, it takes a combination of God's work and our work. It requires us to cooperate with God.

These nine characteristics are "fruit of the Holy Spirit." They grow out of God's Spirit working within us, but to develop them in our lives requires work and effort on our part. Even in the world of nature, for a tree to produce fruit it requires effort on the part of the tree, so much so that after the season of fruit-bearing, the tree has to rest and become dormant for a time or it cannot produce another crop of fruit next season. Bringing forth a child which the Bible refers to as "fruit of the body" (Micah 6:7) requires strenuous effort, labor, and pain on the part of the mother. Just ask any woman who has been through the experience of childbirth.

Salvation is all God's work. Becoming like Jesus by bearing the fruit of the Holy Spirit in our lives is a joint effort of God and ourselves. These qualities of character have their source in God, but they are also things we have to work at for our lives to become more like Jesus.

Now let us consider these nine characteristics, the fruit of the Holy Spirit.

1. LOVE

The Greek language, in which the New Testament was originally written, has four different words translated into English by the one word "love:" (1) *eros*, sexual love; (2) *storge*, love within the family circle; (3) *philia*, social love, affection between friends or brothers and sisters; and (4) *agape*. When the New Testament speaks of "love," it usually means *agape*.

What is *agape* love? It is the love that God has for his creatures, a love that flows from the heart of the very nature of God, a love that overflows with mercy and kindness and goodness toward humans who do not deserve to be loved and who are unworthy of his love, who sin and rebel against him. "The Lord is good to all, and his tender mercies are over all his works" (Ps. 145:9).

God's Holy Spirit is working within us to help us so that, more and more, bit by bit, we are being changed to be more able to love others as God loves us, even as we love ourselves. This love begins with those close to us, family and friends, and widens out in circles like a pebble thrown into a pond, to include our church family, people who live in our own community and beyond, especially strangers, outcasts, poor, needy, helpless folks, and even going so far as to include our enemies. The Lord Jesus taught us: "But I say to you, 'Love your enemies, bless those who curse you, do good to those who hate you, and pray for those who spitefully use you and persecute you'" (Mt. 5:44–45).

It is apparent that God has to do a lot of work in us to get us to the point where we love even our enemies, forgive them, bless them, pray for them, and help them. Yet it is not impossible and there have been many shining examples of Christians showing *agape* love even to enemies throughout Christian history, extending into our own time.

Further, *agape* love is not simply a matter of our emotions, not just having warm fuzzy feelings, but is primarily a matter of treating other people right, with justice, mercy, respect and dignity, as we would like to be treated. It is primarily a matter of the will and doing practical actions of helpfulness (James 2:15–16).

St. John puts it in characteristically blunt fashion: "But whoever has this world's goods, and sees his brother in need, and shuts up his heart from him, how does the love of God abide in him? My little children, let us not love in word or in tongue, but in deed and in truth" (1 Jn. 3:17–18).

2. JOY

Joy, gladness, rejoicing in the biblical sense is not the same as the happiness that comes from some outward circumstance such as getting a promotion, getting a salary increase, acquiring something we have wanted for a long time, having things going well for us. No, joy is an inward thing that is based and grounded in God and what he has done for us in and through Jesus Christ. Christian joy comes not from our human emotions, but from the Holy Spirit (Rom.14:17, 15:13).

The Bible describes joy as being like the rejoicing associated with a wedding (Jn. 3:29), even the joy in heaven:

> "Let us be glad and rejoice and give him glory, for the marriage of the Lamb has come, and his wife has made herself ready."
>
> (Rev. 19:7)

Because our joy does not come from ourselves nor from outward circumstances, Christians can rejoice even in the midst of sorrow and suffering, as St. Paul was enabled to do (Col. 1:24; 2 Cor. 6:10). St. Peter told the Christians not to be surprised at the fiery ordeal that had come upon them, but to "rejoice to the extent that you partake of Christ's sufferings, so that when his glory is revealed, you may also be glad with exceeding joy" (1 Pet. 4:12–13).

Peter and the other apostles knew what they were talking about. By order of the High Priest and the Sanhedrin, they were arrested, imprisoned, and then flogged. "So they departed from the presence of the council, rejoicing that they were counted worthy to suffer shame for his name" (Acts 5:41).

God commands us to rejoice no matter what our circumstances: "Rejoice always" (1 Thes. 5:16; Phil. 3:1, 4:4). If Christian joy were a matter primarily of our emotions, it could not be commanded.

Our joy will be full in heaven, but even here and now, no matter our outward circumstances, with God's help we can rejoice (1 Pet. 1:8).

3. PEACE

Peace in biblical usage is not merely the absence of conflict, but well-being, completeness, fulfillment in every aspect of life, prosperity, health, good family life, wonderful friendships, every blessing. The Hebrew word is *shalom*.

As the Bible sees it, mankind's greatest need for peace is in his relationship with God. Mankind has estranged himself from God, has rebelled against God, and is in conflict with God. But God has provided the way for mankind to be reconciled to himself and have peace with him through the life, death, and resurrection of Jesus Christ. When a person comes to faith in Jesus Christ, he is justified by faith, and his life is brought into union with the life of God, and consequently he has peace with God (Rom. 5:1). Thus, the Gospel is the good news of peace (Rom.10:15).

Having peace with God, we can have his blessed gift of peace even in the midst of adversity, conflict, trials and tribulations. This inexplicable peace in the midst of turmoil is Jesus' special gift to his followers, when he said, "Peace I leave with you, My peace I give to you; not as the world gives do I give to you" (Jn. 14:27).

What does this peace look like? It looks like Jesus asleep on the cushion in the stern of the boat, completely at peace in the midst of the fierce storm raging on the Sea of Galilee (Mk. 4:38).

Yet, even though this *shalom* is the gift of God, it takes work and effort on our part to have it (Eph. 4:3; Heb.12:14). King David in the Old Testament (Ps. 34:14) and St. Peter in the New Testament both say we must *pursue* peace (1 Pet. 3:11). And they both tell us that the primary way to do this is to speak words of sincerity, truth, and blessing, and to live lives that conform to our words by departing from evil and doing good.

Jesus gives us peace not only for our own benefit, but to help bring peace to others, and so far as we have ability and opportunity, to the world. "Blessed are the peacemakers, For they shall be called sons of God" (Mt. 5:9).

4. PATIENCE

Patience in the biblical sense "is a God-exercised, or God-given, restraint in face of opposition or oppression."[21] In dealing with sinful mankind, God is so very patient, forbearing, forgiving, and kind. When we commit wrongs against God, he is most patient with us, restraining his wrath, not striking us down as he would be justified in doing, because he wants to bring us to repentance and new life (2 Pet. 3:9).

Christians are to be like God in being patient with others (1 Cor.13:7; Eph. 4:2; 1 Thes. 5:14). Not only are Christians to be patient with other people, but we are also to be patient in suffering, in the afflictions and trials of this present age. Patience in this sense is usually called "endurance" or "steadfastness" (Rom. 5:3; 1 Cor. 13:7; James 1:3).

How long must we be patient? Until the coming of the Lord (James 5:7–11). The one who endures to the end shall be saved (Mk. 13:13). God calls us to "patient endurance" (Rev. 3:10, RSV).

The more we realize how kind and patient and forgiving God has been with us, the more we are able to treat other people that way, even those who do us wrong. (*See* Parable of the Unforgiving Servant, Mt.18:23–35).

5. KINDNESS

Kindness is being sympathetic, friendly, tender-hearted, generous. Kindness describes the way God treats his people now (Rom. 2:4, 11:22; Tit. 3:4), and in the ages to come he will show us "the exceeding riches of his grace in his kindness toward us in Christ Jesus" (Eph. 2:7).

And God wants us to treat others with kindness, as St. Paul did (2 Cor. 6:6). Indeed, God is working within us, and expects us to co-operate with his work in order that kindness becomes so customary with us that we give it no more thought than putting on our clothes when we get up in the morning. "Therefore, as the elect of God, holy and beloved, put on tender mercies, kindness, humbleness of mind, meekness, longsuffering" (Col. 3:12).

6. GOODNESS

We humans are so certain that we know what "good" and "goodness" are that we try to apply the standard of what we consider good to God himself, and when terrible tragedies happen or when we go through bad times, often we are quick to accuse God of not being good.

The news media and the law go so far as to refer to even terrible destructive natural disasters as "Acts of God." But we sinful humans have it backward. God is the only one who is good. When the rich man greeted Jesus as "Good Teacher," Jesus was quick to correct him: "Why do you call Me good? No one is good but One, that is God" (Mk.10:18). Therefore, we cannot know what is truly good apart from God.

One aspect of the Fall, the sin of Adam and Eve, was the desire to know good and evil for themselves, not being willing to learn it from God himself alone, as symbolized by eating the forbidden fruit of the Tree of the Knowledge of Good and Evil.

God is good in his very nature and being. The Psalms tell us over and over that "The Lord is good" (Ps.100:5, 136:1). He is the one who determines what is good. And he has not hidden his goodness from us. It is displayed in his creation; it is shown in his actions on behalf of his people throughout history; it is revealed to us in his Word and in his Commandments, and supremely in his Son Jesus Christ. God has shown us and told us what is good (Micah 6:8).

In our dealings with others, we are to imitate God (Eph. 5:1). As God's love and goodness overflow with blessings and benefits to people, whether they are good or bad, worthy or unworthy, so should we endeavor to treat others the same way. We are not to judge others; that is God's job. God calls us to love him first and foremost and secondly to love our neighbors as ourselves. We are to love others as God in Christ has loved us (Jn.13:14–34). Christian love is not simply a warm feeling in our hearts for hurting people: it means practical actions to help them, as God gives us opportunity and ability (James 2:15–16).

Loving others as ourselves means doing good in practical ways to:

- Ourselves (Lev.19:18; Mk.12:31)
- Our families (1 Tim. 5:8)
- Our fellow church members (Gal. 6:10)
- Our fellow believers elsewhere in the world (as the Gentile Christians sent money to help the suffering Jewish Christians in Jerusalem) (1 Cor. 16:1–4; 2 Cor. chapters 8 and 9)
- Our fellow human beings all over the world who are suffering and in need ("as we have opportunity, let us do good to all men") (Gal. 6:10, RSV).

Obviously, none of us can do everything, but we can all do something to share God's goodness in this hurting world.

7. FAITHFULNESS

Faithfulness means being trustworthy, reliable, dependable. The character of God is to be faithful. The Scriptures tell us over and over that "God is faithful" (Is. 49:7; 1 Cor.1:9, 10:13). His faithfulness endures forever; He will always be faithful (Ps.100:5, 117:2). God's faithfulness is shown in his keeping his promises (Heb.10:23). If he has promised something, he will do it (Is. 46:11). Therefore, we can trust in God's promises, even when we are in the midst of great suffering (Lam. 3:23; 1 Pet. 4:19).

God wants his people to emulate him. Since faithfulness is such an important aspect of his character, he wants his people to be faithful. He wants us to be reliable. He wants us to be people who are dependable. He wants us to be people who fulfill their obligations and keep their promises, even if it costs them to do so (Ps.15:4).

God wants us to be people who mean what they say, who are straight-forward in their speech and do not try to deceive others with words or with silence. When we say "Yes," we are to mean it, and when we say "No," we are to mean that (Mt. 5:37; James 5:12). God wants us to be faithful and truthful witnesses who do not lie (Prov. 14:5).

In this world so full of lies and deception, it is a great witness to Jesus Christ for Christians to be truthful, to be faithful and reliable and dependable, to be people of honesty and integrity who say what they mean and mean what they say, regardless of whether they are dealing with fellow believers or with unbelievers.

God is working within us by his Holy Spirit to change and transform us so that we become people whose lives are characterized by faithfulness. For those who cooperate with this work of God in their lives, what a blessing it will be at the Last Day for them to hear God himself tell them, "Well done, good and faithful servant... Enter into the joy of your Lord" (Mt. 25:21–23).

8. GENTLENESS

Gentleness means being humble, considerate, unassuming. Its opposite is pride. "A distinctive feature of biblical religion is its teaching about pride and its converse, humility; this is unparalleled in other religions and ethical systems. According to the Bible (and to the classical Christian moral teaching), pride is the very root and essence of sin. Sinfulness consists essentially in the rebellious pride which attributes to self the honor and glory that are due to God."[22]

Jesus' life, more than any other, exemplifies true gentleness and humility. He emptied himself of his heavenly glory and came down from heaven to earth, born in poverty and humble surroundings. (*See,* Phil. 2:5–11). He was "gentle and humble in heart" (Mt.11:29, NRSV). When he came to his people as King on Palm Sunday, he came humbly riding on a donkey, not proudly riding on an impressive white stallion as an earthly king would have done (Mt. 21:5).

Jesus demonstrated his humility to his disciples at the Last Supper by actually taking the part of a servant and washing their feet (Jn.13:1–17). In his trials, sufferings, and death on the cross, Jesus showed the utmost in gentleness and humility, trusting totally in God.

Christians are to follow Jesus' example of gentleness and true humility (Jn.13:17; Tit. 3:2; Eph. 4:2). Even when we are defending ourselves and our faith to opponents, we are to act with gentleness and respect (1 Pet. 3:16). We are to "show by [our] good life that [our] works are done with gentleness born of wisdom" (James 3:13, NRSV).

As we cooperate with the Holy Spirit in his work to produce the fruit of the Spirit within us, gentleness and humility will become as natural to us as putting on our clothes:

"As God's chosen ones, holy and beloved, clothe yourselves with compassion, kindness, humility, [gentleness], and patience. Bear with one another and … forgive each other" (Col. 3:12–13, NRSV).

9. SELF-CONTROL

Self-control, like the other virtues which are fruit of the Holy Spirit, is both God's work in us and something that requires a great deal of effort from us.

God has given us "a spirit of power and of love and of self-discipline" (2 Tim.1:7, NRSV). And God expects us to cooperate with him to grow in self-control and self-discipline. In fact, he instructs us to make every effort to be self-controlled (2 Pet.1:6).

Without self-control, we cannot be very productive in our

work for God and his Kingdom. Without self-control, we are very susceptible to Satan's temptations (1 Cor. 7:5). Without self-control, we have little defense against enemies (Prov. 25:28). Without self-control, if we are self-indulgent and live for pleasure, we are as good as dead even while we are living (1 Tim. 5:6).

St. Paul compares living the Christian life to athletic competition, reminding us of the tremendous discipline and self-control it requires to compete:

> "Do you not know that in a race the runners all compete but only one receives the prize? Run in such a way that you may win it. Athletes exercise self-control in all things; they do it to receive a perishable wreath, but we an imperishable one. So I do not run aimlessly, nor do I box as though beating the air; but I punish my body and enslave it, so that after proclaiming to others I myself should not be disqualified."
>
> (1 Cor. 9:24–27, NRSV)

The virtue of self-control seems to be focused on the self, but if we lack self-control, whether over anger, temper, sexual urges, alcohol, greed (for instance, gambling or dishonest dealings), it will certainly have adverse effects upon other people, especially our families and those close to us. And if we exercise self-control, it is bound to have a positive effect on those around us.

Yes, self-control requires sacrifice on our part. Sometimes it means giving up things we would really like to do. It could involve discomfort, and perhaps pain. But it is necessary as part of the expression of our love for God and love for others.

We are called to be followers of Jesus Christ. We are his students, and we are to learn from him. Like him, we are to keep our eyes on the goal, enduring the discomfort and suffering and pain we must go through for the sake of the joy that is set before us (Heb.12:2).

Summary

Remember, it is God's intention and our destiny that we be conformed to the image of Jesus Christ, so that he might be the eldest in God's family with many brothers and sisters (Rom. 8:29).

In all the things that happen to us in this life, in all circumstances, in our struggles and spiritual warfare, in bad times and in good times, in sickness and in health, God is at work within us to make us more like Jesus. And what will our lives look like as we cooperate with the work of God's Holy Spirit and become more like Jesus? Our lives will be characterized more and more by love, joy, peace, patience, kindness, goodness, faithfulness, gentleness, and self-control.

And then when the Lord Jesus returns to earth to bring his Kingdom in its fullness, whether we are still in the flesh or have fallen asleep, God will complete his good work within us and will transform us so that even our lowly bodies will become like Jesus' glorious body. Then we will shine with the brightness of his glory. Then we will understand that the things we must go through in this life are not worth comparing with the glory which God has in store for us (Rom. 8:18).

H
THE GIFTS OF THE HOLY SPIRIT

Scripture speaks of "the fruit of the Holy Spirit" which God is working to produce in all Christians, those qualities which reflect the image and character of Jesus Christ. However, the Scriptures also speak of the gifts of the Holy Spirit. The Greek word is *charismata* and means "gifts of grace." These are gifts for special service given by the Holy Spirit not to all Christians but "as the Spirit wills" (1 Cor.12:11). They are not given primarily for the benefit of the one who receives them, but "for the common good" (1 Cor.12:7, NRSV), for the building up of the church (1 Cor.14:5). Though they may appear to be quite different, they are unified because they are given by the one Holy Spirit and are the working of the one God (1 Cor.12:4–11).

In 1 Corinthians chapter 12, St. Paul lists nine of these charismatic grace-gifts: the word of wisdom, the word of knowledge, faith, gifts of healing, working of miracles, prophecy, discerning of spirits, different kinds of tongues, and the interpretation of tongues. Let's take a look at each of them.

1. THE WORD OF WISDOM

Wisdom has to do with making wise decisions, deciding what

is better to do when faced with a choice, deciding what is good, what will be beneficial, what will avoid unnecessary danger. God's wisdom may be given directly to an individual, or it may be given to one through another individual or through dreams or visions.

There are many examples in the Bible of God leading his people by a word of wisdom to make a decision that is wise, even though it may not seem so initially. In the Old Testament, for example, when the Hebrews came out of slavery in Egypt, God did not lead them to the Promised Land by the shortest and most direct route but by a much longer way around through the wilderness of the Red Sea. The reason was that if they had gone by the shortest way, they would have had to fight the Philistines, and they were not yet ready to fight and may have changed their minds when faced with war (Ex. 13:17–18). Another Old Testament example is when God told a prophet to return home by the way he came, but he did not do so and was killed by a lion (1 Kings 13:17–24).

Then in the New Testament, when the Wise Men visited the Child Jesus in Bethlehem, God warned them in a dream not to return to King Herod in Jerusalem, so they returned home by a different route (Mt. 2:12). God warned Joseph in a dream to take his family to Egypt to escape from Herod (Mt. 2:13), and then he guided Joseph in another dream to return from Egypt, but not to settle in Judea but rather to make their home in Nazareth (Mt. 2:19–23).

2. THE WORD OF KNOWLEDGE

This is where God gives a person knowledge in a supernatural way, so that he knows something is true although he may not be able to say how he knows. An example of this in the Old Testament is where the prophet Samuel anointed David to be King of Israel. God told Samuel it would be one of the sons of Jesse the Bethlehemite. Samuel told Jesse to bring his sons before him. The oldest son Eliab was tall, strong, and handsome, and Samuel thought he was the one, but God said not. Then five other sons of Jesse came before Samuel, but the Lord said no. Samuel asked Jesse, "Are all the young men here?" and Jesse mentioned the youngest, David. He considered him so unimportant that he had not brought him with the others but left him out in the field tending the sheep. When David came before Samuel, Samuel knew he was the one. God told him, "Arise, anoint him; for this is the one!" (1 Sam.16:1–13).

A New Testament example of the word of knowledge in operation is the story of Ananias and Sapphira. They sold property and only brought part of the sale price to the apostles, representing it to be the total. God gave the Apostle Peter knowledge that the money they brought was not the total, that Ananias was lying, and even the exact amount of the sale price (Acts 5:1–11).

3. FAITH

In the context here, "faith" does not mean "faith unto salvation," for the recipients of the grace-gifts are already Christians. It must mean "faith to move mountains," miracle-working faith that believes God against all obstacles and against all appearances. It is the kind of faith Jesus described: "[F]or assuredly I say to you, if you have faith as a mustard seed, you will say to this mountain, 'Move from here to there,' and it will move; and nothing will be impossible for you" (Mt. 17:20). It is the kind of faith shown by the prophet Elijah against the prophets of Baal in the contest at Mount Carmel (1 Kings 18:20–40).

4. GIFTS OF HEALING

It is significant that this grace-gift is spoken of in the plural: *gifts* of healing, not *the* gift of healing. All health and all healing come from God. "Every good gift and every perfect gift is from above, and comes down from the Father of lights" (James 1:17).

It is amazing how much the Bible is concerned with health. Many of God's laws, statutes, and ordinances for the Israelites are health regulations. Certainly, if we live according to God's rules, follow his instructions in the Wisdom books of the Bible (Proverbs and Ecclesiastes) and eat and drink in moderation, our health will be much better than if we live lives of excess.

All healing comes from God. Often it comes through the specialized knowledge and skill of physicians. Jesus himself said that those who are sick need the physician (Lk. 5:31). St. Luke was a medical doctor, "the beloved physician" (Col. 4:14). Christians who become ill are being disobedient to God not to seek medical help when it is available.

However, God's healing work is not limited to the medical profession. He can work directly through charismatic gifts of healing. Healing has always been a part of the ministry of the church, carrying out Jesus' instruction to his first followers to heal the sick (Lk. 9:1). Usually, healings are worked through prayer with laying-on-of-hands or anointing with oil, although God is certainly not limited to these means. Normally, the church follows the instructions of St. James: "Is anyone among you sick? Let him call for the elders of the church, and let them pray over him, anointing him with oil in the name of the Lord. And the prayer of faith will save the sick, and the Lord will raise him up" (James 5:14–15).

A person does not have to be an ordained minister to exercise the charismatic gifts of healing. God has raised up many lay people to be his ministers of healing throughout the history of the church and in our own time.

5. WORKING OF MIRACLES

The word translated "miracles" in Greek is *dunameis* which means "powers, acts of power, mighty works." Its root is the same as "dynamite." The Christian God—the God of the Bible—is "God All-Mighty," "God All-Powerful." Our God is a miracle-working God. One of the Biblical designations for God is "The Power" (Mk.14:62).

God is the source of all power. Nothing is too hard for

him, nothing is impossible for him (Gen.18:14; Mk.10:27), for he is the One who created heaven and earth (Jer. 32:17). Jesus is the power of God incarnated in human flesh and blood (1 Cor.1:24).

In his ministry on earth, Jesus worked many miracles, performed many "works of power," as we have seen. Jesus shared his miracle-working power with his Apostles while he was alive, and after his ascension into heaven, he empowered his followers with the same miracle-working power: "And these signs [miracles] will follow those who believe" (Mk.16:17). In the Acts of the Apostles, we see them performing the same kinds of miracles that Jesus himself performed. Indeed, the ability to perform "signs and wonders and mighty deeds" was the mark of a true apostle (2 Cor.12:12).

Since "Jesus Christ is the same yesterday, today, and forever" (Heb.13:8), this same miracle-working power has existed in the church throughout its history and is still going on in the world today and will continue to the close of the age. In many parts of the world today, when the Gospel is preached in the power of the Holy Spirit, healings and miracles and deliverances from evil spirits accompany the preaching of the Word and many people are converted to Jesus Christ as Lord and Savior and healed.

6. PROPHECY

Prophecy is God's supernatural action in giving a message to a person to deliver to God's people. The prophetic message sometimes pertains to the present time, applying God's truth to the current historical situation; sometimes it pertains to the future time, foretelling what God will do in time to come; or it may contain both elements. Our common popular understanding of prophecy limits its operation to the future, but this is a great misunderstanding. Biblical prophecy both "forth-tells" and "fore-tells." It includes both proclamation and prediction, as biblical scholars have pointed out. St. Peter gives us the best definition: "...prophecy never came by the will of man, but holy men of God spoke as they were moved by the Holy Spirit" (2 Pet.1:21).

Prophecy was a substantial and essential part of God's Old Testament revelation. The messages of the prophets comprise more than thirty percent of the text. In the New Testament, God has shown that the prophetic Scriptures of the Old Testament find their fulfillment in Jesus Christ, just as the Law was fulfilled in him.

Since God reveals his truth to his prophets (Heb.1:1) and "does nothing, Unless he reveals his secret to his servants the prophets" (Amos 3:7), we should not be surprised that prophecy retains an important place in the revelation of God's New Covenant with mankind in Jesus Christ.

God prepared the way for Jesus through the ministry of John the Baptizer, the last of the prophets in the Old Testament line. Some examples of the gift of prophecy operating in the New Testament are: St. Mary's Song of Praise ("the Magnificat") in Luke 1:46–55; the prophecy of Zechariah (the father of John the Baptizer) in Luke 1:67–79 known as "the Benedictus;" and the prophetic words of Simeon in Luke 2:34–35. Jesus himself was the greatest prophet of all, speaking the messages given him from God his Father (Jn. 8:28; 12:50; 15:15).

The New Testament church had a recognized ministry of prophecy (1 Cor.12:28; Acts 13:1). One well-known prophet from the Jerusalem church was Agabus, who predicted a world-wide famine (Acts 11:27–28) and also predicted that if Paul went to Jerusalem, he would be arrested by the Jews and handed over to the Gentiles (Acts 21:10–14). Both of these prophecies came to pass.

In the New Testament church, the gift of prophecy was not limited to men, but women also prophesied as predicted by the prophet Joel (Acts 2:17–18). Philip the Evangelist had four unmarried virgin daughters who prophesied (Acts 21:8–9).

The most common manifestation of the gift of prophecy in

today's church is the preaching of the Gospel when the message is true to the Scriptures and is empowered by the Holy Spirit, applying God's truth to the hearts and minds and lives of those who hear the message.

The Apostle Paul instructed the Christians at Corinth: "Pursue love, and desire spiritual gifts, but especially that you may prophesy" (1 Cor.14:1) because those who prophesy build up the church (v.4) by speaking encouraging and consoling words to the people (v.3).

However, the Scriptures teach us that there are false prophets as well as true prophets, lying prophets as well as truthful ones, those speaking their own message as well as those speaking God's message. How can we tell the true prophets from the false prophets? We desperately need the spiritual gift of discernment.

7. DISCERNING OF SPIRITS

Discerning of spirits is the supernatural gift of the Holy Spirit whereby Christians are enabled to distinguish God's truth from falsehood, true prophets from false prophets, good spirits from evil spirits, good from evil.

Not everything "spiritual" is good, for there are unclean, evil spirits at work as well as good spirits. In spiritual matters, things are not always what they seem. Even Satan can disguise himself as an angel of light (2 Cor.11:14). Not every preacher who quotes a text from the Bible is proclaiming God's truth, because the devil can quote Scripture as he did at the Temptation of Jesus. The preacher can be stating merely his own opinions rather than God's truth. Not every idea a person gets when he prays and asks for God's guidance is from God. It may be from the devil, or from the influence of others, or from the mind or desires of the person praying.

Christians are not to be gullible in spiritual matters. St. Paul tells us, "Do not despise prophecies. Test all things; hold fast what is good" (1 Thes. 5:20–21). St. John tells us not to believe every spirit, "but test the spirits, whether they are of God; because many false prophets have gone out into the world" (1 Jn. 4:1). Remember that false prophets can even work miracles, as Jesus himself taught (Mk.13:22). *See also,* Deut.13:1–5 and Rev.13:13–14.

Spiritual matters can only be spiritually discerned (1 Cor. 2:14). Only the Holy Spirit can guide us into truth (Jn.16:13). Jesus was filled with the Holy Spirit completely. Thus, Jesus knew even the thoughts of men (Mt. 9:4, 12:25; Jn. 2:25). But unlike Jesus, we are not completely filled with the Holy Spirit. We have a great deal of sin left in us and are susceptible not only to influences from the Holy Spirit, but also from the world, from our own sinful desires and minds, and from the devil. We do not see spiritual matters clearly; our vision is clouded; our knowledge is limited (1 Cor.13:12).

But God has not left us completely in the dark. In the New Testament he has given us some guidelines to help us distinguish the true from the false in spiritual things. J. P. Baker in his illuminating article on "Prophecy" in *The Illustrated Bible Dictionary, p.* 1276 summarizes them:

> "Testing or weighing prophetic utterances is all the more necessary in view of the warning of the New Testament ... against false prophets and false prophecy by which Satan seeks to lead the unwary astray (Mt. 7:15; 24:11,24; 2 Peter 2:1; 1 Jn. 4:1ff), and an example of which appears in Bar-Jesus at Paphos (Acts 13:5ff).
>
> "The testing of any prophetic utterance will be in accordance with our Lord's warning, 'You will know them by their fruits' (Mt. 7:20 *in loc.*) and will include these criteria:
>
> 1. their conformity to the teachings of Scripture, of Christ and of his apostles in both content and character;
> 2. their over-all tendency and results or fruits (e.g., do they glorify Christ and edify the church, as per Jn.16:14 and 1 Cor.14:3 ff.?);

3. the consensus of the recognized prophets, and presumably elders and teachers, in that place weighing and discerning what is said (1 Cor. 14:29,32);

4. the consistency of this utterance with other prophetic utterance in that place (vv.30,31); and

5. the reverent confession of Jesus as the incarnate Lord by the Spirit speaking through the prophet (1 Cor.12:2–3; 1 Jn. 4:1–3)."

8. SPEAKING IN DIFFERENT KINDS OF TONGUES

The term "speaking in other tongues" in the New Testament seems to refer to two different phenomena. At the Day of Pentecost, the Apostles "were all filled with the Holy Spirit and began to speak with other tongues, as the Spirit gave them utterance" (Acts 2:4). Each member of the crowd that had gathered "heard them speaking in the native language of each. Amazed and astonished, they asked, 'Are not all these who are speaking Galileans? And how is it that we hear, each of us, in our own native language?... [I]n our own languages we hear them speaking about God's deeds of power'" (Acts 2:6–11, NRSV).

At Pentecost, the hearers all understood what was being spoken in languages the speakers, the Apostles, did not know.

However, the "speaking in tongues" St. Paul writes about that was taking place in the church at Corinth was a different phenomenon, as Scripture specifically says that "nobody understands them [those who speak in tongues], since they are speaking mysteries in the Spirit" (1 Cor.14:2, NRSV). St. Paul repeats the same point seven verses later, that those speaking in tongues were uttering speech "that is not intelligible" (v.9, NRSV).

It seems that the "speaking in tongues" at Pentecost was quite different from that at Corinth which might more accurately be termed "ecstatic speech," which has a spiritual benefit to the one speaking but not to the entire Christian assembly unless it is interpreted.

St. Paul goes into this matter of "speaking in tongues" in

the Christian congregation in detail in the 14th chapter of 1 Corinthians. He specifically says that it is not to be forbidden (14:39) but encouraged (14:5), and he thanks God that he speaks in tongues more than any of them (14:18). However, he would rather that they prophesy in the language everyone understands so that the whole congregation can be up-built and encouraged and strengthened, and not just the one speaking (14:2–5), and so that outsiders and non-believers can be reached with the Word of God (14:20–25). He says that if everybody in the church assembly is speaking in tongues and outsiders or non-believers come in, "will they not say that you are out of your mind?" (14:23).

St. Paul lays down the rule that "if there is no interpreter, let him keep silent in church, and let him speak to himself and to God" (14:28).

9. INTERPRETATION OF TONGUES

Interpretation of tongues is the God-given spiritual gift of being able to understand the message being spoken by the one speaking in tongues who may not know what he is saying, so that it can be expressed in words which the whole congregation can understand. Thus the church can be built up and encouraged and strengthened. If there is no one present who can interpret, then a person speaking in tongues is to keep silent "and speak to himself and to God" (1 Cor. 14:28).

In his teaching on the nine supernatural spiritual gifts, St. Paul stresses the unity of the Body of Christ in the exercise of its diversity of gifts, that all things must be done in love (1 Cor. chapter 13), that the ministry of prophecy (preaching) is of the greatest priority, and that "…all things [should] be done decently and in order" (1 Cor.14:40).

10. SOME ADDITIONAL SPIRITUAL GIFTS

In Romans 12:6–8, St. Paul mentions some other grace-gifts (*charismata*). He begins by stressing the diversity in unity:

"For as we have many members in one body, but all the members do not have the same function, so we, being many, are one body in Christ, and individually members of one another. Having then gifts differing according to the grace that is given to us, let us use them…"

(Rom. 12:4–6)

Then he mentions some grace-gifts we have not dealt with before.

Serving ("ministry"). The root word is *diakonos* (translated "deacon") which literally means a waiter, one serving food at table. It has come to mean "practical service." The first deacons were set apart to supervise the daily distribution of food (Acts 6:1–6). Then deacon came to be an ordained minister in the church, below the rank of presbyter (elder or priest). It was always part of the deacon's duties to supervise the distribution of charitable gifts ("almsgiving") for the local congregation. But the basic meaning of "deacon" is "one who serves." And whether or not they technically have the title of "deacon," the Holy Spirit chooses particular individuals in the local congregation for the ministry of practical service to help those who are in need.

Encouraging. This is a better translation of the Greek word *paraclesis* than "exhorting" which several Bible translations use. A *paraclete* was a person called in to help another, to stand by his side and speak for him, especially in court. Thus, the ministry of *paraclesis* involves encouraging others, exhorting them, comforting, and strengthening them.

Contributing to the needs of others ("giving"). This is giving goods or money to help needy people and to further the spread of the Gospel. St. Paul says that the person giving should give with generosity. Some translations say "with simplicity." The idea is that a person making the contribution should give generously, but not make any fuss about, it, not drawing attention to himself. This is in accord with Jesus' instructions to give in secret, not letting the right hand know what the left hand is doing (Mt. 6:3–4).

Showing mercy. St. Paul says that the person showing mercy, pity, compassion toward another should do it cheerfully, not grudgingly, but gladly (Rom.12:8).

We need to bear in mind that these charismatic grace-gifts are just as important in the life of the church as the nine "gifts of the Holy Spirit" set forth in 1 Corinthians 12:8–10. These four charismatic grace-gifts, serving, encouraging, giving, showing mercy, are much more humble and quiet and do not attract attention in the way that working miracles and speaking in tongues do. But they are just as essential to the building up of the Body of Christ. Remember the words of the Lord Jesus, that "… whoever gives one of these little ones only a cup of cold water in the name of a disciple, assuredly I say to you, he shall by no means lose his reward" (Mt.10:42).

SOME OTHER WORK OF THE HOLY SPIRIT

In addition to the gifts of the Holy Spirit, the fruit of the Holy Spirit, and the offices in the church for which the Holy Spirit sets Christians apart, the Holy Spirit functions in several other capacities. Let's consider some aspects of his work.

Teacher: The Holy Spirit teaches and instructs us in the things of God, spiritual things (1 Cor. 2:10–13). Jesus comforted his disciples on the night in which he was betrayed by telling them: "But the Helper, the Holy Spirit, whom the Father will send in My name, he will teach you all things, and bring to your remembrance all things that I said to you" (Jn.14:26).

Jesus himself is the Truth (Jn.14:6), and the Holy Spirit is the Spirit of Jesus (Acts 16:7; Rom. 8:9), and so the Holy Spirit is the "Spirit of Truth" (Jn. 14:17, 15:26, 16:13). Therefore, the Holy Spirit leads us to Jesus. If any spirit leads us away from Jesus, leads us to doubt that Jesus is Lord God in human flesh, leads us to think there is any way to God apart from Jesus, it is not the Holy Spirit, but an unholy spirit (*See* 1 Cor.12:3). The Holy Spirit glorifies Jesus and leads us deeper into the truth of

Jesus, not to any supposed "truth" apart from Jesus (Jn. 16:14,15) nor to some supposed wisdom or teaching which "goes beyond" the truth as it is in Jesus (2 John 9, NRSV). Any teaching that claims some way to God apart from Jesus, or that salvation is possible except through Jesus, is from the devil, the deceiver, the liar, the antichrist (2 John).

Witness: The Holy Spirit bears witness to Jesus Christ (Jn. 14:26; Rom.8:9–17; Heb.10:15; 1 Jn. 5:6–8), and seals and confirms that testimony in our hearts (1 Cor.1:6; 1 Jn. 5:10).

Illuminator: It is the Holy Spirit who opens the Holy Scriptures to our minds and hearts, who illuminates the written Word of God, who guides us in applying God's truth to our lives. "All Scripture is God-breathed and is useful for teaching, rebuking, correcting and training in righteousness, so that the man of God may be thoroughly equipped for every good work" (2 Tim. 3:16–17, NIV).

Since the Scriptures were breathed out and inspired by God's Holy Spirit, they must be interpreted and opened to us by the Holy Spirit (1 Pet.1:10–12). St. Peter wrote: "… no prophecy of Scripture is of any private interpretation, for prophecy never came by the will of man, but holy men spoke as they were moved by the Holy Spirit" (2 Pet.1:20–21).

The bare words of the Bible by themselves are lifeless, but interpreted and illuminated to us by the Holy Spirit they bring life and freedom, and joy and peace. "[T]he letter kills, but the Spirit gives life" (2 Cor. 3:6). As Jesus said: "It is the Spirit who gives life; the flesh profits nothing" (Jn. 6:63). Without the Holy Spirit enlightening us, the Bible is merely words and does us no good, but opened to us by the Holy Spirit, God works through its words to bring us his truth and to continue to nourish and strengthen his life within us.

Therefore, our Bible study must be bathed in prayer that God would enlighten us by his Holy Spirit and illuminate and enliven the written words to our minds and hearts and apply them to our lives.

Guide. The Holy Spirit is our guide. He guides us into all truth, truth being centered in Jesus Christ who himself is the Truth (Jn.16:13). And he also guides us in the concrete decisions of our lives, as he led St. Peter to go to the home of the Roman Centurion Cornelius, thus bringing the Gospel to Gentiles for the first time (Acts chapter 10; 11:12), and as he led St. Paul not to go into the Roman provinces of Asia, Mysia, and Bithynia but instead to go into Greece (Roman province of Macedonia), thus bringing the Gospel into Europe for the first time (Acts 16:6–10).

Helper. The Holy Spirit also helps us in many different ways. He is known as the Helper, the Holy Comforter, the Advocate. These are all translations of the Greek word *paraclete*, which means one called to stand beside us, help us, and speak for us, like our lawyer in court (Jn.14:16). He even helps us in our weakness, helps us pray, and even prays for us:

> "Likewise the Spirit also helps us in our weaknesses. For we do not know what we should pray for as we ought, but the Spirit himself makes intercession for us with groanings which cannot be uttered. Now he who searches the hearts knows what the mind of the Spirit is, because he makes intercession for the saints according to the will of God."
>
> (Rom. 8:26–27)

And the Holy Spirit helps us witness to Jesus Christ, all the time, but especially in the time of trial. Jesus specifically instructed his disciples: "But when they deliver you up, do not worry about how or what you should speak. For it will be given to you in that hour what you should speak; for it is not you who speak, but the Spirit of your Father who speaks in you." (Mt. 10:19,20 *See also*, Mk.13:11; Lk.12:12).

Other work. Some of the other things the Holy Spirit works in the lives of Christians:

convicts of sin (Jn.16:18)
brings hope (Rom.15:13)
brings freedom (2 Cor. 3:17)

brings joy (1 Thes.1:6)
delivers from fear (Rom. 8:15)
renews us (Tit. 3:5)
makes Christians more holy, sanctifies us (1 Pet. 1:2, 2 Thes. 2:13), making us more like Jesus

Summary

We cannot become Christians without the Holy Spirit working within us (1 Cor. 12:3); and we cannot continue living the Christian life without his continual help.

How can we have the Holy Spirit with us and in us? The Lord Jesus has told us:

> "If a son asks for bread from any father among you, will he give him a stone? Or if he asks for a fish, will he give him a serpent instead of a fish? If you then, being evil, know how to give good gifts to your children, how much more will your heavenly Father give the Holy Spirit to those who ask him!"
>
> (Lk. 11:11–13)

Part Five: God will Save His People

There are three time dimensions to God's salvation of his people: past, present, and future. In the life, ministry, death, and resurrection of Jesus Christ, God has redeemed his people through these mighty works of God in the past. Through his Holy Spirit working in the lives of his people, God is applying to our lives here and now the salvation won for us by Jesus Christ, and he is working within us to transform us gradually to be more like Jesus. So, we are now being saved in the present. However, we know that this process will never be complete in our earthly lives. Sin will remain in us as long as we live in this world.

But in the magnificent future God has planned for his people, we will be saved fully and finally. Our redemption will be complete. Our struggles will be over. Our sorrows, griefs, trials, and tribulations will be no more. God will bring to completion the redemption and salvation of his people in life with him forever, in a life so wonderful that we can only get fleeting glimpses of how great it will be.

Although we separate various aspects of the Last Things into sub-parts to discuss and consider them, this is misleading in a sense, because the various events of the Last Times really constitute parts of one mighty work of God. They are not separate, isolated, unrelated events. Often, two or more aspects of the Last Things will be mentioned in the same sentence or the same verse of Scripture.

This completion and fulfillment of God's work will be inaugurated by the return to earth of Jesus Christ in his Second Coming.

A

THE SECOND COMING OF JESUS CHRIST

1. THE REALITY OF HIS RETURN

The New Testament tells us over and over again that Jesus Christ will return in person to this earth again. Jesus himself said so; His apostles said so; the Christian church through the centuries has said so as an essential article of the faith: "We believe... He will come again in glory to judge the living and the dead, and his Kingdom will have no end" (Nicene Creed).

It might be helpful to consider this matter under the heading of the questions: Who? What? Where? Why? and When?

Who is it that will return? Forty days after his Resurrection from the dead, immediately after Jesus had been taken up into heaven, two angels appeared to the dumbfounded apostles standing and looking up to the skies and told them: "This same Jesus, who was taken up from you into heaven, will so come in like manner as you saw him go into heaven" (Acts 1:11). The One who shall return is the same Jesus who was conceived by the Holy Spirit, born of the Virgin Mary in Bethlehem, grew up in Nazareth, preached the Kingdom of God, taught God's truth, worked miracles, was crucified under the Roman Governor Pontius Pilate, was dead and buried in the tomb, rose again from the dead on the third day, appeared to his Apostles and many of his followers, and was taken up from the earth into heaven where he had come from. It is this same Jesus who will return to earth.

What is the Second Coming? How will it be different from his first coming? Here a few of the many contrasts between the two:

At His First Coming	At His Second Coming
He was born as a helpless baby.	He will return as the mighty King of Kings and Lord of Lords (Rev. 19:16).
His birth was in obscurity, observed only by Mary and Joseph.	His Return will be a cosmic event, unmistakable, like lightning flashing from east to west (Mt. 24:27).
He came to earth all alone, as a baby.	He will be accompanied by multitudes of his mighty angels (2 Thes. 1:7) and saints (1 Thes. 3:13).
He came to earth quietly.	His coming will be with a shout of command and the trumpet of God heard all over the world (1 Thes. 4:16).
His life was one of humility and humiliation.	He will come in power and great glory (Mt. 25:31).

He came to be judged and condemned to death as a criminal.	He will come in flaming fire and will be the one to judge all mankind (Mt. 25:31; 2 Thes.1:7–10).
He came to save, not to condemn (Jn. 3:17).	He will judge the living and the dead, reward those who believe in him and inflict "vengeance on those who do not know God and on those who do not obey the gospel" (2 Thes.1:8).

Where will Jesus' return to the earth take place? Surprisingly, the Bible specifically answers this question. The prophet Zechariah tells us that when the Lord comes with all his holy ones to rule and reign over all the earth, "… in that day his feet will stand on the Mount of Olives, Which faces Jerusalem on the east" (Zech. 14:4). This is supported by the prophet Ezekiel who wrote that when the glory of God returns to the Temple, it will come from the east and enter by the gate of Jerusalem facing east (Ezek. 43:1–5). This is the gate called "The Golden Gate."

These prophecies are consistent with St. Luke's account of the Ascension of Jesus. He ascended into heaven from the Mount of Olives, specifically from the village of Bethany which lies on the eastern slope of the Mount, only three kilometers from the eastern wall of Jerusalem (*See* Lk. 24:50). Since the angels told Jesus' on-looking apostles that Jesus would return in the same way he had been taken up into heaven (Acts 1:11), it is only to be expected that he will return to earth where he departed, on the Mount of Olives.

Centuries ago, when Jerusalem was under Muslim domination, they knew the Jewish and Christian expectation that when he came to earth, the feet of Messiah would stand on the Mount of Olives and that he would enter Jerusalem through the "Golden Gate," and so they closed it up and put a Muslim cemetery east of that gate, thinking that this would prevent the Messiah from entering Jerusalem. Of course, such a hope is vain, for Jesus will return as the Almighty Ruler of all things and nothing can stop him. Nothing can prevent him from fulfilling the Scriptural prophecies. Nothing can stand in the way of his omnipotent power.

Why will Jesus come back to earth? What is the purpose of his Second Coming? His return will accomplish several purposes, including:

1. To bring his Kingdom in its fullness and to reign as absolute sovereign forever (Rev. 11:15)

2. To bring to a close this present temporary evil age and inaugurate in its fullness the eternal life of "the age to come" and God's new creation (2 Pet. 3:11–13)

3. To sit in judgment of each one of us, living and dead, so as to punish and execute vengeance on the ungodly and to vindicate and reward the godly (2 Cor. 5:10; 2 Thes.1:5–10; Rev. 20:11–13)

4. To fulfill all the prophecies concerning the Messiah, for the Scriptures cannot be broken or annulled (Jn.10:35; Acts 3:21)

5. To complete the salvation of believers (Heb. 9:28; 1 Pet.1:5)

6. To destroy the power of sin (Rev. 21:27), death (1 Cor.15:25–26;Rev. 20:14), and the devil (Rev. 20:10)

When is Jesus going to return to earth as King of Kings and Lord of Lords? As Christians of the 21st century, we would very much like to know the answer to this question, just as much as Jesus' earliest disciples did (Mk.13:3). But Jesus is absolutely clear on this point: we cannot know when it will be.

Surprisingly, Jesus said that even he himself did not know. It is a secret known only to God the Father. "But of that day and hour no one knows, no, not even the angels of heaven, but My Father only" (Mt. 24:36). Just before Jesus ascended back into heaven, his apostles asked him again when it would be (Acts 1:6). And Jesus told them the same thing he had taught them earlier: "It is not for you to know times or seasons which the Father has put in his own authority" (Acts 1:7).

However, he has given us some signs of his coming, which we will consider in the next section.

Jesus taught very clearly that his Return would be sudden, unexpected, and therefore entirely unpredictable, just as we don't know the exact time a burglar might break into our house ("like a thief in the night").

Has the Second Coming been delayed? Jesus made statements that some scholars have interpreted to mean that he expected to return in a very short time, during the lifetime of the Apostles (Mk. 9:1; Mt. 10:23; Mk. 13:30). Was Jesus mistaken? No, not at all. As a leading modern theologian writes:

> "Precisely because the Second Coming will be unexpected in the strictest sense of the word, we are not to speculate as to whether it is near at hand or far in the future. Precisely because the Second Coming is the end of the history of this world, it is always equally near at hand. It is therefore absurd to suggest that Jesus miscalculated the nearness of his Second Coming... He was not mistaken, as no one else can be mistaken in awaiting the Second Coming at every moment... The suggestion that it has been delayed presupposes that it is conceived to be an event which in some way will transpire within the course of world history. But according to the New Testament it marks the end of time, and this is the meaning of its unexpected character. And since it marks the end of time, it makes no sense to speak of its having been delayed 2, or 200, or 2000 years. The idea that the return of the Lord has been delayed can prevail only where men have ceased to watch and pray and instead have given themselves to speculation about the time of His return. The New Testa-

ment says, therefore, that this idea is entertained by 'scoffers' (2 Pet. 3:3–10)."[23]

We must not forget that since God is eternal, to him time is totally different than it is for us. What we count as a thousand years may be like one day to God (Ps. 90:4; 2 Pet. 3:8). God dwells above the realm of space and time. He sees everything from the beginning to the end (Is. 46:10).

In considering when he will return again, we need to bear in mind continually the clear and plain words of the Lord Jesus himself: "… you know neither the day nor the hour in which the Son of Man is coming" (Mt. 25:13).

However, he has given us some signs of his coming.

2. THE SIGNS OF HIS COMING

Although the Scriptures tell us explicitly that we cannot know when Jesus will return to earth, Jesus and his Apostles have given us some signs, pointers, indicators, road markers, as it were.

These signs can be grouped under seven headings for purposes of consideration, namely:

a. The preaching of the Gospel to all the world

b. Persecution of Christians

c. Apostasy

d. Disasters

e. The appearance of the Antichrist

f. The conversion and ingathering of the Jews

g. Disorder and chaos in the universe.

The preaching of the Gospel to all the world

Jesus said specifically that before the end comes, the Gospel must first be preached to all nations (Mk.13:10; Mt. 24:14). Since the Lord Jesus began his public ministry, the preaching of the Good News of the Kingdom of God has been underway. In the Acts of the Apostles, St. Luke tells us of the beginnings of the spread of the Gospel after Jesus' Ascension, first in Jerusalem, then in Judea and Samaria; first among the Jewish people, then extending to the Gentiles; around parts of the Mediterranean world all the way to Rome, the capital of the Roman Empire.

Christian history tells us of the spread of the Gospel all around the Mediterranean world by the end of the 1st millennium reaching from Spain around to Africa; into Europe, the British Isles, Scandinavia; into Eastern Europe (Armenia became the first Christian nation in AD 294), Russia (around AD 988), Poland (around AD 1000), through the Middle East, as far East as India.

With Columbus' discovery of the New World in 1492, North and South America were opened to the Christian faith. Missionaries went as far as China, Japan and the Philippines. In the 19th century, the powerful surge of the foreign mission movement carried the Gospel to many parts of the world where it had previously been unknown, such as deep into Africa, to China, and Southeast Asia.

And in the 20th century with the advent of world-wide means of communication such as radio and television, the Gospel message has been spread farther into previously non-Christians areas of the world.

However, the task has not yet been completed. There are many places in the world where the name of Jesus Christ is not known.

Thus, we see that the preaching of the Gospel to all nations is not something that takes place only at the end of this age, but rather has been going on ever since Jesus began his public ministry and will continue until the time is fulfilled and the Lord returns to earth.

Persecution of Christians.

In the ministry of Jesus, in the ministry of the Apostles, and throughout Christian history, whenever and wherever the Gospel is preached, some are stirred up to faith and newness of life in Jesus and others are stirred up with hatred, anger, and fury to the point of persecuting the evangelists and the converts.

Jesus came in love; He never hurt anybody; He did nothing but help people; He "went about doing good"; He did nothing wrong; He spoke nothing but God's truth. And yet the leaders of God's own people, the Jews, hated Jesus and stirred up the mob to demand Jesus' death. The same crowds that welcomed Jesus on Palm Sunday with shouts of "Hosanna to the Son of David" were screaming "Crucify him!" just a few days later.

Jesus told his disciples plainly that they could expect no better treatment. "If they persecuted Me, they will also persecute you" (Jn. 15:20). "… [T]hey will hand you over to be tortured and will put you to death, and you will be hated by all nations because of My name" (Mt. 24:9, NRSV). Jesus' Apostles said the same thing: "We must through many tribulations enter the kingdom of God" (Acts 14:22). "[A]ll who desire to live godly in Christ Jesus will suffer persecution" (2 Tim. 3:12).

Persecution takes a variety of forms. It covers a spectrum from being harassed and threatened; to being driven out of places as happened to Paul and his missionary companions on several occasions; to losing business and property, or having property seized or confiscated (Heb.10:34); to being imprisoned; to being beaten, flogged, tortured; all the way to being put to death as were Stephen and James the son of Zebedee. We must never forget that all of the Apostles were put to death for their faith, except for the Apostle John who died an old man, according to church tradition.

Persecution against Christians has been continuing since New Testament times. It has been estimated that by AD 313 when the Emperor Constantine issued the Edict of Toleration, 100,000 Christians had been put to death. In Christian history, frequently the missionaries who carry the Gospel into a new area are persecuted severely, often murdered. Historians have said that in the supposedly enlightened 20th century, more people were killed because of the simple fact that they were

Christians than in all the preceding centuries added together. And persecution continues in our 21st century, particularly from militant Muslims and Hindus and secularists. One example: estimates are that in Sudan over two million Christians have been killed by Muslims and countless others enslaved in recent years.

Why is it that the Good News of Jesus Christ stirs up such blind, fanatical, unreasoning hatred and fury that incites the enemies of the Gospel to persecute Jesus' followers? What is the spiritual dynamic at work in this situation?

- People don't like to be disturbed or forced to question their deeply held beliefs; Jesus' people "turn the world upside down" (Acts 17:6).

- Sometimes the motive is jealousy, when the religious leaders see their followers deserting them and turning to Jesus and his way (Acts 5:17).

- When devotees of idols, whether physical images or non-biblical ideas about God, are confronted with God's truth that Jesus is the *only way* to the true God, oftentimes they react with furious rage (Acts 19:23–41, the riot at Ephesus).

- Jesus' way is a judgment upon the values of this world. The things that worldly people prize so highly and invest so much time, money, and effort in pursuing (such as possessions, power, prestige, pleasure) are worthless in God's sight and have no value whatsoever in eternity. As Jesus said: "What will a man gain by winning the whole world, at the cost of his true self?" (Mt.16:26, NEB). And people do not want to be told that.

- Underlying and motivating the world's persecution of Christians is the power of the devil. Satan hates God, but he cannot reach God, so he turns his cruel rage against God's people on earth, both Jews and Christians (Rev. 12:12).

Although persecution has been going on through the centuries, Scripture teaches that it will intensify as the end of the world approaches.

Apostasy:

(1) resulting from persecution.

When persecution comes upon Christians, some will fall away from the faith and turn away from the living God (Heb. 3:12). In Jesus' Parable of the Sower, he tells us that there are some who hear the Gospel and right away receive it with joy, yet "when tribulation or persecution arises because of the word, immediately he stumbles" (Mt. 13:20–21).

"Apostasy" originally meant rebellion against rightful authority, especially rebellion against God. Literally, it means to defect, to withdraw, to separate from, to desert. Some English versions of the Bible translate it as "falling away," others as "rebellion." One poignant example occurred in the ministry of Jesus after he had given some very strong teaching, and as a result, "many of his disciples went back and walked with him no more" (Jn. 6:66).

"To be an apostate is to enter into unbelief and to dissolve any union one might have had with God in Christ. The normal mark of a genuine apostate is his denial that Christ is very God or his repudiation of Christ's atoning work on the cross (Phil. 3:18; 2 Pet. 2:1; 1 John 4:1–3)."[24]

(2) resulting from false teaching.

However, persecution is not the only cause of apostasy. It also can result from heresy (false teaching) in the church. Jesus' teaching against false messiahs and false prophets is very forceful. He warned that it would occur (Mt. 7:15–20; 24:4,5,11,23–25; Mk.13:5,6,21,22; Lk. 21:8) but that the punishment would be horrible for false teachers who led his people astray: "[W]hoever causes one of these little ones who believe in Me to stumble, it would be better for him if a millstone were hung around his neck, and he were thrown into the sea" (Mk. 9:42; *see also,* Mt.18:6; Lk.17:2).

The New Testament is replete with warnings of the Apostles against false teachers who lead people away from Jesus Christ. For example, St. Paul said:

> "The coming of the lawless one [antichrist] is apparent in the working of Satan, who uses all power, signs, lying wonders, and every kind of wicked deception for those who are perishing, because they refused to love the truth and so be saved. For this reason God sends them a powerful delusion, leading them to believe what is false, so that all who have not believed the truth but took pleasure in unrighteousness will be condemned."
>
> (2 Thes. 2:9–12, NRSV)

(*See also,* 2 Peter chapter 2; 1 John 4:1; Epistle of Jude.)

The Apostle John tells us that we must test the spirits to see whether the teaching is from God (1 Jn. 4:1). The Scriptures give us some criteria for discerning false teachers:

1. Do they teach the Incarnation of Jesus Christ, namely, that he is God in human flesh? (1 Jn. 4:1–3).

2. Do they teach the centrality of Jesus' atoning death on the cross, for us, in our place? (Phil. 3:18–19).

3. Is their teaching in accordance with the generally accepted Christian doctrine, "the faith which was once for all [time] delivered to the saints"? (Jude v.3).

4. Do they teach that Christians should live moral lives in accord with the Commandments of God, or rather, do they teach sensuality and immorality, taking "pleasure in unrighteousness;" 2 Thes. 2:12); "licentiousness" (Jude 4,7,16); "teaching and beguiling [His] servants to commit fornication"? (Rev. 2:20–23).

5. Are their lives characterized by greed, "imagining that godliness is a means of gain" (1 Tim. 6:5), in their covetousness exploiting God's people with "deceptive words" (2 Pet. 2:3)?

Jesus summed up the test of false teachers by saying "You will know them by their fruits" (Mt. 7:16). It takes time for fruit to develop on trees; we may not be able to discern false prophets immediately. But later we can see whether the teaching leads to goodness or evil, toward God or away from him, toward righteousness or unrighteousness.

Throughout Christian history, there has been apostasy. People who had been members of the church, who had confessed their faith in Jesus Christ, whose lives had given evidence of being Christians, even teachers and leaders in the church, have fallen away and rebelled against Jesus Christ. This has been the situation from New Testament times through the centuries and in our own time. But the Scriptures tell us that at the end of this age, apostasy will be widespread. (2 Tim. 3:1–13 paints a vivid picture). Jesus and his apostles teach us that a great apostasy is one of the signs of his Return to earth (2 Thes. 2:3; Mt. 24:9–10).

Apostasy is an extremely serious matter. The New Testament contains several strong warnings against Christians departing from Christ, falling away from him, for example:

1 Timothy 4:1–3
2 Thessalonians 2:3
2 Peter 3:17 and chapter 2
Hebrews 6:4–6; 10:26–31.
Epistle of Jude.

Our attitude should be like that expressed by Simon Peter in the 6th chapter of John's Gospel. Because of Jesus' strong teaching, many of his disciples had turned away and left him. Jesus asked the Twelve: "'Do you also want to go away?'" Then Simon Peter answered him: "'Lord, to whom shall we go? You have the words of eternal life. Also we have come to believe and know that You are the Christ, the Son of the living God'" (Jn. 6:67–69).

Disasters

Several signs of Jesus' return to earth can be listed under the heading of "disasters."

(1) *Earthquakes.* Jesus said that there would be earthquakes in various places, as one element of "the beginning of the birth pangs" (Mt. 24:7; Mk.13:8; Lk. 21:11, NRSV).

Earthquakes have occurred in various parts of the world since Jesus said these words. A few of the many on record are:

Year (AD)	Location	Number killed (estimate)
1201	Upper Egypt and Syria	1.1 million
1556	Shansi, China	830,000
1737	Calcutta, India	300,000
1755	Lisbon, Portugal (extending into North Africa)	70,000
1906	San Francisco, California [city almost destroyed by ensuing fires]	3,000
2004	ocean off North coast of Sumatra causing a tsunami	280,000
2005	Kashmir	87,000
2008	Sichuan Province, China	70,000

However, it appears that the earthquakes at the end of this age will be even more dreadful. The Book of Revelation tells of "a great earthquake" which will occur when the sixth seal is opened (Rev. 6:12); another which will destroy ten percent of

Jerusalem with 7,000 deaths, terrifying the survivors (Rev.11:13); and a final "violent earthquake, such as had not occurred since people were upon the earth, so violent...that the great city was split into three parts, and the cities of the nations fell" (Rev.16:18–19, NRSV).

Fierce storms. Among the signs of his Return given by Jesus is "distress among nations confused by the roaring of the sea and the waves..." (Lk. 21:25, NRSV).

Apparently, these fierce storms will be wide-spread and not localized like the tropical storms and hurricanes that hit the Atlantic and Gulf coasts of North America, Central America, and the Caribbean islands every year. Possibly, they may be tsunamis resulting from severe earthquakes.

In May 2008 a huge tsunami struck Myanmar (formerly Burma), killing perhaps as many as 100,000 people and devastating huge areas.

Famines are also a sign of the end-times. *See* Mt. 24:7; Mk. 13:8; Lk. 21:11.

Famines have recurred throughout recorded history, such as:

- In Western Europe and England, the "Great Famine" of 1315–1322 in which untold millions of people died of starvation; in attempting to survive, many people turned to crime; peasants ate their seed grain and livestock, killed their own children, and resorted to cannibalism, even digging up dead bodies
- In Ireland, the potato blight of 1845–55 killed an estimated million people, the worst famine in proportion to population in history
- In China, a series of crop failures led to severe famines in 1976–79 causing 9 million deaths (est.)
- In India, there were ten major famines between 1860 and 1900 resulting in 15 million deaths (est.)
- In the Soviet Union in 1932–33, between 7 and 10 million people starved to death, mostly in the Ukraine, as

a result of deliberate Communist government policies forcing the peasants into agricultural collectives and seizing food supplies.

In present day Africa, there are severe recurring famines almost every year, resulting from drought, locusts, governmental corruption, and deliberate policies of genocide, especially of Islamic governments against non-Muslim citizens, particularly Christians.

(4) *Plagues, pestilence, and epidemics.* These also are signs of the tribulations of the Last Days (Lk. 21:11). Jesus' Revelation to the Apostle John says that a third of humanity will be killed by plagues (Rev. 9:18; *see* Rev. chapter 16).

However, plagues, pestilence, and epidemics are not limited to the end of the present age; they have been recurring throughout human history. A few well-known examples: a terrible outbreak of bubonic plague ("the Black Death") struck Europe in the 14th century, beginning in 1348, resulting in the horrible death of one-third of the people; in the early 20th century, an estimated 11 million people were killed by plague in India; the "Spanish Influenza" following the First World War was a world-wide epidemic which killed an estimated fifty million people.

AIDS is a recent phenomenon, another world-wide epidemic which has killed an estimated twenty-five million people thus far and has devastated entire nations of Africa. And there are numerous other diseases which strike various parts of the world from time to time such as cholera, typhus, typhoid, malaria, smallpox, yellow fever, polio, anthrax, Ebola (a flesh-eating disease), and new forms of potential epidemics such as SARS and Avian flu which seem to be developing constantly.

(5) *Wars and rumors of wars.* Jesus said: "The time is coming when you will hear the noise of battle near at hand and the news of battles far away" (Mt. 24:6, NEB); "[D]o not be troubled; for such things must happen, but the end is not yet" (Mk. 13:7. *See also,* Lk. 21:9–10).

Wars have been going on since the start of human history.

At the end of the year 2006, there were twenty-one wars going on in various parts of the world.[25]

Some of the most disastrous wars in history:

- In the Napoleonic Wars (1799–1815) there were 2.5 million military deaths and 1 million civilian deaths.
- In the American Civil War (1861–1865) 360,000 Union soldiers and 260,000 Confederates were killed.
- In the First World War (1914–1918) more than 15 million people lost their lives, 8.5 million members of the military and 6.5 million civilians.
- In the Second World War (1939–1945), which was probably the most devastating war in human history thus far, the deaths are mind-boggling: 12.7 million military deaths on the Allied side and 7.2 million on the Axis side totaling nearly 20 million military deaths, and 45.5 million civilian deaths on the Allied side (20 million in Russia alone) and 3.8 million on the Axis side, totaling 49.3 million civilian deaths; all deaths in WWII 68.8 million people. [All figures are the best estimates.]

But, according to Jesus' teaching, although wars are a sign of his Coming, they are not the final sign.

(6) *Disintegration of human society and morality.* Jesus spoke these powerful words:

"And because lawlessness will abound, the love of many will grow cold" (Mt. 24:12).

The Apostle Paul spells it out in more detail:

> "You must understand this, that in the last days distressing times will come. For people will be lovers of themselves, lovers of money, boasters, arrogant, abusive, disobedient to their parents, ungrateful, unholy, inhuman, implacable, slanderers, profligates, brutes, haters of good, treacherous, reckless, swollen with conceit, lovers of pleasure rather than lovers of God, holding to the outward form of godliness but denying its power."
>
> (2 Tim. 3:1–5, NRSV)

Simply observing the world around us gives convincing evidence that we are truly living in the Last Days. Jesus warned his people to prepare them for the terrible tribulations of the End Days: "For then there will be great tribulation, such as has not been since the beginning of the world until this time, no, nor ever shall be" (Mt. 24:21; Mk. 13:19). It will be a time of "great distress" (Lk. 21:23). "People will faint from fear and foreboding of what is coming upon the world..." (Lk. 21:26, NRSV).

The antichrist

Hundreds of years before Jesus was born, God had revealed through his prophets that before he brings his kingdom in its fullness and destroys his enemies, there will be a period of time when the forces of evil are unleashed in the world in a concentrated and intense way, causing great destruction and extreme suffering, persecution, torture, and death to many of his people. "It is that, as the darkest hour is that which precedes the dawn, so before the final victory of God and the establishment of his Kingdom, all the forces of evil must be unleashed and do their worst."[26]

This immense evil and great rebellion against God will be concentrated and focused in an individual known in the New Testament as "the man of sin," "the man of lawlessness," "the abomination of desolation," "the beast," or simply "the antichrist."

The principal Old Testament passages on this theme are the 38th and 39th chapters of Ezekiel, chapters 9 through 14 of Zechariah (especially the 14th chapter), and the 7th through 12th chapters of Daniel. Jesus and his Apostles restated the Old Testament teaching concerning this final rebellion against God led by the antichrist.

Although there will be one immensely powerful evil being known as "the antichrist" who will appear near the end of the closing period of this present age, the Apostle John makes the point that the forces opposing and rebelling against the Lord God and his Christ were already present and active during the

New Testament period. St. John writes: "Little children, it is the last hour; and as you have heard that the Antichrist is coming, even now many antichrists have come, by which we know that it is the last hour" (1 Jn. 2:18).

These persons opposing Christ ("anti-Christ") are not the final, immensely powerful "antichrist" of the Last Days, but rather are persons manifesting "the spirit of the Antichrist, which you have heard was coming, and is now already in the world" (1 Jn. 4:3).

John the Apostle tells us two of the distinguishing characteristics of "the spirit of antichrist": (1) denial that Jesus is the Christ ("Who is a liar but he who denies that Jesus is the Christ? He is antichrist who denies the Father and the Son" (1 Jn. 2:22); and (2) denial that in Jesus, God took human flesh upon himself ("For many deceivers have gone out into the world who do not confess Jesus Christ as coming in the flesh. This is a deceiver and an antichrist" (2 Jn. 7).

What are some characteristics of the end-time "antichrist," "the man of sin," "the abomination of desolation," the man of lawlessness," "the beast"?

1. *Self-deification:* He will put himself in the place of God, requiring worship of himself, and opposing all other religions and worship (2 Thes. 2:4).

2. *World-wide worship:* The whole world will worship the antichrist ("the beast") except for the elect of God, those whose names are written in the Lamb's Book of Life (Rev. 13:8).

3. *Coerced worship:* Antichrist will use coercion of all kinds to enforce worship of himself, including political and economic pressure. Those who do not receive the mark of the beast will be prohibited from engaging in business, from buying and selling (Rev. 13:16–17). And he will not hesitate to exercise the most severe penalty available to him: death (Rev.13:15).

4. *Satanic empowerment:* Antichrist is not Satan, but will operate by the authority and with the power of Satan, "the dragon" (Rev. 13:4). Thus, he will use evil spiritual "...power, signs, and lying wonders, and with all unrighteous deception..." (2 Thes. 2:9–10. *See also,* Rev. 13:13–14).

5. *Lies, deception, and murder:* Like Satan who empowers him, antichrist will operate through lies, deceit, and murder (2 Thes. 2:9–11; Rev. 13:15).

6. *Unbelief in Jesus and hatred of him:* Antichrist hates Jesus and cannot stand even the mention of his name. He cannot abide the truth that in Jesus, God has come down to this world in human flesh (1 Jn. 2:22; 4:2–3; 2 Jn. 7).

7. *Rage and hatred against God's people:* Because antichrist cannot reach Jesus who is now in heaven and thus beyond his power, antichrist turns his malicious hatred of Jesus against Jesus' people on earth, both Jews (God's chosen race, Jesus' brethren) and Christians (Rev. 12:17), despises them, pours out his blind rage against them, and makes war on them (Rev. 13:7).

Ever since New Testament times and continuing throughout Christian history, "the spirit of antichrist" has been working like a malignant cancer within the Body of Christ through unbelief, sowing doubt and discord, seeking subtly to turn Christians away from the wisdom of God as revealed in the Holy Scriptures and in Jesus Christ, and to turn them to the shallow and superficial wisdom of man, to substitute lies for God's truth.

Those with eyes to see can discern these trends in the church of their day, whether they lived in the past or live in the present time. God's true believers must pray for the continual guidance of the Holy Spirit to discern teachers and preachers operating in the spirit of antichrist, and they must do all in their power assisted by the wisdom and power of Almighty God to reject the unbiblical and ungodly teachings infecting and poisoning the church with the lies and deceptions of the anti-christ forces. And God's people must strive to live lives worthy of the Gospel of Jesus Christ.

Jesus' word to us is the same as to the early Christians: "Be faithful until death, and I will give you the crown of life" (Rev. 2:10).

The conversion and ingathering of the Jews

The Bible indicates that before the end of time and history, at or before Jesus' return to earth, there will be a widespread conversion of the Jewish people to faith in Jesus Christ as the Messiah of Israel.

God had revealed to his prophets that he would convert the Jews, his chosen people, from their sinful and rebellious ways to love and serve him with all their hearts, that he would gather them together and bring them back to their homeland, the Holy Land. Old Testament prophets both before and after the two exiles foresaw that the scattered, exiled Jewish people would be reunited and restored to their homeland, both those from the Northern Kingdom ("Israel") and the Southern Kingdom ("Judah"). Some examples are:

> "… I will bring you home, at the time when I gather you; for I will make you renowned and praised among all the peoples of the earth, when I restore your fortunes before your eyes, says the Lord."
>
> (Zeph. 3:20, NRSV)

> 'I will strengthen the house of Judah [the Southern Kingdom] and I will save the house of Joseph [the Northern Kingdom]. I will bring them back because I have compassion on them… Though I scattered them among the nations, yet in far countries they shall remember me… I will bring them home… I will make them strong in the Lord, and they shall walk in his name, says the Lord."
>
> (Zech. 10:6,9,10,12, NRSV)

Some similar passages are Isaiah 35:10 and 51:11; Jeremiah 24:4–7, 29:10–14, chapters 30 and 31, 32:26–44, and 33; and Ezekiel 39:25–29.

These prophecies have been partially fulfilled in the return of the Jews from captivity in Babylon beginning in the year 538 BC (Isaiah chapters 40–55) and also, in the return of the Jews to Israel in modern times. But it is obvious that there has not yet been complete fulfillment because the Jewish people are still scattered all over the earth.

In Jesus' earthly ministry, many of the Jewish people accepted him as the Messiah, but many rejected him. Then in the early days of the Christian faith, when the Gospel began spreading among the Gentiles but was rejected by many of the Jews, this created a dilemma for the Church: Since Jesus was the true Messiah, why was he rejected by so many of the Jews?

The Apostle Paul wrestled with this dilemma in his Epistle to the Romans, specifically dealing with this issue in Romans chapters 9 through 11. In these chapters he sets forth God's master plan for salvation and shows where the Jewish people fit into it.

First, he says that he has "great sorrow and continual grief in [his] heart"

> "For I could wish that I myself were accursed from Christ for my brethren, my kinsmen according to the flesh, who are Israelites, to whom pertain the adoption, the glory, the covenants, the giving of the law, the service of God, and the promises; of whom are the fathers and from whom, according to the flesh, Christ came, who is over all, the eternally blessed God. Amen."
>
> (Rom. 9:3–5)

Then he says that the word of God has not failed, because not all Israelites truly belong to Israel, "and not all of Abraham's children are his true descendants" but rather only those who are "children of the promise," that is, only those descended from Isaac, Abraham's son by Sarah. But God is not unjust, because he is sovereign and salvation depends on his mercy: "... it depends not on human will or exertion, but on God who shows mercy" (Rom. 9:6–16, NRSV).

Next, St. Paul explains that the Jews have been seeking salvation in the wrong way, "striving for the righteousness that is based on the law" through their works. They have stumbled over Jesus Christ by rejecting him Who has completely and perfectly fulfilled the law of God so as to provide "righteousness for everyone who believes." The Jews have not turned to Jesus Christ for salvation, but the believing Gentiles have done so and have been saved because "'Everyone who calls on the name of the Lord shall be saved.'" Thus, the Jews have rejected God's New Covenant of salvation which is based on "believing, not on achieving" (J.B. Phillips' marvelous translation; Rom. 9:17–10:21).

Moreover, says St. Paul, God has not rejected his chosen people, the Jews. He himself was an Orthodox Jew, a "Hebrew of the Hebrews," and originally all the Christians were Jews who had come to faith in Jesus as the Messiah, "a remnant chosen by grace" (Rom. 11:1–10, NRSV).

Then he raises the question whether the rest of the Jews who have rejected Jesus have fallen irretrievably so as to be ineligible for salvation. "Certainly not!" he replies (Rom. 11:11–12).

Rather, it seems that the way God is working in this situation, giving the Gospel such success in the Gentile world, is to make the Jews jealous of God's blessings being poured out on the Gentiles, so that at least some of the Jews will want that for themselves (Rom. 11:11).

Then Paul turns to address the Gentiles and tells them not to become proud but to stand in awe of God's work. He then uses an analogy to explain what God is doing: Israel is God's cultivated olive tree; He broke off some of the branches and grafted in wild olive branches in their place, but they (Gentiles, the wild olive branches) are supported by the root (Israel). The Gentiles must not become proud that they are now part of God's olive tree while most of the Jews are not, because it is only by faith that they stand. And, he says that if the Jews do not persist in unbelief, God will graft them back into the original olive tree, which is much easier than grafting wild branches into a cultivated olive tree (Rom. 11:13–24).

Finally, the Apostle Paul explains a great mystery which God has now revealed:

> "For I do not desire, brethren, that you should be ignorant of this mystery, lest you should be wise in your own opinion, that hardening in part has happened to Israel until the fullness of the Gentiles has come in. And so all Israel will be saved, as it is written... Concerning the gospel they are enemies for your sake, but concerning the election they are beloved for the sake of the fathers. For the gifts and the calling of God are irrevocable."
>
> (Rom.11:25–29)

These chapters in Romans (chapters 9–11), together with the Old Testament prophecies that God will gather his chosen people, the Jews, are the basis for the Christian belief that as part of God's mighty work in the end times, overwhelming numbers of the Jewish people will be converted to faith in Jesus the Messiah, the Savior.

St. Paul concludes his discourse on this issue by writing this magnificent doxology:

> "Oh, the depth of the riches both of the wisdom and knowledge of God! How unsearchable are his judgments and his ways past finding out!
> "'For who has know the mind of the Lord?'
> 'Or who has become his counselor?'
> 'Or who has first given to him, and it shall be repaid to him?"
> "For of him and through him and to him are all things, to whom be glory forever. Amen."
>
> (Rom.11:33–36)

The signs of Jesus' return to earth are already in process and have been taking place since he ascended into heaven, namely, the preaching of the Gospel to all the world, persecution of Christians, apostasy, disasters, anti-Christs (although the end-time antichrist, the beast, has not yet appeared), even the conversion and ingathering of the Jews. It is estimated that there are about 20,000 "Messianic Jews," several congregations of them, in the land of Israel now. But there is one sign, or group of signs, that has not yet taken place, namely:

Disorder and chaos in the universe

In teaching about his Second Coming, Jesus said that "[i]mmediately after the tribulation of those days the sun will be darkened, and the moon will not give its light; the stars will fall from heaven, and the powers of the heavens will be shaken" (Mt. 24:29) These events will fulfill the prophecies that God gave centuries ago by the prophets Isaiah (Is. 13:10), Ezekiel (Ezek. 32:7–8), and Joel (Joel 2:10,30–31).

"Then," said Jesus, "the sign of the Son of Man will appear in heaven, and then all the tribes of the earth will mourn, and they will see the Son of Man coming on the clouds of heaven with power and great glory" (Mt. 24:29–30. *See also*, Mk.13:24–25; Lk. 21:11, 25–26).

The picture the Lord Jesus gives us is that after all the tribulations are completed, immediately before his triumphal return, there will be such chaos and disorder in the physical universe, the sun, moon, stars, and planets, that the very structure of the created universe will be falling apart.

The Apostle Peter put it this way: "... the day of the Lord will come as suddenly and unexpectedly as a thief. In that day the heavens will disappear in a terrific tearing blast; the very elements will disintegrate in heat and the earth and all that is in it will be burned up to nothing" (2 Pet. 3:10, J.B. Phillips).

The Last Day will be terrifying to many of the earth's people. As Adam and Eve scrambled to hide in the bushes from the presence of the Lord God after they sinned in the Garden of Eden, those who are ungodly people will be panic-stricken, mourning and crying, and calling out for the very mountains and rocks to fall upon them to hide them from the glorious presence of Jesus Christ. Then they will know that the Almighty and All-Holy God lives and governs all things and that they have not believed in him and have not tried to live according to his ways and his Law, and that now it is too late to repent, to look to Jesus and be saved.

Not so for God's faithful people. When these terrible events of the Last Day begin to take place, they will stand and lift up their heads, knowing that their redemption is drawing near (Lk. 21:28). On That Day the Lord will give the crown of righteousness, the crown of eternal life, not only to the greatest Christians like the Apostle Paul and God's choice saints, but also to all those ordinary Christians who have been longing for Jesus' return (2 Tim. 4:8).

3. ARE WE LIVING IN THE LAST DAYS?

How can it be that the signs of Jesus' return to earth are signs of the end times when many of them have been going on ever since Jesus left this earth to ascend back to heaven? Some of these signs have been occurring throughout human history.

This seeming dilemma is solved when we realize that it bears out Jesus' explicit, clear teaching that we cannot know when he will return, that it will be sudden and unexpected, that he will return at a day and hour that we cannot know, that it will take place in God's own good time.

Thus, in the New Testament view, we have been living in "the Last Days" ever since Jesus departed from this earth to return back up to his throne in heaven. Here are a few verses of Scripture that bear out this statement:

- "God, who at various times and in different ways spoke in time past to the fathers by the prophets, has in these last days spoken to us by his Son... (Heb. 1:1–2).

- "Little children, it is the last hour..." (1 Jn. 2:18).
- "Now all these things happened to them as examples, and they were written for our admonition, on whom the ends of the ages have come" (1 Cor.10:11).
- "He indeed was foreordained before the foundation of the world, but was manifest in these last times for you..." (1 Pet. 1:20).
- "But the end of all things is at hand..." (1 Pet. 4:7).
- "...the coming of the Lord is at hand... Behold, the Judge is standing at the door!" (James 5:8–9).
- In his sermon at the Day of Pentecost, the Apostle Peter quoted the Prophet Joel ("In the last days it will be, God declares..." Joel 2:28, NRSV) and stated that this prophecy was being fulfilled on Pentecost (Acts 2:16–17), thus indicating that they were living in "the last days").

However, the New Testament is replete with references to the effect that the completion of our redemption and "the restoration of all things" (Acts 3:21) still lies in the future. So what we are experiencing now in the present time is best understood as "the Overlap of the Ages," this present evil age being overlapped by the "last days." The present evil age and the new age of the eternal life to come are existing side by side.

The new age of the Kingdom of God is already present, but its complete fulfillment still lies in the future, from our human point of view (See further discussion of this topic in Part III under "The Teachings of Jesus," earlier in this book.).

4. WHAT SHOULD BE OUR ATTITUDE TOWARD JESUS' SECOND COMING?

The way we should live in the light of his Coming is spelled out in many parts of the New Testament, especially in some of Jesus' parables such as the Ten Bridesmaids (Mt. 25:1–13), the Talents (Mt. 25:14–30), and the Fig Tree (Mt. 24:32–35), and in his teachings such as the Sermon on the Mount (Mt. chapters 5–7) and the Olivet Discourse (Mt. chapters 24 and 25; Mk. chapter 13: Lk. chapter 21), as well as in the portions of the Epistles dealing with Christian living.

Some points the Scriptures emphasize are these:

a. In contrast to the ungodly, unrepentant people who are afraid, even terrified, or simply apathetic, Christians long for, eagerly look forward to, indeed love his appearing (2 Tim. 4:8).

b. We are to watch and live in patience as we await his Coming (James 5:7–8).

c. We are to be ready and prepared for his Return by living lives that glorify him, lives that are pure and holy, lives that are worthy of our calling (Eph. 4:1; 2 Thes. 1:11), as best we can, and when we fail, to ask for and receive his forgiveness (1 Jn. 1:8–9).

d. We are to keep our hearts and minds on the goal—the magnificent future God has for us—and live in self-control and godliness (Tit. 2:12; 1 Pet. 2:11), not fall into sinful, self-indulgent lives of dissipation and drunkenness, and not let our hearts be weighed down with the worries of this life (Lk. 21:34).

e. Our waiting for the Lord's Return is not to be a passive, sitting down, taking-it-easy kind of waiting, but rather an active, working waiting, diligently doing the work God has given us to do (2 Thes. 3:6–15). "Blessed is that servant whom his Master will find at work when he arrives" (Mt. 24:46, NRSV).

f. While we are waiting and working, the Lord expects us to do what we can to help people in need, as God gives us opportunity and ability, especially our Christian brothers and sisters wherever they are (Gal. 6:10).

g. And we are to continue to pray with our fellow Christians of all times and places, "Even so, come, Lord Jesus!" (Rev. 22:20).

To a considerable extent, Christians' attitude toward the Second Coming of Jesus Christ influences and even determines the way they live their lives in the present time. As the Apostle John writes: "And everyone who has this hope in him purifies himself, just as he is pure" (I Jn. 3:3).

B
THE RESURRECTION OF THE DEAD

When Jesus returns to earth as the triumphant Messiah, the King of the universe, he will raise the dead to life by his omnipotent power. Let us consider this matter under the headings: Who? When? What? and How?

Who will be resurrected from death? The Scripture is clear: All the dead, both those who will enter into eternal life and those who will not. This is what the Lord Jesus taught: "... the hour is coming in which all who are in the graves will hear his voice and come forth,—those who have done good, to the resurrection of life, and those who have done evil, to the resurrection of condemnation" (Jn. 5:28–29). The Apostles taught the same. St. Paul said: "... there will be a resurrection of the dead, both of the just and the unjust" (Acts 24:15).

When will the resurrection from the dead take place? Again, the Scripture is clear: it will be at Jesus' Return to earth. Jesus himself emphasized this by stating it not once, but four times, in one discourse: "I will raise him up at the last day" (Jn. 6:39, 40, 44, 54). The Apostles taught the same thing as their Master (*See* 1 Thes. 4:13–18 and 1 Cor. 15:23, 52).

What will the resurrection be like? First, we must stress that it will be a bodily resurrection. We believe in "the resurrection of the body," Christians state in the Apostles' Creed.

The Christian belief is not the Greek pagan philosophical belief in "the immortality of the soul," that some spirit or essence of the person has the quality of never dying ("immortality") and thus lives on forever after death. Only God has immortality (1 Tim. 6:16). Rather, Christians believe in the resurrection of the body, that is, the restoration to life again of the entire, complete human being who has been dead, with his or her distinctive, unique and individual soul, body, and personality.

What will the resurrection body be like? The Bible does not tell us all we would like to know, but it tells us all that God has determined we need to know. Scripture does give us some clues to help us understand as much of this mystery as our limited understanding is capable of.

A fair summary of Scriptural teaching is to say that there will be continuity of the resurrection body with our earthly body and also discontinuity: they will be alike in some ways and different in some ways.

We get some indication of this from the resurrection of Jesus Christ himself, because the New Testament tells us that our resurrection bodies will be like his (Phil. 3:21; Rom. 6:5). In the forty days between Jesus' Resurrection and Ascension, he could be seen; He could speak; He could be touched; He could eat food, as he did to prove that his resurrection body was a real physical body and not a ghost or spirit (Lk. 24:36–43). Indeed, his resurrected body still bore the marks and scars of his crucifixion: the nail wounds in his hands and feet and the spear wound in his side (Jn. 20:24–29; Lk. 24:39). And yet his body could pass through locked doors and he could suddenly appear (Jn. 20:19) and vanish (Lk. 24:31). His resurrection body was the same as his earthly body, and yet it was different. His disciples had spent three years with him, and yet sometimes they recognized him immediately, and sometimes they did not.

Like Jesus, our resurrection bodies will be the same as our

earthly bodies but different. The Apostle Paul goes into this matter in detail in the 15th chapter of 1 Corinthians and gives us the illustration of the seed and the plant. The bare grain that is planted does not look at all like the plant that springs forth into life from it, and yet it is the same in essence.

The resurrected body will not be simply a re-animated corpse but will be a glorious new re-creation by God. The Apostle Paul strains to explain the mystery of the resurrected body in its continuity and discontinuity with the earthly body and actually invents a term to try to express this truth by calling it "*a spiritual body*" (1 Cor. chapter 15). This is a seeming contradiction in terms, because spirits don't have bodies. To paraphrase the meaning, we can say that the resurrection body will be fitted for life in eternity with God just as the earthly body is fitted for life on this earth.

The Apostle Paul gives us another clue to help us understand what our resurrection bodies will be like when he writes:

> "from [heaven]...we are expecting a Savior, the Lord Jesus Christ. He will transform the body of our humiliation that it may be conformed to the body of his glory, by the power that also enables him to make all things subject to himself."
>
> (Phil. 3:20,21, NRSV)

Other versions translate this phrase as "our vile body" (KJV), "our lowly body" (RSV), "these wretched bodies of ours" (J.B. Phillips). A good paraphrase would be "these humiliating bodies of ours."

And our earthly bodies do humiliate us, not allowing us to do the things we would like to do, shaming and humiliating us as we get older and our bodies deteriorate and decay with sickness, disease, or simply the aging process, causing us eventually to lose control of bodily functions. To see evidence of this, all one has to do is walk down the hall of a total care nursing facility and observe the people in the hallways and lying in their beds, humiliated by the gradual disintegration of their bodies, helpless in their misery.

But when God gives us our resurrection bodies, our "spiritual bodies," they will no longer be subject to the ravages of sin, sickness, disease, deterioration, decay, and death. We will each be ourselves with our own unique individual personalities but will be transformed to be like Jesus' glorious body. And what was Jesus' body like when his life on this earth ended? He was in his early 30's, in the full and radiant health of maturity. He was never sick a day in his life. He was physically strong, having worked as a carpenter and walking long distances. (For example, it is about 100 miles from Caesarea Philippi to Jerusalem). And our resurrection bodies will be like his.

Those who are ill will be completely healthy. Those who are deformed will be whole as God intended them to be. Those who are retarded or mentally defective will be so no more but will have perfectly sound minds. Babies who have been stillborn or aborted or miscarried will have the full, whole, and healthy bodies that God originally intended them to have before their development was cut short. In the resurrection, God will transform our humiliating earthly bodies to be like Jesus' glorious body.

Those Christians who are alive at Jesus' return will not have to go through death, but will be transformed instantaneously into their resurrection bodies. The Apostle Paul describes this transformation in 2 Cor. 4:16–5:5.

How will God bring about the resurrection and transformation of our bodies? The same way he brought his creation into being out of nothingness: by speaking his mighty word of power that accomplishes his purposes. The Lord Jesus himself revealed this to us:

> "Most assuredly, I say to you, the hour is coming, and now is, when the dead will hear the voice of the Son of God; and those who hear will live ... Do not marvel at this; for the hour is coming in which all who are in the graves will hear his voice and come forth—those who have done good, to the resurrection of life, and those who have done evil, to the resurrection of condemnation."
>
> (Jn. 5:25, 28–29)

The Apostle Paul tells us that the Lord Jesus himself will descend from heaven "with a cry of command, with the archangel's call and with the sound of God's trumpet ... and the dead in Christ will rise first" (1 Thes. 4:16, NRSV). Just as Jesus called Lazarus out of death and into life with his loud voice (Jn.11:43), by his mighty shout of command at his Second Coming he will call the dead into the new life of the age to come.

What a magnificent future awaits us! The Apostle Paul puts it this way:

> "The whole creation is on tiptoe to see the wonderful sight of the sons of God coming into their own ... And the hope is that in the end the whole of created life will be rescued from the tyranny of change and decay, and have its share in that magnificent liberty which can only belong to the children of God! ... [W]e who have a foretaste of the Spirit are in a state of painful tension, while we wait for that redemption of our bodies which will mean that at last we have realized our full sonship in him."
>
> (Rom. 8:19–23, J.B. Phillips)

For that mighty work of God, we patiently wait and work and pray, as did the early Christians: "Even so, come, Lord Jesus!" (Rev. 22:20). Yes, come quickly, Lord.

C

THE FINAL JUDGMENT

When Jesus returns to earth in power and great glory as the victorious King of Kings and Lord of Lords, raises the dead to life and transforms those who are living at his Return, then comes the Final Judgment. "When the Son of Man comes in his glory, and all the holy angels with him, then he will sit on the throne of his glory. All the nations will be gathered before him, and he will separate them one from another, as a shepherd divides his sheep from the goats..." (Mt. 25:31–32).

Jesus Christ, the Lord of heaven and earth, will be the Judge, as he himself explained: "For the Father judges no one, but has committed all judgment to the Son, that all should honor the Son just as they honor the Father... [God the Father] has given him [the Son] authority to execute judgment also, because he is the Son of Man" (Jn. 5:22,23,27).

1. WHAT WILL THE JUDGMENT BE?

In considering this matter, at the outset we need to correct two widespread misunderstandings of the Final Judgment by stating two things that it is not.

One common, but erroneous, idea is that in the Judgment

our good deeds and our bad deeds will be weighed and compared, and if we have more good deeds than bad ones, we will go to heaven, but if our evil deeds predominate, then we will be sent to hell. Unfortunately, this idea of weighing merits against demerits crept into Christianity at an early date and is common in medieval Christian art. For example, the sculptures over the central doors of many ancient cathedrals in Europe, like Notre Dame of Paris, depict the scene of Christ sitting in judgment, with himself or an angel holding a pair of scales to weigh good deeds against bad ones. Muslims think of the Last Judgment in these same terms, based on Mohammed's teaching.

But this idea of judgment is not biblical. It simply is not true. Why? For one thing, Jesus taught that if we did everything God requires of us, if that were possible, we get no merits; we have only done our duty. Jesus said: "…when you have carried out all your orders, you should say, 'We are servants and deserve no credit; we have only done our duty'" (Lk.17:10, NEB).

Neither is there any biblical basis for the idea that the saints have accumulated surplus merits, over and above what they themselves need to be saved, which can be applied to our account at the Judgment. With the exception of Jesus' atonement for our sins, the Bible clearly teaches that the righteousness of one human being cannot be transferred to another. The prophet Ezekiel wrote that even the righteousness of Noah, Daniel, and Job, considered the most righteous men of the Old Testament, could save only themselves, not even their own sons and daughters, but "they would deliver only themselves by their righteousness" (Ezek.14:14).

Furthermore, the biblical attitude is that even the best things we do are polluted with sin, as expressed by the Prophet Isaiah in graphic language: "But we are all like an unclean thing, And all our righteousnesses are like filthy rags" (literally, *menstruous rags*) (Is. 64:6).

So, the idea of merits and demerits, of God weighing our good deeds against our bad ones at the Judgment, is not biblical at all.

Another common misconception of the Final Judgment is that it will be like the trial of lawsuits that we are familiar with. This is also unbiblical and erroneous. The Last Judgment is not a trial to find out the facts of our lives because God already knows everything about us, every detail of our lives, what we have done, what we have failed to do, even our motives and the secrets of our hearts. God is omniscient, all-knowing.

"[God] knows all things" (1 Jn. 3:20). "Even before a word is on my tongue, O Lord, You know it completely" (Ps. 139:4, NRSV).

God knows all our foolishness and sins. (Ps. 69:5). He knows even our thoughts. (Ps. 94:11; 139:2). Jesus, who was God in human flesh, demonstrated this truth in his earthly ministry. In the Gospels we read that Jesus knew what people were thinking. (Mt. 9:4; 12:25; Mk. 12:15; Lk. 11:17). God knows the secrets of our hearts. (I Kings 8:39; Lk. 16:15; Acts 1:24, 15:8). Since God already knows everything about us, the Judgment is not a fact-finding inquiry or trial.

The clearest proof of this is Jesus' own teaching on the Last Judgment, the Parable of the Sheep and the Goats (Mt. 25:31–46). The Lord Jesus, the Son of Man, sits as Judge and separates people one from another as a shepherd separates the sheep from the goats. There is no fact-finding inquiry or trial to determine whether one is a sheep or a goat. There is absolutely no doubt as to who is a sheep and who is a goat; there is no possibility of confusing the two. We are either sheep who belong to the Good Shepherd or not. "The Lord knows those who are his" (2 Tim. 2:19).

Having considered some erroneous ideas of the Last Judgment, what it is not, now let us turn to what the Last Judgment is according to the Bible's teaching.

First, it is certain. As the Apostle Paul preached in his sermon at Athens: "... [God] has appointed a day on which he will judge the world in righteousness by the Man whom he has ordained" (Acts 17:31). Also, as St. Paul wrote: "For we must all appear before the judgment seat of Christ, that each one may receive the things done in the body, according to what he has done, whether good or bad" (2 Cor. 5:10).

And as we have seen, Jesus Christ, God the Son, will be the Judge on behalf of God the Father, and the Judgment will take place when Jesus returns to earth.

Second, the Last Judgment will be thorough. When we stand before Christ at the Last Judgment, we will be called upon to give an account of every aspect of our lives:

- our thoughts (Heb 4:12,13; 1 Cor. 4:5; Rom. 2:16)
- our words [Jesus said: "I say to you that for every idle word men may speak, they will give account of it in the day of judgment. For by your words you will be justified, and by your words you will be condemned" (Mt.12:36–37).]
- our deeds (2 Cor. 5:10)
- our secrets (Rom. 2:16)
- our motives, "the counsels of the heart" (1 Cor. 4:5).

At the Last Judgment, God will call us to account to him for our management of the gifts and resources he entrusted to us (*See,* The Parable of the Talents, Mt. 25:14–30; and The Parable of the Ten Pounds, Lk. 19:11–27).

Third, the Judgment will be universal. Every nation, every person who has ever lived, and those who are living at his Coming, will be required to appear before Jesus Christ, the Judge of all. "For we must all appear before the judgment seat of Christ" (2 Cor. 5:10).

Fourth, the Judgment will be impartial. "[God] judges all people impartially according to their deeds…" (1 Pet. 1:17, NRSV). "God shows no partiality" (Acts 10:34; Rom. 2:11; Gal. 2:6. *See also,* Eph. 6:9; Col. 3:25).

God is no respecter of persons. To him, it doesn't matter who you were, whether you were educated or not, whether you were rich or poor, what position you may have held in society, what reputation you may have had. To him, it doesn't even matter whether you are one of his chosen people, the Jews, or a Gentile (Rom. 2:1–16). The Jews knew the law of God; they will be judged by the law. The Gentiles did not know God's law, but they knew right from wrong and had their conscience and the natural law to guide them. God will judge us by the light we had, by the knowledge we had of his Holy will. But the problem is that none of us has lived up to the knowledge and light that we had. Therefore, we are all guilty sinners, deserving of condemnation. God is completely impartial in his judgments.

Fifth, the Judgment will be entirely and completely just. The Judge of the whole earth will do right and will do justice (Gen. 18:25). To him every knee will bow and every tongue will confess that Jesus Christ is Lord, not only those who have believed in him but also those who have rejected him and those who did not believe that God even existed (Phil. 2:10–11). Even the nonbelievers will be forced by the fact of Jesus' glorious appearance to admit that there is One Almighty God and that Jesus Christ is his only-begotten Son with all power and authority in heaven and on earth. And they will admit that they are guilty and without excuse.

> "For what can be known about God is plain to them, because God has shown it to them. Ever since the creation of the world his eternal power and divine nature, invisible though they are, have been understood and seen through the things he has made. So they are without excuse; for though they knew God, they did not honor him as God or give thanks to him, but they became futile in their thinking, and their senseless minds were darkened."
>
> (Rom. 1:19–21, NRSV)

When they are face to face with God's truth in the person of Jesus Christ, even the nonbelievers will know that their condemnation is right and just. There will be no room for complaints that God is unfair and unjust. Before God, every mouth will be stopped (Rom. 3:19). "True and righteous are his judgments" (Rev. 19:2).

Note that in Jesus' account of the Last Judgment, contrary to much Christian art, the accursed (the goats) are not forcibly dragged off to hell by demons, kicking and screaming as they go, but rather Jesus tells them to depart (Mt. 25:41) and they simply "go away into eternal punishment" (Mt. 25:46). They know who they are, what they deserve, and where they belong.

Sixth, the Final Judgment of each person will be based on his or her deeds. "For we must all appear before the judgment seat of Christ, that each one may receive the things done in the body, according to what he has done, whether good or bad" (2 Cor. 5:10). At his Return, Jesus the Judge of all "will reward each according to his works" (Mt. 16:27). God "without partiality judges according to each one's work" (1 Pet. 1:17). At the Day of Judgment, God "'will render to each one according to his deeds':

> "eternal life to those who by patient continuance in doing good seek for glory, honor, and immortality; but to those who are self-seeking and do not obey the truth, but obey unrighteousness—indignation and wrath, tribulation and anguish, on every soul of man who does evil, of the Jew first and also of the Greek: but glory, honor, and peace to everyone who works what is good, to the Jew first and also to the Greek. For there is no partiality with God."
>
> (Rom. 2:6–11)

Saved by Faith, Judged by Works?

There seems to be a problem of inconsistency here because the New Testament clearly teaches that we are saved through faith alone—that is, by believing in Jesus Christ as our Lord and Savior, not by our works (Rom. 3:28), but it also clearly teaches that we will be judged on the basis of our works, by the deeds done in this life. Saved by faith, but judged by works? How can that be?

First, we need to consider what saving faith is. It is not simply making a "profession of faith" in Jesus because our "faith" may be self-deluding. We may be deceiving ourselves into thinking we are Christians when we are not. Our profession may only be empty words without having any effect on the people we are and the lives we live. Jesus himself taught us this in the Sermon on the Mount:

> "Not everyone who says to Me, 'Lord, Lord,' shall enter the kingdom of heaven, but he who does the will of My Father in heaven. Many will say to Me in that day [the Judgment], 'Lord, Lord, have we not prophesied in Your name, cast out demons in Your name, and done many wonders in Your name?' And then I will declare to them, 'I never knew you; depart from Me, you who practice lawlessness!'"
>
> (Mt. 7:21–23)

Furthermore, saving faith is more than simply believing the facts about Jesus to be true. The kind of "faith" we have may be simply an intellectual faith that is superficial, a "faith" that is in our minds but has not gotten down into our hearts and lives.

We may know and believe all the basic Christian teachings, for example, that Jesus was conceived by the Holy Spirit and born of the Virgin Mary, that he is both fully and truly God and fully and truly human, that he worked all the miracles written in the Gospels, that he died on the Cross and was raised from the dead, that he ascended into heaven and now rules and reigns at the right hand of God the Father over all things both in heaven and on earth, and that he will return to this earth—but yet not have a living saving faith. The Apostle James makes this clear: "Even the demons believe [intellectually, the facts of the Christian faith]—and shudder" (James 2:19, NRSV). Without a life-transforming faith that leads us into loving God and our fellow human beings with a love manifested in doing what we can to help needy, suffering people, such "faith" is not a living faith, but is dead (James 2:17).

If it is possible for us to have a sort of "faith" which is really a false faith or a dead faith, "holding to the outward form of godliness but denying its [life-changing] power," as the Apostle Paul described it (2 Tim. 3:5, NRSV), then what is a true, living and saving faith?

The best explanation is given by Jesus himself in the analogy of the tree and its fruits. A tree produces fruit according to its nature. In the Sermon on the Mount, Jesus said:

> "Do men gather grapes from thornbushes or figs from thistles? Even so, every good tree bears good fruit, but a bad tree bears bad fruit. A good tree cannot bear bad fruit, nor can a bad tree bear good fruit. Every tree that does not bear good fruit is cut down and thrown into the fire."
>
> (Mt. 7:16–19))

Jesus amplified this analogy in his teaching to his disciples in the upper room on the night he was betrayed. He put it this way:

> "I am the true vine, and My Father is the vinedresser. Every branch in Me that does not bear fruit he takes away; and every branch that bears fruit he prunes, that it may bear more fruit ... Abide in Me, and I in you. As the branch cannot bear fruit of itself, unless it abides in the vine, neither can you, unless you abide in Me. I am the vine, you are the branches. He who abides in Me, and I in him, bears much fruit; for without Me you can do nothing. If anyone does not abide in Me, he is cast out as a branch and is withered; and they gather them and throw them into the fire, and they are burned."
>
> (Jn. 15:1–6)

If Jesus lives in us by the Holy Spirit, if our lives are connected in a vital, life-giving union with his life, then God is at work within us, changing and transforming us to be more like Jesus, and thus love for God and for our neighbors will flow freely from deep within us (*See* Jn. 7:37–39).

What it means to love God and our fellow human beings is not simply having warm feelings toward them, but rather love is defined by keeping God's Holy Law, summarized in the Ten Commandments and in the Law of Love. "By this we know that we love the children of God, when we love God and keep his commandments. For this is the love of God, that we keep his commandments" (1 Jn. 5:2–3).

This is why there is no inconsistency when the Bible insists that we are saved by faith alone, but will be judged by our works. The kind of fruit manifest in our lives shows what kind of tree we are, whether a good tree or a bad tree, a good tree that has God's eternal life within it, or a bad tree fit for nothing but to be burned in the fire. The lives we live and the things we do evidence whether we have true faith or not.

Thus, the seventh characteristic of the Final Judgment is that it is two-fold; it will have two totally different outcomes. Either acquittal (justification) or condemnation; either eternal life or death; either heaven or hell. In his most extensive teaching on the Last Judgment, the Lord Jesus said that the end result would be the unrighteous goats going away into eternal punishment but the righteous sheep entering into eternal life (Mt. 25:46).

2. THE URGENCY OF BEING PREPARED FOR THE FINAL JUDGMENT

The great prophets of the Old Testament preached the inevitability of God's judgment of destruction coming upon the people if they did not repent and return to God and forsake their sins. But far more forcefully than any of the prophets, Jesus preached and taught with extreme urgency of the judgment of God falling on unrepentant sinners and the Good News that in him, God had provided a way for them to be forgiven of their sin and be rescued from the wrath to come and consequently saved from destruction.

Thus, the necessity for repentance and receiving him as the God-sent Messiah and Savior was the theme of Jesus' earthly ministry. "Jesus came to Galilee, preaching the gospel of the kingdom of God, and saying, 'The time is fulfilled, and the kingdom of God is at hand. Repent, and believe in the gospel'" (Mk. 1:14–15).

The Greek word translated "to judge" means to separate; to distinguish between; to sift as with a sieve; to divide out; thus, to decide.[27] It is both a legal term used in courts of law and a theological term, for God himself is the Judge of all people and of all nations. Judgment always has a two-fold outcome: guilty or not guilty, being convicted or acquitted, being condemned or vindicated.

Jesus' earthly ministry certainly had the effect of separating and dividing people, and this intensified as his ministry continued. His teaching and preaching and miracles resulted in a division between those who accepted him and those who rejected him, between those who thought he was filled with the Holy Spirit and those who thought he was possessed by a demon, between those who thought he was the true Messiah and those who thought he was a false imposter, between those who thought he was the Son of the Living God and those who considered him a blasphemer, between those who believed in him and those who did not.

Jesus recognized that his ministry had this effect on people when he said, "Do not think that I came to bring peace on earth. I did not come to bring peace but a sword. For I have come to 'set a man against his father, a daughter against her mother, and a daughter-in-law against her mother-in-law'" (Mt.10:34–35).

In Jesus' preaching and teaching, "the thought of judgment is central. Jesus' call to repentance is urgent because God's judgment hangs over every man. The task of Jesus is continually to impress on men the seriousness of this judgment and to awaken fear of the judge."[28]

Any form of Christianity which does not hold to the centrality of God's judgment is deceptive and false to Gospel truth because it does not confront people with the most important question of life: "What must I do to be saved and not be condemned at the last judgment?"

The centrality of God's judgment is shown in the Sermon on the Mount. Consider these strong words of Jesus:

> "If your right eye causes you to sin, tear it out and throw it away; it is better for you to lose one of your members than for your whole body to be thrown into hell. And if your right hand causes you to sin, cut it off and throw it away; it is better for you to lose one of your members than for your whole body to go into hell."
>
> (Mt. 5:29–30, NRSV)

> "Not everyone who says to Me, 'Lord, Lord,' shall enter the kingdom of heaven, but he who does the will of My Father in heaven. Many will say to Me in that day, 'Lord, Lord, have we not prophesied in Your name, cast out demons in Your name, and done many wonders in Your name?' And then I will declare to them, 'I never knew you; depart from Me, you who practice lawlessness!'"
>
> (Mt. 7:21–23)

Jesus stressed this urgent theme of judgment in his interactions with people. To his disciples he said:

> "… do not fear those who kill the body but cannot kill the soul. But rather, fear him who is able to destroy both soul and body in hell."
>
> (Mt. 10:28)

> "Therefore whoever confesses Me before men, him I will also confess before My Father who is in heaven. But whoever denies Me before men, him I will also deny before My Father who is in heaven."
>
> (Mt. 10:32–33)

To the people ("the crowds") he said:

> [To the cities where he had worked great miracles but the people did not repent:] "Woe to you, Chorazin! Woe to you,

Bethsaida! For if the mighty works which were done in you had been done in Tyre and Sidon, they would have repented long ago in sackcloth and ashes. But I say to you, it will be more tolerable for Tyre and Sidon in the day of judgment than for you. And you, Capernaum, who are exalted to heaven, will be brought down to Hades; for if the mighty works which were done in you had been done in Sodom, it would have remained until this day. But I say to you that it will be more tolerable for the land of Sodom in the day of judgment than for you."

(Mt.11:21–24)

In the Parable of the Wicked Tenants who not only refused to pay the landlord [God] his share of the crops but also abused and killed his agents, and finally killed his Son, Jesus asked those who were listening: "Now when the owner of the vineyard comes, what will he do to those tenants? They said to him, 'He will put those wretches to a miserable death...'"

(Mt. 21:33–44, NRSV)

To the Jewish leaders ("the scribes and Pharisees") Jesus said:

"'...whoever blasphemes against the Holy Spirit can never have forgiveness, but is guilty of an eternal sin'—for they had said, 'He has an unclean spirit.'"

(Mk. 3:29, NRSV)

[This makes it clear that the "unforgiveable sin," "blasphemy against the Holy Spirit," is to refuse to believe that Jesus was sent from God and was filled with the Holy Spirit, and thus to say in effect, "Jesus has an evil spirit; He is not from God but from the Devil," thereby rejecting the one and only Savior God has sent to save mankind.]

Although Jesus' teaching had much in common with the Pharisees such as the resurrection of the dead, the reality of angels and demons, the entire Old Testament being the Word of God, he was unsparing in his denunciation of their perversion of true godliness, pronouncing "Woes" upon them (Mt. 23:13–36) because he knew men's hearts and minds and thus knew that they would not change their minds about him and repent.

When he said "Woe to you" it expressed two ideas: "first, grief or indignation at the sin which is defined in the following clause; secondly, a warning of punishment from God for those who have committed this sin."[29]

However, it is in the Parables that we have some of the most forceful teaching of Jesus on the judgment to come and the two-fold nature of the judgment, eternal life or eternal death, heaven or hell.

In the *Parable of the Weeds among the Wheat,* often called the Parable of the Wheat and the Tares, Jesus told the story of a farmer who planted good wheat seed in his field, but during the night his enemy sneaked into the field and sowed darnel ("tares," in KJV), which is a noxious, poisonous weed. The wheat and the darnel plants look alike until they put up seed stalks and then the difference between them becomes plain. This is one of the few parables of which Jesus gave a full explanation. "The harvest," he said, "is the end of the age ... Just as the weeds are collected and burned up with fire, so will it be at the end of the age ... [when the angels] will collect out of his kingdom all causes of sin and all evildoers, and they will throw them into the furnace of fire, where there will be weeping and gnashing of teeth. Then the righteous will shine like the sun in the kingdom of their Father" (Mt.13:24–30, 36–43, NRSV).

In his discourse on the Last Things, Jesus told three powerful parables. First, *the Parable of the Faithful or the Unfaithful Servant.* A master who was going away for a time entrusted his household into the care of his chief servant. When the master returns, said Jesus, if the servant has been faithful in carrying out his responsibilities, the master will reward him. But if he has been unfaithful and has taken advantage of his authority over the other servants and become self-indulgent, when the master returns, he will mete out punishment in severe and horrible fashion: "He will cut him in pieces and put him with the hypocrites, where there will be weeping and gnashing of teeth" (Mt. 24:45–51, NRSV).

Second, *the Parable of the Ten Bridesmaids,* also known as the Parable of the Wise and the Foolish Virgins. In accordance with the wedding customs of Jesus' time, ten bridesmaids were waiting for the groom to come to the wedding feast, with festive lamps to light the path in welcome. Five of them were wise and brought extra oil; five of them were foolish and brought no extra oil, only what was in their lamps. The groom was delayed, and the bridesmaids became drowsy and fell asleep. At midnight the bridesmaids were suddenly awakened when the shout went up that the groom was coming! Panic! The five foolish bridesmaids found that the oil in their lamps was about gone and their lamps were about to go out. "Give us some of your oil, for our lamps are going out," they asked the five wise ones who replied, "No! There will not be enough for you and for us; you had better go to the dealers and buy some for yourselves." While they were gone to buy more oil, the groom arrived for the wedding banquet, and the door was shut and locked. When the five foolish bridesmaids arrived, they knocked on the door and shouted, "'Lord, lord, open to us.' But he replied, 'Truly I tell you, I do not know you'" (Mt. 25:1–13, NRSV).

The point of the parable is that Jesus Christ, the Bridegroom, is coming back to earth to celebrate the wedding banquet with his bride, his beloved people, and if we are not prepared to greet him, the door will be shut, and then it will be too late to get into the Kingdom of Heaven.

Third, *the Parable of the Talents.* A man going away on a journey entrusted his property to three of his servants, according to their respective abilities, five talents to one of them (a talent was an enormous amount of money, roughly equal to nineteen years' income for a day laborer), two talents to another, and one talent to the third one. While the master was gone, the first two servants invested the money and doubled it. The third servant was afraid to risk losing any of the money, and so he hid it in the ground to keep it safe. When the master returned, he called the three servants to account. He was well pleased with the first two for their wise management of the money he had entrusted to them. However, he was extremely angry with the third one, and denounced him as a wicked, lazy, and worthless servant, and said that he should at least have deposited the money into a savings account at the bank where it would have drawn some interest. The master ordered the third servant thrown "into the outer darkness, where there will be weeping and gnashing of teeth" (Mt. 25:14–30, NRSV).

The point of this parable is that at the Last Judgment, Jesus the Judge will call each one of his servants to account: "What did you do with the gifts I gave you? How did you manage the blessings I bestowed upon you? What use did you make of the abilities I entrusted to you? What did you do to further My Kingdom?"

Then Jesus concluded his discourse on the Last Things with his teaching on the Last Judgment, often called *"the Parable of the Sheep and the Goats."* (Mt. 25:31–46). Here he makes crystal clear what he had implied in the previous parables, that he himself will be the Judge on the Last Day, that all the nations will be gathered before him, and that he will separate people one from another as a shepherd in Bible times separated the sheep from the goats every night. The sheep, placed at his right hand, receive God's blessing, inherit the Kingdom prepared for them from the foundation of the world, and enter everlasting life. However, the goats, placed at his left hand, are cursed forever and go away into the eternal fire prepared for the devil and his evil angels.

What is the basis of the Judgment? It is whether they were sheep or goats, people who belonged to God and followed the Good Shepherd, or whether they were not God's people. This difference was manifested in their lives by the way they treated Jesus' brothers and sisters, whether they fed the hungry, gave drink to the thirsty, welcomed the stranger, gave clothing to the needy, cared for the sick, and visited the prisoners, or failed to do so. This does not mean that we will be saved because of our good deeds, but rather because the deeds we do show what kind of people we are. The fruits of our lives will show whether we are good trees or bad ones.

When we citizens of the 21st century seriously consider Jesus' teaching on the Last Judgment, we are struck, even shocked, by its severity, its harshness, its uncompromising nature, its strictness, its rigidity. We moderns, even many in the church, find it out of line with our idea of the God of love. It certainly does not fit with the stereotype of "Gentle Jesus, meek and mild." Perhaps the reason we find Jesus' teaching on the Judgment so hard to accept is that we do not consider sin to be nearly so serious a matter as God does.

Jesus did not mince words in speaking of the judgment to come. He did not soft-pedal this aspect of God's truth, but he fully intended to confront us with the urgency of the question: What will be the outcome of the Final Judgment for *you:* everlasting destruction in hell, or everlasting life and blessedness in heaven?

3. HOW CAN WE ESCAPE CONDEMNATION AND BE ACQUITTED AT THE LAST JUDGMENT?

Because of the sin and rebellion against God which has infected all of humanity since the Fall, no one, not even the best of us, deserves anything other than being condemned and sentenced to eternal destruction, because none of us is perfect as God requires. None of us has fully kept the Law of God. None of us has fully and completely loved God with all our hearts and with all our souls and with all our minds and with all our strength. None of us has fully and completely loved others as we love ourselves. We have all lived our lives trying to please ourselves first and foremost, rather than God. Thus, none of us deserves anything other than a guilty verdict at the Last Judgment.

However, in his unimaginably great love and mercy, God has had mercy and compassion upon us and has provided a way for us to avoid condemnation at the Last Judgment and be saved. He has done this by sending Jesus, his beloved Son, to take our human flesh upon himself and live life as one of us, subject to all the temptations that we have. God's Son, Jesus Christ, has lived a life of perfect obedience to the Law of God without committing any sin whatsoever. And he has taken our sins upon himself in his death on the cross and has paid the price for our sins, not for his own, for he had none of his own. There on the cross he made the one full, perfect, and sufficient sacrifice, offering, and satisfaction for the sins of the whole world, for us, on our behalf, in our place, to set things right between God and the human race, to reconcile us to God and him to us.

Jesus' resurrection from the dead is the proof that he has truly borne the sins of the world in his own body in his death on the cross, has paid the price for our sins, and has won the victory over sin, death, and the devil.

Then, in God's plan, when the Good News of what Jesus has done for us in his life, death, and resurrection is preached or witnessed to us and we believe the message and are baptized, then God works an amazing miracle. He forgives our sins and remembers them no more. He takes our sin and gives us Jesus' righteousness. He takes our depravity and gives us Jesus' purity. He takes our death and gives us Jesus' eternal life. We are born again from above by water and the Holy Spirit. He adopts us into God's own family. He gives us newness of life.

When this tremendous change takes place in our lives, we are so united and identified with Christ that when God looks at us, he does not see us in our sinfulness and weakness, but he sees only Jesus Christ, his dearly beloved Son, for then we are "in Christ," members of his very body.

Considered from another point of view, when we are brought

to repentance and converted and come to faith in Jesus, we realize the truth that we are sinners by nature and have sinned in actuality, and that our sin against God and others is so grievous that we deserve the death penalty for our sin. And we come to realize that God in his mercy has provided Jesus as the sacrificial Lamb without spot and without blemish, who has suffered death on the cross for us and in our place, and that through the sufferings and death of Jesus, God has given us forgiveness of all our sins and newness of life

Therefore, we have already accepted the judgment of God upon our sins, and that if it were not for Jesus dying for us on the cross, making us his own people, and uniting his life with ours, we would have deserved eternal death and destruction. But because Jesus died for us and in our place, God's justice has been satisfied, and we go free. Because Jesus' merits have been transferred to our account, God considers and accounts us as "Not guilty!" Thus, we will be justified, acquitted, at the Last Judgment, rather than being found "guilty as charged" and condemned to eternal death. Jesus said:

> "Most assuredly, I say to you, he who hears My word and believes in him who sent Me has everlasting life, and shall not come into judgment [condemnation], but has passed from death into life."
>
> (Jn. 5:24)

However, some of those who have heard the Good News of the salvation God offers them through Jesus Christ have not accepted it. Perhaps they thought the Gospel is foolishness. Perhaps they thought they have often tried to do the right thing and should get some credit for that. Perhaps they thought they are pretty good people and not nearly so bad as others. Perhaps they thought that their good deeds outweigh their bad ones. For whatever reason, they have rejected the salvation God has offered through Jesus Christ. They have turned their backs on the only way God has provided for them to be saved. Thus they have condemned themselves. They have remained the goats they are, rather than accepting the way God has provided for them to be converted and changed into his sheep. And so, at the Last Judgment they go away into eternal death rather than into eternal life.

Thus, in a sense his verdict upon us reflects our verdict upon him. Jesus himself set out the alternatives very plainly:

> "For God so loved the world that he gave his only begotten Son, that whoever believes in him should not perish but have everlasting life. For God did not send his Son into the world [at his First Coming] to condemn the world, but that the world through him might be saved. He who believes in him is not condemned; but he who does not believe is condemned already, because he has not believed in the name of the only begotten Son of God ... He who believes in the Son has everlasting life; and he who does not believe the Son shall not see life, but the wrath of God abides on him."
>
> (Jn. 3:16–18, 36)

God doesn't want you to be lost and perish. He is merciful and gracious, abounding in steadfast love. He takes no pleasure in the death of any sinner (Ezek. 18:23, 32; Mt. 18:14). He pleads with you to accept his love and the salvation he offers to you in Jesus Christ. Turn to him in prayer and ask him to forgive your sin and have mercy upon you. Accept Jesus Christ as your Lord and Savior and ask him to come into your heart and life and to live his life in you by his Holy Spirit.

For God's sake, and for your own sake, don't let your pride or anything else get in the way and keep you from asking God to save you.

God is full of love and compassion. If you turn to him, don't be afraid of being rejected. He will not turn away anyone who calls upon him and prays to him for salvation. To be sure we know that, God has told us three different times in his Holy Word that he will save everyone who calls on the name of the Lord [Jesus]. (Joel 2:32; Acts 2:21; Rom. 10:13).

Jesus Christ himself stands before you with his arms of love open wide to welcome you and draw you to himself and embrace you with his love. If you, like the prodigal son, turn and begin to walk toward God, you will be surprised to find him running toward you to welcome you home to himself. And God and the angels in heaven will rejoice and celebrate your homecoming, and God will give you his salvation and richest blessings.

This salvation, which we do not deserve, which we could never merit no matter how hard we tried, God offers to us as a free gift through Jesus Christ, "without money and without price," (Is. 55:1, KJV), and saves us now and forever.

"How shall we escape if we ignore such a great salvation?" (Heb.2:3, NIV).

D
HELL

It is a startling fact that of the twelve times the word "hell" (*Gehenna* in Greek and Hebrew) appears in the New Testament, all but one of them is from the lips of the Lord Jesus himself, as well as all three references to hell as "outer darkness." This teaching of Jesus seems harsh, severe, and oppressive to us citizens of the 21st century, quite contrary to our idea of Jesus embodying the love of God. "How could a loving God consign anybody to the fires of hell?" we ask.

The problem is that we have created our own ideas of what God ought to be like, which is a sin the Scriptures condemn as idolatry, rather than believing and accepting God as he has revealed himself to us in the Holy Scriptures and in his Only-begotten Son Jesus Christ. Yes, God is love, but he is also holy. Therefore, his love is a holy love that hates sin and cannot abide it, not the sentimental warm feeling that we think love is.

Perhaps the basic reason we have trouble with the doctrine of hell is that we think we know what is good and evil for ourselves rather than looking to God to teach us what is truly good for us and what is harmful for us. This was the attitude underlying the sin of Adam and Eve, wanting to know and decide for themselves what is good and what is evil, rather than believing and accepting God's word and obeying his commands, looking to him to teach them what is good and what is evil.

Therefore, we do not take sin with the utmost seriousness that God does. We blind ourselves to the destructive nature of sin. Sin is dreadfully destructive of human life and happiness. Why does God hate sin so fiercely? Because he loves us humans so fiercely and wants us to have the best life possible.

1. HELL: A REAL PLACE

When Jesus spoke of hell, he was referring to an actual place located Southwest of Jerusalem known as "*Gehenna*" in Hebrew. (There is another Hebrew word, *Sheol*, which the King James Version also translates as "hell," but these are two different things. Most of the modern translations clear up this problem and reserve the word "hell" for *Gehenna*, the place of eternal punishment; *Sheol* means simply the place of the dead, in Greek, *Hades*.)

Why did Jesus refer to Gehenna to teach us what hell is like? For two reasons: (1) because of what it had been used for in the ancient past, and (2) what it was being used for during his earthly ministry.

In ancient times, when the Israelites had fallen away from true faith and had adopted the religious practices of the pagan peoples around them, they would offer their children as sacrifices to the pagan god Moloch by killing them in the fire, referred to as making the child "pass through the fire." The primary place where this ghastly sin took place was in the Valley of Hinnom, called "Gehenna" in the Bible, just outside the city of Jerusalem. Sometimes even the kings sacrificed their own children to Moloch in this way, such as King Ahaz did (2 Kings 16:3; 2 Chron. 28:3) and also King Manasseh (2 Kings 21:6; 2 Chron. 33:6).

Child sacrifice was so horrible a thing and so contrary to the faith of Israel and the Law of Moses (Lev. 18:21; Deut. 18:10) that the prophets considered it the ultimate depth of sin and rebellion against God (Jer. 7:31; 32:35). In fact, the abominable atrocity of child sacrifice was one of the main reasons that God's judgment fell upon Israel, the Northern kingdom, carried out by the Assyrians who conquered its capital Samaria in 721 BC Its surviving people were taken away captive into Assyria (located in northern Iraq) (2 Kings 17:17). The same was true of Judah, the southern kingdom with its capital at Jerusalem which fell to the Babylonians in 586 BC when the Temple and the city of Jerusalem were destroyed and the leaders of the nation and many of the people were carried away captive into Babylon (*See* 2 Chron. 36:11–21).

Since Gehenna was the location where the Jews had practiced the despicable crime of child sacrifice in ancient times, it held grim, grisly, hideous, and horrible associations in the minds of the Jews, so much so that by the time of Jesus it had become the symbol of hell, the terrible place of eternal punishment.

In our time, a comparable symbol of hell might be the Nazi concentration camps like Auschwitz and Dachau where the Nazis tortured people, used them for horrible medical experiments, and finally killed them and buried or cremated their bodies. The awful mental and emotional associations that the mention of these Nazi death camps brings to us are comparable to those raised by the mention of Gehenna to the Jews in Jesus' time. Gehenna ("Hell") is an unutterably horrible place.

In later centuries the Valley of Hinnom ("Gehenna") was used as the garbage dump and trash pile for the city of Jerusalem, and this was the case in Jesus' time. It was a nasty place, constantly burning, smoking and smoldering, inhabited by maggots, rats and other vermin. It was the place where human and animal excrement from the city was taken. The bodies of donkeys, dogs, and other dead animals lying on the streets of Jerusalem were hauled to Gehenna. The bodies of executed criminals were sometimes thrown there. The stench of Gehenna was awful. It was a foul, nauseating, disgusting, repulsive place.

So when Jesus taught about hell ("Gehenna"), the people had a very clear idea of what he was talking about. If they went outside of Jerusalem to the edge of the Valley of Hinnom, they could see the fires burning constantly, see the vermin scurrying around in the piles of garbage and trash, and smell the stench.

No wonder Jesus warned people about Gehenna. What a horribly tragic thing it would be for people to live such ill-spent, purposeless, pointless, ungodly lives that at the end, they would be fit for nothing but to be thrown on the garbage dump of the universe.

2. SOME CHARACTERISTICS OF HELL

Jesus' teachings and other Scriptures give us a picture of some characteristics of hell, all of which are consistent with the real place known as Gehenna ("hell") located in the Valley of Hinnom southwest of the ancient city of Jerusalem. For example:

a. It is a place of unquenchable fire (Is. 66:15–24; Mt. 5:22; Mk. 9:43–48), a lake burning with fire and sulfur (Rev. 21:8).

b. It is a place infested with maggots continually (Is. 66:24; Mk. 9:48: "where their worm never dies").

c. The fire of hell is eternal (Mt. 13:42–50; 18:8).

d. Hell is eternal punishment, the opposite of eternal life (Mt. 25:46).

e. Hell is also described as the outer darkness (Mt. 25:30), the deepest darkness (2 Pet. 2:17).

f. Hell is eternal destruction (2 Thes. 1:9).

g. Hell is described as a bottomless pit (Rev. 9:1, 11:7).

h. Hell is being excluded from the presence of God (Mt.7:21–23; 2 Thes.1:9).

Jesus' teaching indicates that there are degrees of punishment in hell, depending on the degree of one's knowledge of God's will. "[T]hat servant who knew his master's will, and did not prepare himself or do according to his will, shall be beaten with many stripes. But he who did not know, yet committed things worthy of stripes, shall be beaten with few" (Parable of the Faithful or the Unfaithful Servant, Lk. 12:47–48).

How can we escape being condemned to hell at the Last Judgment? We can only escape condemnation if our names are "written in the Lamb's Book of Life" (Rev. 21:27). "And anyone not found written in the Book of Life was cast into the lake of fire" (Rev. 20:15).

What makes the difference whether our names are written there or not? Jesus himself has told us: "He who believes and is baptized will be saved; but he who does not believe will be condemned" (Mk. 16:16).

What does it mean to believe in Jesus? The Apostle Paul has explained it plainly: "...if you confess with your mouth the Lord Jesus [that is, that Jesus is God] and believe in your heart that God has raised him from the dead, you will be saved" (Rom.10:9).

HEAVEN

The Bible does not tell us a great deal about heaven, and for a very good reason: we would not be able to comprehend it. How could our finite minds grasp the infinite glory of heaven? How could we possibly understand how absolutely marvelous it would be to live in the presence of God and behold his face?

An example may help illuminate this truth. Suppose that you were a child still in your mother's womb but you could hear and understand what people said to you. Suppose that someone tried to tell you in detail what life would be like in the outside world after you were born. In the dark and constricted world you were in, you would be unable to form any idea of what life would be like outside the womb or how different but wonderful it would be.

When you are born, you are the same person you were in the womb, but now everything is so different. What is the first thing you would do when you were born into this world? You would cry, so that your lungs would begin to work, taking in oxygen from the air which you previously received from your mother's blood through the umbilical cord. Instead of darkness, there is now light. Instead of a constricted space, now you are living in freedom. Immediately, you start moving your arms and kicking with your feet. The freedom feels so wonderful! Then reflexively you want to suck to take in nourishment. In the womb, you were fed from your mother's body through the umbilical cord.

But if you were to try to tell the child in the womb what life would be like outside the mother's body, even if it understood your words, there would be no way he or she could comprehend how wonderful and different life outside the womb would be, what freedom, what joy, what delight.

For us in our limited and restricted earthly condition, there is no way we can comprehend what heaven is like. So what God has done is to give us some glimpses, some pictures, of heaven to excite our imagination and give us some preview of the glory that will be revealed to us in heaven (Rom. 8:18).

1. SOME GLIMPSES OF WHAT HEAVEN IS LIKE

Scripture teaches us that the sin of humankind has corrupted and polluted and disrupted the order and beauty of God's creation. And so, part of God's process of redemption and salvation at the end of time will be that "… the creation itself also will be delivered from the bondage of corruption into the glorious liberty of the children of God" (Rom. 8:21).

God has revealed to us that as part of the renewal of all things, "… the heavens and earth which now exist are … reserved for fire" (2 Pet. 3:7) and that when the Day of the Lord comes, "… the heavens will pass away with a great noise, and the elements will melt with fervent heat; both the earth and the works that are in it will be burned up" (2 Pet. 3:10). Then God will create "… new heavens and a new earth in which righteousness dwells" (2 Pet. 3:13).

Actually, centuries before Christ, God revealed part of his plan to the prophet Isaiah in exalted language and marvelous imagery (*See* Is. 65:17–25, "new heavens and a new earth").

After his resurrection and ascension into heaven, Jesus Christ showed the Apostle John a vision of the Holy City, the

New Jerusalem, coming down out of heaven to the re-created earth (Rev. chapter 21).

So the eternal heaven will not be far off "up there" somewhere, but rather will be down here on God's newly re-created earth where God will make his home and live among his people forever (Rev. 21:3).

Really, the basic definition of heaven is that it is God's home, the place where he lives. It is the place where his will is always done perfectly, fully, and completely, as the Lord Jesus taught us in the Lord's Prayer: "Thy will be done on earth, as it is [done now, always, fully, and completely] in heaven" (Mt. 6:10). In the world to come, God will come down from highest heaven to live with his loved ones in the Holy City, the New Jerusalem, on the re-created earth. "Now the dwelling of God is with men, and he will live with them. They will be his people, and God himself will be with them and be their God" (Rev. 21:3, NIV).

Let's take a look at some of the characteristics of heaven, first, some things that will be absent from heaven, then, some things that will be present in heaven.

2. SOME THINGS THAT WILL NOT BE IN HEAVEN

First, none of God's enemies, which are also our enemies and the enemies of our happiness, will be there, for they will be no more. These enemies are the world, the flesh, and the devil. The devil (which we may think of as evil *beyond* us, in the spiritual realm) will not be there to tempt, torment, and accuse God's people anymore, for he will have been cast into the lake of fire (Rev. 20:10).

The present world (which we may think of as evil *around* us, evil coming through other people to tempt us or to oppress us) will be no more, for it will have been destroyed, burned up, and consumed with fire (2 Pet. 3:10) and will have been replaced by the New World, the new heavens and the new earth.

The flesh (which we may think of as evil *within* ourselves, in other words, sin) will no longer be our enemy, for all sin has been forgiven, forgotten, done away with, and atoned for by the blood of the Lamb of God shed on the cross. Sin will be eliminated and God's people will live in the new earth in which no sin, but only righteousness dwells (2 Pet. 3:13).

We cannot even imagine how wonderful it will be to live in a world free of the power of the devil, free of the power of the present evil world, completely free of our own sin, and not subject to temptation and oppression coming from others. We have never lived in such a condition, and we cannot imagine living in a world where there is nothing but love and joy and peace.

Second, there will be no death there, for God will have cast death into the lake of fire (Rev. 20:14). Since death is the wages of sin (Rom. 6:23), where there is no sin, there will be no death. Death has been the lot of all mankind since the Fall when Adam and Eve sinned and were expelled from the Garden of Eden and prevented from having access to the Tree of Life (Gen. 3:24). But now in heaven, in the New Jerusalem, God's people will live forever, for they will have free access to the Tree of Life watered by the river of life flowing from the throne of God (Rev. 22:1–2).

We in our present situation cannot imagine how wonderful it would be to live in a world without the specter of death staring us in the face.

Third, in heaven there will be no pain, no suffering, no grief, no sorrow, for "God himself will be with [His people]; He will wipe every tear from their eyes. Death will be no more; mourning and crying and pain will be no more, for the first things have passed away" (Rev. 21:3–4, NRSV).

Now in the present time we cannot imagine how great it would be to live in such a world.

Fourth, there will be no oppression nor persecution of God's people, for Christ has won the eternal victory over our enemies.

Fifth, in heaven the curse and the effects of the Fall of mankind and of our own sin will have been removed and done away (Rev. 22:3). Everything will have been put right, and there will be no disorder nor separation. "Also there was no more sea" (Rev. 21:1), the sea symbolizing separation and chaos.

The sin of mankind had resulted in mankind's separation (a) from God, (b) from one another, and (c) from the environment (nature). Now in heaven there will be no separation:

a. God and mankind are completely reconciled, all sin has been atoned for, and now, rather than hiding from God in guilt and shame, redeemed mankind will rejoice in God's presence.

b. No longer are people separated from each other; there is no competition, no jealousy, no misunderstandings between people and thus nothing to impede the free flow of love among and between God's people.

c. In heaven, no longer is mankind separated from nature, from the environment. No longer can mankind pollute the earth, for nothing unclean or polluting will be found in heaven (Rev. 21:27). There will be complete and perfect order and peace in the environment, with no destructive or harmful elements whatsoever.

The Bible pictures this in beautiful poetic language depicting what has been called "The Peaceable Kingdom:"

"The wolf also shall dwell with the lamb,
The leopard shall lie down with the young goat,
The calf and the young lion and the fatling together;
And a little child shall lead them.
The cow and the bear shall graze;
Their young ones shall lie down together;
And the lion shall eat straw like the ox.
The nursing child shall play by the cobra's hole,
And the weaned child shall put his hand in the viper's den.
They shall not hurt nor destroy in all My holy mountain;
For the earth shall be full of the knowledge of the Lord
As the waters cover the sea."

(Is. 11:6–9)

Turning from the negative to the positive, let us consider:

3. SOME THINGS THAT WILL BE IN HEAVEN

First and foremost, God will be there, God the Father, God the Son (Jesus Christ), and God the Holy Spirit, for heaven is God's home. And we will be privileged to behold something no mortal has ever seen before: the face of God himself. As David said, "As for me, I shall behold Your face in righteousness; when I awake I shall be satisfied, beholding Your likeness" (Ps. 17:15, NRSV). We will be privileged to see what people through the ages have longed to see: the unveiled face and glory of God himself. "[W]e shall see him as he is" (1 Jn. 3:2).

Second, since God will be present in all his glory, worship and praise of God will be there. We will worship God with magnificent exalted worship, together with all God's people and "with angels and archangels and all the company of heaven." The worship of God in heaven is pictured most magnificently in the Book of Revelation, especially in chapters 4, 5, and 7.

In our present circumstances, we cannot even imagine how magnificent the worship of God will be.

Third, all God's redeemed people will be there, a throng so vast we could not count them (Rev. 7:9), God's saints from every age and generation. Therefore, heaven will be immense in size to accommodate such a multitude of people. John's vision in Revelation 21:16 pictures heaven as being a cube about 1,500 miles in each dimension.

Will we recognize and know our redeemed loved ones in heaven? Yes! *(See* Jesus' Parable of the Rich Man and Lazarus, Lk. 16:19–31.)

Fourth, Scripture seems to indicate that in addition to worshipping God, we may have tasks to do and responsibilities to carry out in heaven. Several biblical references say that God's redeemed people will rule and reign with Jesus. "If we suffer with him, we shall also reign with him" (2 Tim. 2:12, KJV; *see also,* Rev. 5:10).

Jesus taught that we would have differing levels of responsibility in God's kingdom depending on how faithful we were in carrying out our earthly responsibilities (*see* Parable of the Talents, Mt. 25:14–30).

The Apostle Paul wrote that the only foundation for our lives and work is Jesus Christ, but what we build on that foundation varies. Some build lives that are pure gold, or silver, or precious stones, while others build with wood, or hay, or straw. The fire of the Last Judgment will test what sort of work each one has done. "If anyone's work which he has built on it endures, he will receive a reward. If anyone's work is burned, he will suffer loss; but he himself will be saved, yet so as through fire" (1 Cor. 3:10–15). That is, in the latter case, it is like a family whose house has been totally destroyed by fire and they have lost everything, all their clothes, furniture, and earthly belongings, but they have escaped with their lives.

Fifth, there will be unimaginable beauty in heaven. The holy city, the New Jerusalem "has the glory of God and a radiance like a very rare jewel, like jasper, clear as crystal" (Rev. 21:11, NRSV). "The wall is built of jasper, while the city is of pure gold, clear as glass" (Rev. 21:18, NRSV). The foundations of the wall are adorned with jewels and the twelve gates are each made of a single pearl and the street is "pure gold, transparent as glass" (Rev. 21:18–21, NRSV).

These pictures stir our imaginations. How fantastic it will be to live in the midst of such beauty!

Sixth, in ways that we cannot comprehend, the very best of earth will be there. In God's economy, nothing that is truly good and righteous will be lost but will be present in heaven: (1) the good deeds of God's people ("'Blessed are the dead who from now on die in the Lord.' 'Yes,' says the Spirit, 'they will rest from their labors, for their deeds follow them" Rev.14:13, NRSV); (2) the glory and honor of the nations, brought by the kings of the earth (Rev. 21:24) and the people (Rev. 21:26).

Seventh, in heaven there will be joy that we cannot fathom with our present limitations. In two of his parables, Jesus compared the kingdom of heaven to a wedding banquet and to a magnificent feast, "the Messianic Banquet" (Mt. 22:2–14; Lk.14:15–24. *See* Is. 25:6–10). Jesus taught that believing Gentiles as well as believing Jews will be present at the feast: "I say to you that many will come from east and west, and sit down with Abraham and Isaac, and Jacob in the kingdom of heaven" while the Jews who should have been heirs of the kingdom but did not believe in him "will be cast out into outer darkness. There will be weeping and gnashing of teeth" (Mt. 8:11–12). And the celebration and rejoicing in heaven after the defeat of all God's enemies is pictured as the marriage feast of the Lamb, when Jesus takes his bride, his church, consisting of all true believers, unto himself (Rev. 19:7–9).

What a wonderful privilege it will be to be invited to be a guest at the marriage feast of the Lamb!

Some Christians are disappointed to find out that there will be no sex in heaven, for in God's plan sex and marriage are restricted to life on this earth. Once the Sadducees tried to catch Jesus in a trap with their concocted story of a woman who had been married seven times and they asked him whose wife she would be in the resurrection. Jesus told them they were wrong because they did not know the Scriptures nor the power of God: "For when they rise from the dead, they neither marry nor are given in marriage, but are like angels in heaven" (Mk.12:18–27).

One Christian writer points out that sex is the greatest thing God has created on this earth, and that if there is no sex in heaven, God must have something unimaginably more wonderful for us there.[30]

Certainly, the greatest momentary pleasure we ever experience from sex in this present life is not worth comparing to the joy—yes, ecstasy—of heaven, which lasts forever. God revealed this a thousand years before Christ to David who wrote:

> "In Your presence is fullness of joy; At Your right hand are pleasures forevermore."
>
> (Ps.16:11)

The greatest joys of this life are finite and short-lived; the joys of heaven are infinite and last forever.

There is no way that we in our present limited human condition can comprehend or even imagine the glory and joy of heaven. To get to heaven will be worth all the trials and tribulations we undergo on earth. "… [t]he sufferings of the present time are not worth comparing with the glory about to be revealed to us," wrote the Apostle Paul (Rom. 8:18 NRSV).

Life with God in heaven will be infinitely more wonderful than we can think or even imagine.

> "'Things beyond our seeing,
> things beyond our hearing,
> things beyond our imagining,
> all prepared by God for those who love him."
>
> (I Cor. 2:9, NEB)

CONCLUSION

God wants you to be with him in heaven forever. He does not desire that anyone should perish but on the contrary, he desires that you and all the people he has created should repent and find fullness of life with him forever (2 Pet. 3:9). God "desires everyone to be saved and to come to the knowledge of the truth" (I Tim. 2:4 NRSV).

Near the end of the Revelation, the last book in the Bible, it is as if God is extending an invitation to us, holding out his open arms toward us as wide as Jesus' arms were extended on the Cross, inviting all of us to come to himself and enjoy the love and joy and peace and glory of heaven with him forever:

> "And the Spirit and the bride [the Church, his people] say, 'Come!
> And let him who hears say, "Come!"
> And let him who thirsts come.
> And whoever desires, let him take the water of life [salvation] freely."
>
> (Rev. 22:17)

Accept God's gracious offer of salvation *now*, for this present moment of time may be all you have, for the Lord Jesus is surely coming soon (Rev. 22:20).

Join with all God's people through the ages in praying, "AMEN. Even so, come, Lord Jesus" (Rev. 22:20). Yes, come quickly, Lord Jesus.

As we began our meditation upon these revealed mysteries of God with the very first words of the Holy Scriptures, "In the beginning God created the heavens and the earth" (Gen.1:1), so it is most fitting that we conclude with these final words of the Holy Bible:

"The grace of our Lord Jesus Christ be with you all. Amen" (Rev. 22:21).

ABOUT THE AUTHOR
HENRY SUMMERALL, JR.

BACKGROUND:
Born at Aiken, SC June 22, 1936. Attended public schools in Aiken.

HIGHER EDUCATION:

College:

University of Wisconsin, Madison, WI (B.S., major in English, 1956), Phi Beta Kappa, active in Baptist Student Fellowship.

Law School:

University of South Carolina School of Law (LL.B. 1959).

Seminary:

Virginia Theological Seminary (Episcopal), Alexandria, VA (B.D. 1969).

FAMILY:
Married with two children and two grandchildren. A widower since 2000.

CHURCH AFFILIATIONS:
First Baptist Church, Aiken, SC, 1936–1952 (baptized 1944), 1956–1963.

First Baptist Church, Madison, WI, during college years, (1952–1956).

St. Thaddeus Episcopal Church, Aiken, SC 1963–1969, 1974–1977.

All Saints Anglican Church (Traditional Anglican), Aiken, SC, 1978–1994

St. James Lutheran Church (ELCA), Graniteville, SC, 1994–2005.

St. Paul Lutheran Church (ELCA), Aiken, SC, 2006–2007

Bethlehem Lutheran Church (LC-MS), Aiken, SC, 2007-

VOCATIONS:

Law:

Private practice of law in Aiken, SC 1959–1966 and 1974–2000 (attorney for City of Aiken, 1975–1985). Retired June 30, 2000.

Ministry:

Ordained Deacon in 1969 and Priest in 1970 by the Rt. Rev. John Adams Pinckney, Bishop of Diocese of Upper South Carolina (Episcopal)

Deacon-in-Training at Christ Church (Episcopal), Greenville, SC 1969–1970.

Minister of Holy Cross Episcopal Ch., Simpsonville, SC 1969–1973 (full-time)

Asst. to Rector, St. Thaddeus Episcopal Ch., Aiken, SC 1974–1977 (part-time)

Rector of All Saints Anglican Church, Aiken, SC or Asst. to Rector, 1978–1994 (part-time).

As layman, Sunday School teacher and Bible teacher at St. James Lutheran Church during membership there.

Military service:

Six years with S.C. Air National Guard, McEntire Air Base, SC, of which 13 months were active duty including basic training and active Federal service during the Berlin Wall Crisis of 1961–1962, stationed in Spain.

SELECTED BIBLIOGRAPHY

The Analytical Greek Lexicon (Grand Rapids: Zondervan, 1967).

J. P. Baker. "Prophecy" in *The Illustrated Bible Dictionary, p.*1276 (Wheaton:Tyndale, 1980).

R. T. Beckwith, "Sacrifice and Offering" in *The Illustrated Bible Dictionary, pp.* 1358–1368 (Wheaton: Tyndale, 1980).

J. W. Bowman, "The Life and Teaching of Jesus" in *Peake's Commentary on The Bible, pp.*733–747 (London: Nelson, 1962).

Friedrich Buchsel, "Krino" in *Theological Dictionary of the New Testament,* ed.

Gerhard Kittel, trans. Geoffrey W. Bromiley, vol III:921–941 (Grand Rapids:Eerdmans, 1965).

Anthony M. Coniaris, *Introducing the Orthodox Church: Its Faith and Life* (Minneapolis: Light and Life Pub. Co.1982).

Larry Crabb, *The Silence of Adam* (Grand Rapids: Zondervan, 1995).

Anthony DeStefano, *A Travel Guide to Heaven* (New York: Doubleday, 2003).

J. R. Dummelow, ed. *A Commentary on the Holy Bible* (New York: Macmillan, 1958).

J. D. G. Dunn, "Baptism" in *The Illustrated Bible Dictionary, pp.*172–175 (Wheaton:Tyndale, 1980).

J. C. Fenton, *Saint Matthew,* The Pelican Gospel Commentaries (Baltimore: Penguin, 1963).

Langdon Gilkey, *Maker of Heaven and Earth: The Christian Doctrine of Creation In the Light of Modern Knowledge* (Garden City: Doubleday, 1958).

Ralph Gower, *The New Manners and Customs of Bible Times* (Chicago: Moody, 1987).

H. W. L. Hoad, "Patience" in *The New Bible Dictionary* (Grand Rapids: Eerdmans, 1962).

Joachim Jeremias, "Gehenna" in *Theological Dictionary of the New Testament,* ed.

Gerhard Kittell, trans. Geoffrey W. Bromiley, vol I:657–658 (Grand Rapids:Eerdmans, 1965).

Walter C. Kaiser, Jr., et al., *Hard Sayings of the Bible* (Downers Grove: InterVarsity, 1996).

Frank C. Laubach, *Did Mary Tell Jesus Her Secret?* (London: Marshall, Morgan & Scott, 1970).

Harold Lindsell, *Harper Study Bible* (Grand Rapids: Zondervan, 1965).

Martin Luther, *Lectures on Genesis: Chapter Three* in *Luther's Works,* vol. 1:141–236 (Saint Louis: Concordia, 1958).

L. L. Morris, "Atonement" in *The Illustrated Bible Dictionary, pp.*147–150 (Wheaton:Tyndale, 1980).

Regin Prenter, *Creation and Redemption* (Philadelphia: Fortress, 1967).

———*The Church's Faith: A Primer of Christian Belief* (Philadelphia: Fortress, 1968).

Alan Richardson, ed., *A Theological Word Book of the Bible* (New York: Macmillan, 1956).

Time Almanac 2005 (New York: Time, 2004).

Webster's New World Dictionary of the American Language, College Edition (Cleveland and New York, 1966).

ENDNOTES

1. Regin Prenter, *The Church's Faith: A Primer of Christian Belief,* p.28 (Philadelphia: Fortress, 1968).
2. Martin Luther, *Lectures on Genesis: Chapter Three* in *Luther's Works,* vol. 1, p. 155 (Saint Louis: Concordia, 1958).
3. *Tabletalk,* Feb. 2006, p. 22.
4. Martin Luther, *op. cit.,* p. 176.
5. Martin Luther, *op. cit.,* p. 179.
6. Martin Luther, *op. cit.,* p. 151.
7. Walter C. Kaiser, Jr., *Hard Sayings of the Bible,* p. 96-97 (Downers Grove: InterVarsity, 1996).
8. *Ibid.,* p. 98.
9. Anthony M. Coniaris, *Introducing the Orthodox Church: Its Faith and Life* (Minneapolis: Light and Life Pub. Co., 1982).
10. Frank C. Laubach, *Did Mary Tell Jesus Her Secret?* (London: Marshall, Morgan & Scott, 1970).
11. Ralph Gower, *The New Manners and Customs of Bible Times,* p. 62 (Chicago: Moody, 1987).
12. R. T. Beckwith, "Sacrifice and Offering" in *The Illustrated Bible Dictionary,* pp. 1358-1368 (Wheaton: Tyndale, 1980).
13. Regin Prenter, *Creation and Redemption,* p. 220 (Philadelphia: Fortress, 1967).
14. Friedrich Buchsel, "Krino" in *Theological Dictionary of the New Testament,* ed. Gerhard Kittel, trans. Geoffrey W. Bromiley, vol. III:559-564 (Grand Rapids: Eerdmans, 1965).
15. *Ibid.,* p. 561.
16. Cologne, 1695, Hymn No. 135 in *The Lutheran Book of Wor-*

ship, trans. Francis Pott, verses 1 and 2 (Minneapolis: The Augsburg Press, 1978, 10th ed. 1990).

17. Ralph Gower, *The New Manners and Customs of Bible Times,* p. 73 (Chicago: Moody, 1987).
18. *The New Encyclopedia of Christian Quotations,* compiled by Mark Water, pp. 864, 866 (Grand Rapids: Baker Books, 2000).
19. J. D. G. Dunn, "Baptism" in *The Illustrated Bible Dictionary,* p. 173 (Wheaton: Tyndale, 1980).
20. L. H. Brockington, "Presence" in *A Theological Word Book of the Bible,* ed. Alan Richardson, p. 176 (New York: Macmillan, 1956).
21. J. W. L. Hoad, "Patience" in *The Illustrated Bible Dictionary,* p. 1159 (New York: Macmillan, 1956).
22. Alan Richardson, "Pride" in *A Theological Word Book of the Bible,* p. 176 (New York: Macmillan, 1956).
23. Regin Prenter, *Creation and Redemption,* pp. 551-552 (Philadelphia: Fortress, 1967).
24. Harold Lindsell, ed. *Harper Study Bible (*RSV*),* note on 2 Timothy 2:18 (Grand Rapids: Zondervan, 1965).
25. *Time Almanac* 2005, p. 715 (New York: Time, 2004).
26. A. G. Herbert, "Antichrist, Man of Sin" in *A Theological Word Book of the Bible,* p. 19 (New York: Macmillan, 1956).
27. *The Analytical Greek Lexicon* (Grand Rapids: Zondervan, 1967).
28. Friedrich Buchsel, "Krino" in *Theological Dictionary of the New Testament,* ed. Gerhard Kittel, trans. Geoffrey W. Bromiley, vol. III, p. 936 (Grand Rapids: Eerdmans, 1965).
29. J. C. Fenton, *Saint Matthew,* The Pelican Gospel Commentaries, p. 368 (Baltimore: Penguin, 1963).
30. Anthony DeStefano, *A Travel Guide to Heaven,* pp. 74-76 (New York: Doubleday, 2003).